Glenn's RENAULT Repair and Tune-up Guide

HAROLD T. GLENN

Member, Society of Automotive Engineers; Formerly, Instructor in Long Beach Unified School District, Long Beach, California

Portland Public Library

ILLUSTRATED

CHILTON BOOK COMPANY
Philadelphia   New York   London

Acknowledgments

The author wishes to thank the RENAULT COMPANY for their assistance in furnishing technical information and illustrations and *Road & Track* magazine for permission to use their road test data. Special thanks are due to DON BOLZ, service representative, for his kind assistance in checking the copy for accuracy and for suggestions for improvement. The author also wishes to express special thanks to his wife, ANNA GLENN, for her devoted assistance in proofreading and revising the text.

HAROLD T. GLENN

In many sections the reader will note step-by-step illustrated instructions. These picture series can be identified by a circled number in the lower right-hand corner of each illustration. The numbers agree with the numbered instructions in the text, and are so correlated that no legends are required.

Copyright © 1964 by Harold T. Glenn. Published in Philadelphia by Chilton Book Company, and simultaneously in Ontario, Canada, by Thomas Nelson & Sons, Ltd. All rights reserved. Manufactured in the United States of America.

ISBN 0-8019-1346-2

Library of Congress Catalog Card No. 64-12776

Second Printing, August 1964
Third Printing, August 1965
Fourth Printing, June 1966
Fifth Printing, June 1967
Sixth Printing, August 1968
Seventh Printing, June 1970

Contents

1. **TROUBLESHOOTING** 1
   Basic starting trouble tests.................. 1
   Detailed starting trouble tests............... 2
      Cranking system........................... 2
      Ignition system........................... 4
      Fuel system............................... 6
   Troubleshooting the mechanical parts
      of the engine............................. 8
      Low compression troubleshooting chart..... 10
   Troubleshooting for excess oil consumption... 10
      Excessive oil consumption troubleshooting
        chart 11
   Troubleshooting for engine noises............ 12
      Engine noise troubleshooting chart........ 13
   Troubleshooting for poor performance
      due to excessive friction................. 14
      Excessive friction troubleshooting chart..... 14
   Troubleshooting the cooling system........... 14
      Cooling system troubleshooting chart...... 15
   Troubleshooting the fuel system.............. 16
      Fuel system troubleshooting chart......... 17
   Troubleshooting the carburetor............... 18
      Carburetor troubleshooting chart.......... 18
   Troubleshooting the electrical system........ 18
      Troubleshooting the battery............... 19
      Troubleshooting the cranking system....... 19
      Troubleshooting the charging system....... 20
      Troubleshooting the ignition system....... 22
      Troubleshooting the clutch................ 25
      Troubleshooting the transmission.......... 25
      Troubleshooting the rear axle............. 26
   Troubleshooting the front end................ 26
   Troubleshooting a hydraulic brake system..... 27
   Troubleshooting the caliper disc brake system.. 28

2. **TUNING AND IDENTIFICATION**.............. 29
   Model Identification......................... 29
   General Information—4CV, Dauphine,
      Gordini, and Caravelle.................... 29
   General Information—R-8 and Caravelle "S".. 30
   Ignition Service Notes....................... 30
   Road Tests................................... 30
   Commonly Used Specifications................. 33
   Capacities 33
   General Engine Specifications................ 34
   Car Life Road Tests.......................... 34

3. **THE FUEL SYSTEM**......................... 39
   Overhauling a Solex 28 IBT Carburetor........ 39
   Solex Carburetor Specifications.............. 39

4. **THE ELECTRICAL SYSTEM**................... 48
   Light Bulbs.................................. 48
   Generator and Regulator Specifications....... 49
   Starter and Battery Specifications........... 49
   Chassis Wiring Diagrams...................... 50
   Distributor Specifications................... 52

5. **ENGINE SERVICE**........................... 59
   Engine Service Notes—4CV, Dauphine,
      Gordini, and Caravelle.................... 59
   Mechanical Engine Specifications............. 61
   Valve Specifications......................... 61
   Powerplant, Trans-Axle, and Sub-Frame
      Assembly Removal.......................... 62
   Engine Torque Specifications................. 65

6. **CLUTCH AND TRANSMISSION SERVICE**... 68
   Clutch Pedal Adjustment...................... 68
   Overhauling a Trans-Axle..................... 68
   Rear Axle Specifications..................... 69
   Ferlec Automatic Clutch...................... 78
   Automatic Transmission....................... 83

7. **RUNNING GEAR SERVICE**.................... 86
   Steering Gear Overhaul....................... 86
   Front Axle Specifications.................... 88
   Brake Service—4CV, Gordini, Dauphine,
      and Caravelle............................. 88
   Disc Brake Service—Caravelle "S" and R-8... 90

1
Troubleshooting

Troubleshooting is done before a unit is disassembled so that the mechanic can give the car owner an estimate of the cost of the repair job. It helps the mechanic to pinpoint the trouble so that he will know what to look for as the unit is being disassembled. Then, too, troubleshooting will frequently cut down on the amount of time spent on repair, provided that the defective section can be pinpointed accurately.

BASIC STARTING TROUBLE TESTS

When an engine is difficult to start, or does not start at all, it is necessary to use a logical procedure to locate the trouble. Basically, the problem of hard starting can be broken down into four areas of trouble: cranking, ignition, fuel, and compression. The tests are made in that order, as shown on the roadmap.

When the trouble is localized to one of these four areas, the mechanic can then proceed to make one of the more detailed tests described for each area in order to locate the exact source of trouble.

THE CRANKING SYSTEM (TEST 1)

Turn on the ignition switch and energize the starting motor. If the starting motor cranks the engine at a normal rate of speed, it is an indication that the battery, cables, starting switch, and starting motor are in good shape. A defective cranking system is evidenced by failure of the cranking motor to spin the engine at a normal rate of speed.

If the cranking system is operating satisfactorily, go on to the second test, the ignition system. If it is not operating properly, proceed to the more Detailed Tests of the cranking system which follow this section in order to isolate the trouble.

THE IGNITION SYSTEM (TEST 2)

Disconnect one spark plug wire and hold it about ¼" (12 mm.) from the plug terminal while cranking the engine with the ignition switch turned on. A good, constantly occurring spark to the plug means that the ignition system is in good shape. No spark, a weak spark, or an irregularly occurring one means ignition trouble.

If the ignition system is operating satisfactorily, go on to the third test, the fuel system. If it is not operating properly, proceed to the more Detailed Tests of the ignition system which follow this section in order to isolate the trouble.

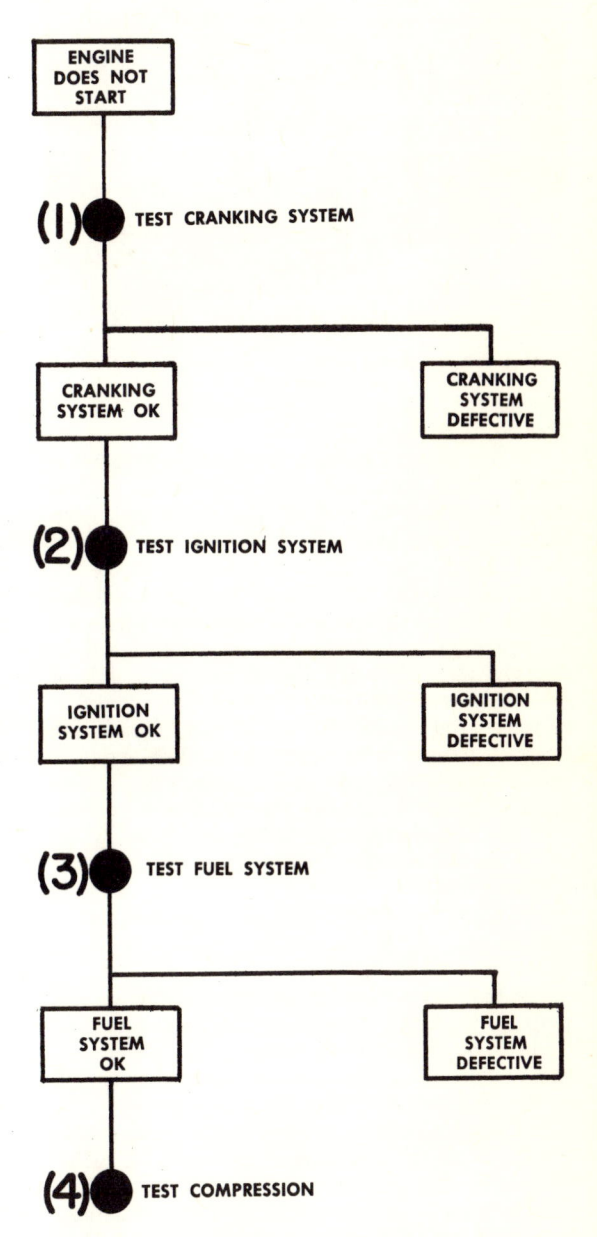

Roadmap for emergency troubleshooting when an engine does not start. The four numbered tests are referred to in the text.

2 Troubleshooting

Testing the ignition system for a spark to the spark plug terminal.

that it can almost be ruled out as a condition causing starting trouble.

DETAILED STARTING TROUBLE TESTS

The more detailed tests which follow are to isolate the starting trouble in the defective system located by the first series of tests. Each of the four general areas of trouble is broken down further to tests of individual components. In this manner, the exact part causing the trouble can be located and replaced.

CRANKING SYSTEM

The cranking system consists of a battery, cables, starting switch, and the starting motor. Failure of the starting motor to spin the engine, or turning it too slowly, is an indication of a defect in one of the above parts.

Battery (Test 1). The battery supplies electric current for the starting motor, lights, ignition, and other electrical accessories. If the starting motor spins the engine at a fairly good rate of speed and then rapidly slows down, the battery is discharged. Turn on the lights while cranking the engine. If the lights go out, the battery is discharged. There is not enough current in a partially charged battery to supply both the starting motor and the lighting system.

A 6-volt battery with a defective cell (shorted separator) usually will not turn the starting motor at all, although it may do so for a very short period if the battery has been charged by a recent run of the engine. If such a battery is allowed to

The Fuel System (Test 3)

Remove the air cleaner to uncover the carburetor throat. Then open and close the throttle several times. A stream of fuel will be discharged from the accelerating jet if the fuel system is in good shape. No discharge indicates that there is no fuel in the carburetor, which means trouble in the fuel system. In rare instances, the carburetor accelerating system may be defective and no fuel will be discharged even though the carburetor is full of gasoline. Usually there is a decided resistance to movement of the throttle when such a condition exists. On some carburetors, there is no acceleration pump; in this case, it is necessary to remove the float bowl cover to see whether fuel is present.

If the fuel system is operating satisfactorily, go on to the fourth test, compression. If it is not operating properly, proceed to the more Detailed Tests of the fuel system to isolate the trouble.

Compression (Test 4)

Compression can be checked by removing a spark plug and holding a thumb over the spark plug hole while the engine is being cranked. Good compression produces a distinct pressure under your thumb as the piston rises to the top of its stroke.

Failure of an engine to start due to compression trouble is rarely encountered in the field. Most frequently, compression trouble will show up as defects in but one or two cylinders. No compression in all cylinders of an engine may occur from improper mating of the timing gears when the engine is rebuilt. It can happen on the road through jumping of a loose timing chain or the snapping of a camshaft—but this is so infrequently the case

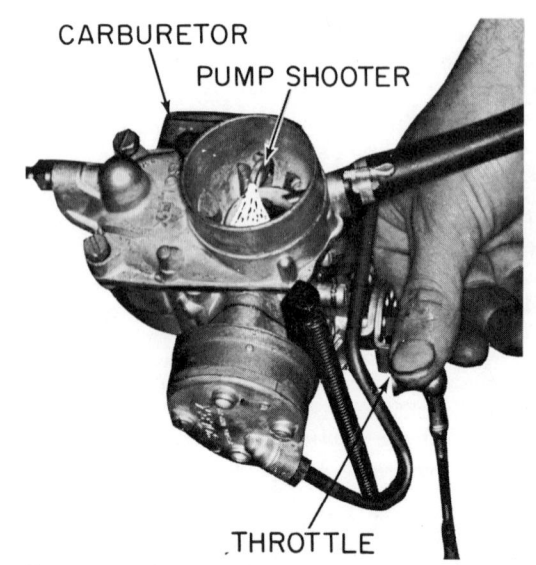

Testing the fuel system. If there is fuel in the carburetor, it can be seen as a discharge from the pump jet. Generally, it is not necessary to remove the top of the carburetor, because the fuel stream can be seen through the choke bore.

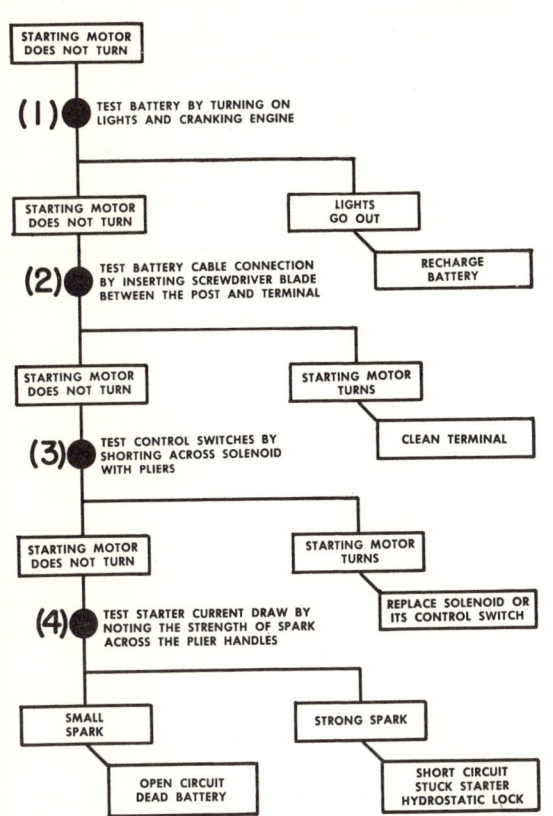

The Cranking System

Roadmap for emergency troubleshooting of the cranking system when the starting motor does not turn. The four numbered tests are referred to in the text.

Testing a cable connection by inserting a screwdriver blade between the battery terminal and the cable connector (Test 2). If the terminal is corroded, the screwdriver blade will make contact between the two parts of the connection and the cranking motor will operate.

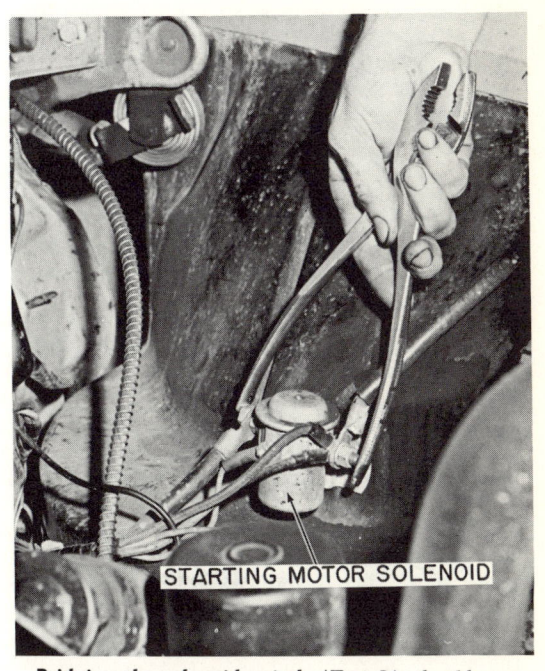

Bridging the solenoid switch (Test 3) should cause the starting motor to operate unless the trouble is in the starting motor itself.

stand for a short time, it will lose this surface charge. A 12-volt battery may operate the starting motor with a defective cell, but it will not spin the starting motor fast enough, and starting troubles will result.

Battery Cables (Test 2). Quite frequently, a bad connection between the battery post and the battery cable will show up as a dead battery. To check this condition, insert a screwdriver blade between the battery post and the cable while having an assistant operate the starting motor switch. Try the blade on each terminal connection. Now, if the starting motor turns, evidently the connection is bad. It should be cleaned by removing the cable terminal and scraping it and the battery post until clean metal appears. Then replace and tighten the terminal securely.

Switches (Test 3). A defective switch in the starting circuit can be checked by bridging each switch in turn with a jumper wire or a pair of plier handles. Bridging the solenoid switch by-passes all other control switches and should energize the starting motor regardless of any other defect in the starting motor control circuit. Use a heavy piece of wire for this test as a thin one will become very hot

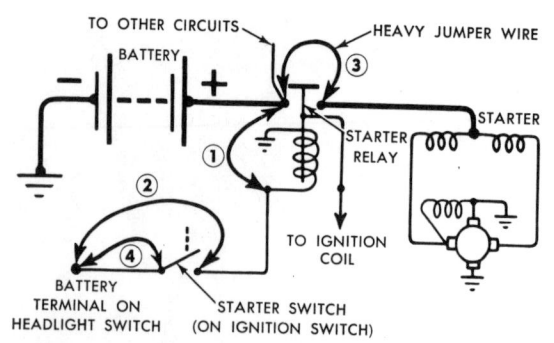

Troubleshooting

Use a jumper wire to bridge each switch in turn to find an open circuit in the starting motor control system.

from the large amount of current drawn through this circuit. Holding a hot wire may cause a serious hand injury.

If the starting motor does not operate with the solenoid switch shorted, and a fully charged battery, then the trouble must be in the starting motor itself.

Starting Motor (Test 4). The size of the spark across the plier handles in the previous test is an indication of the kind of trouble to be expected. If there is a heavy spark across the handles of the pliers, and the starting motor does not turn, it is possible that the starting motor is stuck to the flywheel, the starting motor has a short circuit, or there is a hydrostatic lock in the engine.

If there is little or no spark across the plier handles as they are moved across the solenoid switch terminals, there is an open circuit present with little or no electricity flowing. This condition can be caused by a dead battery, a poor battery terminal connection, or poor connections at the starting motor brushes due to a burned commutator or one with oil on it. If the starting motor spins, but does not crank the engine, the starting motor drive is defective.

IGNITION SYSTEM

The ignition system furnishes the electric spark which fires the mixture. Absence of a spark, or a weak spark, will cause starting trouble. Ignition troubles should be isolated by logical testing. For this purpose, the system is broken down into its smaller circuits: primary and secondary. Each of these should be broken down further and individual components tested separately.

To Test the Entire Ignition System. Remove one spark plug wire and hold it about ½" (12 mm.) away from the base of the spark plug or any metallic part of the engine. Crank the engine with the ignition switch turned on. A good spark from the wire to the metal means that the entire ignition system is in good working order. No spark, or a weak, irregularly occurring spark, means ignition trouble which must be traced by means of the following tests:

To Test the Primary Circuit (Test 1). Loosen the distributor cap retaining bails and move the cap to one side. Remove the rotor. Turn the engine over by means of the fan belt or starting motor until the contact points close. Turn on the ignition switch. Remove the high tension wire leading to the center of the distributor cap; this is the main wire from the ignition coil which supplies the high voltage to the rotor for distribution to the spark plugs. Hold this wire about ½" (12 mm.) from any metallic part of the engine. Open and close the contact points with a screwdriver. Hold the screwdriver against the movable point only as shown. A good, regularly occurring spark from the high tension wire to ground means a good primary circuit and a good ignition coil. No spark, or a weak erratic one, from the high tension wire to ground means primary circuit trouble or a bad ignition coil.

To Test the Ignition Contact Points (Test 2). To test the condition of the ignition contact set, turn the engine over with the fan belt or starting motor until the contact points are separated. Slide

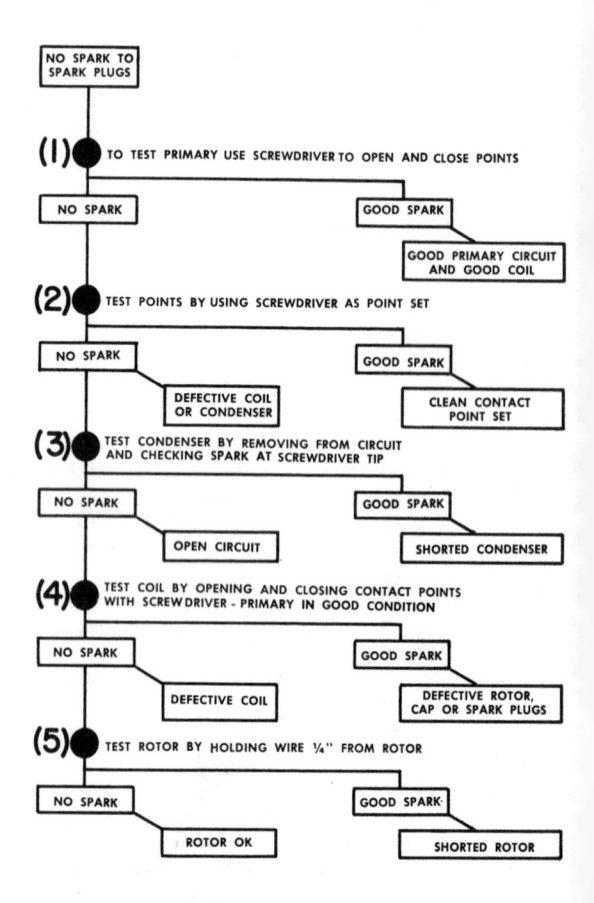

Roadmap for emergency troubleshooting of the ignition system. The five numbered tests are referred to in the text.

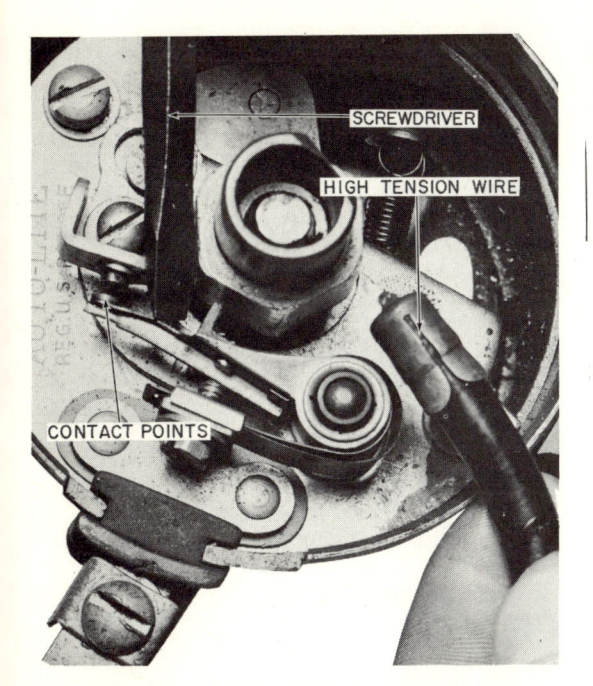

The Ignition System 5

Opening and closing the ignition points with a screwdriver (Test 1), while holding the main high tension wire close to a metallic part of the engine, is a simple test of the primary circuit efficiency.

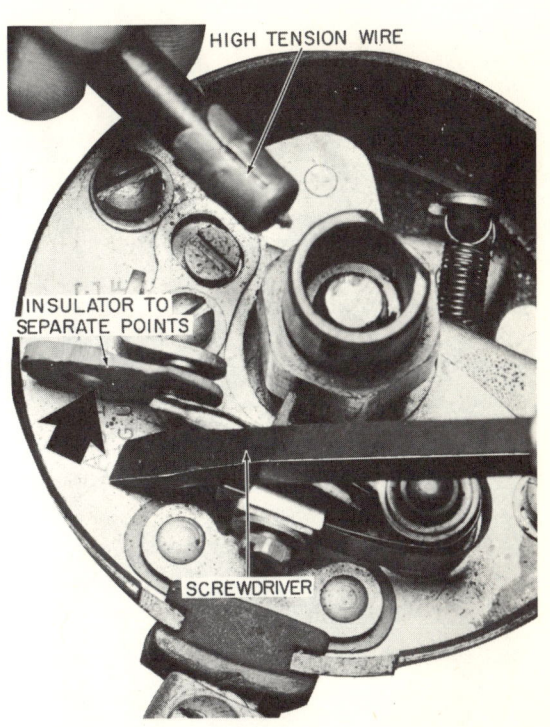

Using the screwdriver as a set of points (Test 2). Use a cleaned insulator (arrow) to keep the points apart, and then slide the screwdriver blade up and down to make intermittent contact with the point plate.

the screwdriver blade up and down, making contact between the movable point and the bottom plate of the distributor, as shown. You are now using the screwdriver tip and the bottom plate of the distributor as a set of contact points. A good spark from the high tension wire to the ground, after having had no spark in Test 1, means that you have a defective set of contact points. No spark, or a weak one, means primary circuit trouble, other than the ignition contact points, or a bad ignition coil.

To Test the Condenser (Test 3). A shorted condenser can be checked by noting, in the previous ignition contact point test (Test 2), whether or not the tip of the screwdriver blade sparked against the ground plate as it was slid up and down. No spark at the tip of the blade means either a shorted condenser or a break in the primary circuit.

This can be checked further by disconnecting the condenser case where it is screwed to the distributor (do not disconnect the condenser wire lead). Hold the condenser so that its case does not make contact with any metallic part of the distributor. Repeat the test of moving the screwdriver blade up and down while holding it against the movable point. Be sure that the contact points are open while making this test. A spark at the screwdriver tip now, which was not present with the condenser in the circuit, means that the condenser is shorted out.

No spark at the screwdriver tip with the con-

A sample of good ignition contact points (top), and a bad set (bottom) for comparison. A light gray contact surface is indicative of a set of contact points working at high efficiency. The lower set is burned black from either high voltage or oil.

Troubleshooting

A broken primary lead may not show up until you pull on it. The insulation hides the damage.

denser out of the circuit means that there is an open circuit somewhere in the primary. Check the small wire lead from the primary terminal to the movable contact point. This wire lead sometimes parts under the constant flexing of operation.

To Test the Secondary Circuit (Test 4). The secondary circuit cannot be tested until the primary circuit is functioning perfectly. If the primary circuit tests good, or after the necessary repairs have been made to the primary circuit, then the secondary circuit can be tested.

To test the secondary circuit, turn the engine over until the contact points close. Then turn on the ignition switch. Hold the main high tension wire (from the center terminal of the distributor cap) about ½″ (12 mm.) from any metallic part of the engine. Open and close the contact points with a screwdriver blade held against the movable contact point only. No spark, or a weak one, from the wire to the block (*with a good primary circuit*), means a bad ignition coil or a defective main high tension wire from the coil to the distributor (especially where it runs through metal conduit). A good spark here (with no spark to the spark plugs) means that the trouble must be in the distributor cap, rotor, or spark plugs. It is seldom that spark plug high tension wires (unless obviously rotted) will keep an engine from starting. To check the main high tension wire, from the coil to the center of the distributor cap, replace it with a new piece of high tension wire, or remove the old wire from the metal conduit and repeat Test 4 while keeping the suspected wire away from any grounded surface.

To Test the Distributor Rotor (Test 5). Test the distributor rotor by replacing it on the distributor shaft and holding the main high tension wire (from the coil) about ¼″ (6 mm.) from the top of the rotor. With the ignition switch turned on, crank the engine with the starter. If the high tension spark jumps to the rotor, it is grounded (defective); if not, the cap must be defective. Inspect the cap for carbon tracks which indicate the passing of high voltage electricity.

FUEL SYSTEM

The purpose of the fuel system is to bring a combustible mixture of gasoline and air into the cylinders. The fuel system consists of the fuel tank, the fuel pump, and the carburetor. Troubles in the fuel system can be caused by too little fuel in the combustion chambers—or too much.

A cracked distributor cap always shows these characteristic carbon tracks. A crack between two terminals will cause misfiring, but a crack from the center terminal to the outside will prevent the engine from starting. Cracks often start from moisture on the surface of the insulating material.

The Fuel System 7

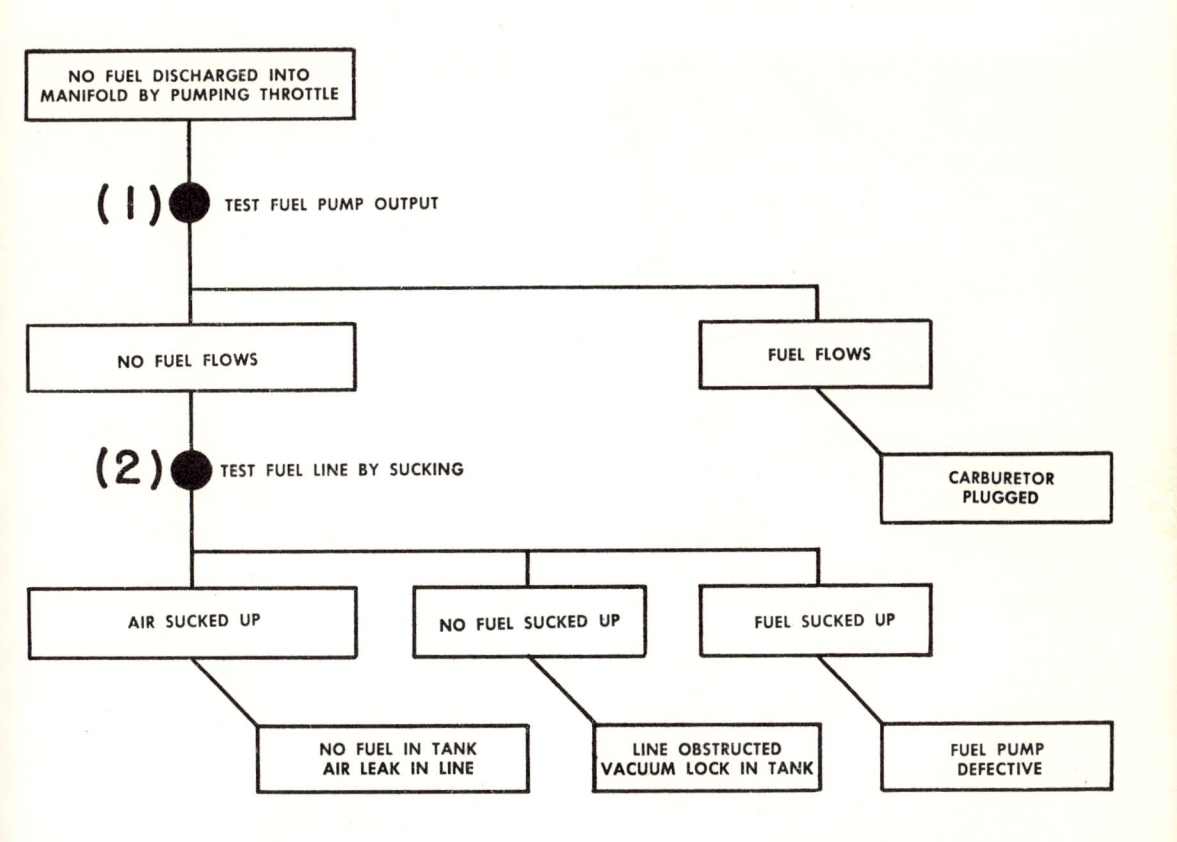

Roadmap for emergency troubleshooting of the fuel system. The two numbered tests are referred to in the text.

Too Little Fuel: TESTING THE FUEL PUMP OUTPUT (TEST 1). Disconnect the fuel line leading into the carburetor bowl and hold a container under the line to catch the gasoline as it spurts from the open end. (The ignition switch should be off; otherwise, the high tension wire should be removed from the center of the distributor cap to prevent the possibility of the engine starting and spraying gasoline all over the engine compartment.) If a good size stream of fuel flows from the pipe, and the trouble has been isolated to the fuel system, the defect must be in the carburetor. If no fuel flows, the trouble must be in the pump, lines, or gas tank.

Some European-built cars have an electric fuel pump, in which case it is necessary only to disconnect the fuel line and turn on the ignition switch for testing purposes.

It is seldom that the carburetor itself causes starting trouble. Instances have been found of an inlet strainer plugged, or the float valve needle stuck in the closed position, but these are exceptions. Cases of an automatic choke not functioning are encountered more frequently in starting trouble. If the automatic choke does not close on a cold engine being cranked, hold your hand over the top of the carburetor bore to restrict the flow

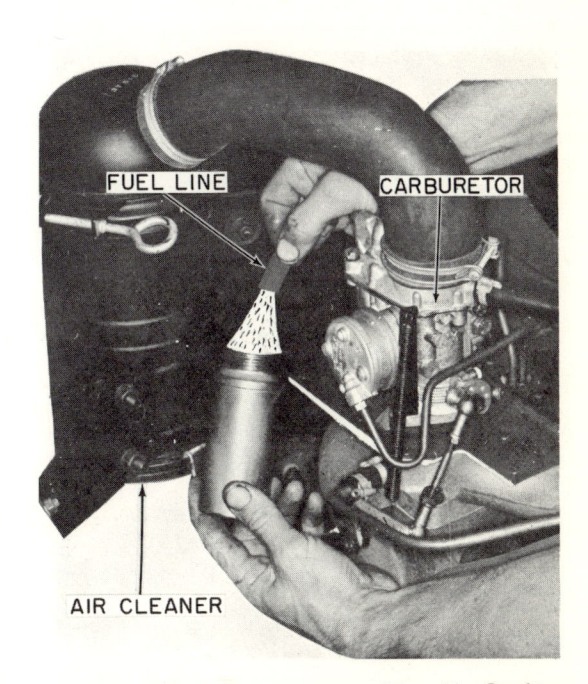

Testing the fuel pump output (Test 1). Cranking the engine with the starting motor should produce a full-sized stream of fuel each time the pump pulses.

Troubleshooting

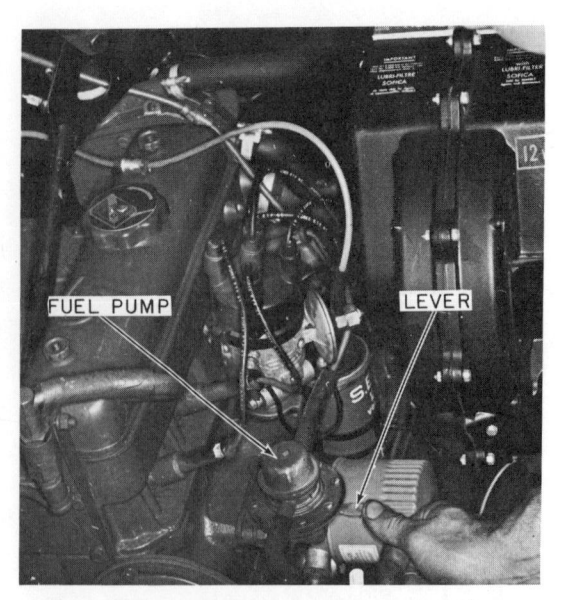

Some fuel pumps have levers to prime the carburetor in the event that you run out of fuel. The lever can also be used to test the fuel pump.

of air, which will assist in starting the engine. Where the choke sticks in the closed position, it can be opened with your fingers and held open until the engine is firing properly.

TO TEST THE GAS TANK AND LINES (TEST 2). To check the gas tank and lines, the fuel line should be disconnected at the inlet side of the fuel pump and sucked on to check for obstructions. Sucking on this line should bring up a mouthful of liquid fuel if there are no defects in the line or tank. Be sure to empty your mouth immediately and wash it out with water, if possible. If liquid fuel can be sucked up, and there is no flow out of the fuel pump, then the fuel pump is defective and must be repaired or replaced.

If only air is obtained by sucking on the line, then there is no fuel in the tank or there is an air leak in the line, probably at the flexible line leading into the fuel pump. If sucking on the line feels solid, and no fuel can be drawn up, the trouble is due to an obstruction in the line or a plugged gas tank vent.

Too Much Fuel. Too much fuel can be caused by overchoking, a defective float, or a defective needle and seat in the carburetor allowing fuel to by-pass the needle and overflow into the intake manifold. This can be seen as a steady stream of raw gasoline coming out of the main jet when the engine is being cranked. Raw gasoline may also enter the intake manifold in excessive amounts when the engine is stopped after a very hard and prolonged pull. In this case, the heat developed by the engine may cause the fuel to boil within the float chamber of the carburetor and percolate over the top of the main delivery tube into the intake manifold. Some carburetors are vented to prevent this possibility, but there are times when this vent is not functioning properly. Excessive amounts of raw gasoline can be seen by opening the throttle fully and looking down into the intake manifold through the carburetor bore.

Sometimes black smoke coming from the exhaust pipe while the engine is being started is another sign of too much fuel. The best test, however, is the removal of a spark plug. An overchoked engine will have spark plugs wet with raw gasoline while a normal engine will have dry spark plugs.

To start an engine which has been overloaded with fuel, it is necessary first to remedy the condition causing the trouble, and then the engine can be started by opening the throttle fully, which opens the choke. Under no circumstances should the throttle be pumped, as this will force additional quantities of raw fuel into the intake manifold.

TROUBLESHOOTING THE MECHANICAL PARTS OF THE ENGINE

Troubleshooting is performed before the engine is disassembled so that the mechanic can give the car owner an estimate of the cost of the repair job before work is started. This troubleshooting mate-

The spark plugs of an overchoked engine will be wet with fuel.

The Mechanical Parts of the Engine

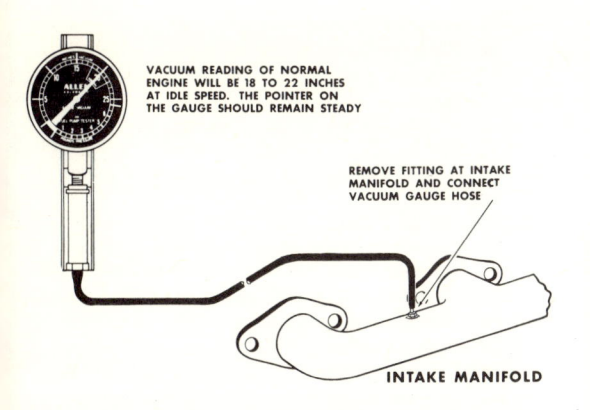

A vacuum gauge is a very important testing device. It is connected to the intake manifold.

rial will also be useful in assisting a mechanic to solve those few minor defects which sometimes occur after a reconditioning job, even after meticulous care has been taken in rebuilding the engine. In most cases, it is just some little thing causing the engine to lose power, overheat, knock, pump oil, or lose compression.

Two very important gauges are needed to locate mechanical engine defects: a vacuum and a compression gauge. The vacuum gauge measures the amount of vacuum in the intake manifold and is an excellent indicator of the over-all efficiency of the engine. Many engine mechanical defects can be identified with a vacuum gauge. The compression gauge is used to identify the exact cylinder in which a compression defect exists.

USING A VACUUM GAUGE

The vacuum gauge is connected to the intake manifold through the windshield wiper hose fitting. The engine should be run until it is at operating temperature and then idled to obtain a reading.

CORRECTIONS. A vacuum gauge indicates the difference between the pressure inside the intake manifold and the atmospheric pressure outside. It is calibrated in inches of mercury (Hg). Consequently, the reading will be affected by any variation in atmospheric pressure, such as altitude and weather conditions; therefore, the most important thing about a vacuum gauge is the action of the needle rather than a theoretical numerical reading. Generally speaking, the vacuum gauge reading will be 1″ lower for each 1000′ of elevation.

NORMAL ENGINE. A normal engine will show a gauge reading of 18″–22″ Hg with the pointer steady. Eight-cylinder engines will read toward the high side whereas 6- and 4-cylinder engines will read closer to the low side. On many later model cars, with overlapping valve timing, the gauge needle will fluctuate widely. To overcome this, many gauges have a constrictor valve which can be adjusted until the fluctuations are reduced to the width of the pointer tip. On gauges without this valve, the hose can be pinched until the undesirable fluctuations cease.

LEAKING VALVE. If a valve is leaking, the pointer will drop from 1″–7″ at regular intervals whenever the defective valve attempts to close during idle.

STICKING VALVE. A sticking valve is indicated by a rapid, intermittent drop each time the valve is supposed to close when the engine is idling. A sticky valve condition can be pinpointed by applying a small amount of penetrating oil or lacquer thinner to each guide in turn. When the sticky valve is reached, the situation will be remedied temporarily.

WEAK OR BROKEN VALVE SPRING. If the pointer fluctuates rapidly between 10″–22″ Hg at 2,000 rpm, and the fluctuations increase as engine speed is increased, weak valve springs are indicated. If a valve spring is broken, the pointer will fluctuate rapidly every time the valve attempts to close at idle.

WORN VALVE GUIDES. Worn valve guides admit air which upsets carburetion. The vacuum gauge reading will be lower than normal with fluctuations of about 3″ Hg on each side of normal when the engine is idling.

PISTON RING DEFECTS. Open the throttle and allow the engine to pick up speed to about 2,000 rpm, and then close the throttle quickly. The pointer should jump from about 2″–5″ Hg or more above the normal reading if the rings are in good condition. A lower gain should be investigated by making a compression test to localize trouble.

BLOWN CYLINDER HEAD GASKET. The pointer will drop sharply 10″ Hg from a normal reading and return each time the defective cylinders reach firing position with the engine idling.

INCORRECT IDLE AIR-FUEL MIXTURE. When the needle drifts slowly back and forth on idle, the fuel mixture is too rich. A lean mixture will cause an irregular drop of the needle.

INTAKE MANIFOLD AIR LEAKS. If there are any air leaks in the induction system, the needle will drop from 3″–9″ Hg below normal with the engine idling, but will remain quite steady.

RESTRICTED EXHAUST SYSTEM. Open the throttle until about 2,000 rpm is reached. Close the throttle quickly. If there is no excessive back pressure, the pointer will drop to not less than 2″, increase to 25″ Hg, and then return to normal quickly. If the gauge does not register 5″ Hg or more above the normal reading, and the needle seems to stop momentarily in its return, the exhaust system is partially restricted.

LATE IGNITION TIMING. A low steady reading on idle indicates late ignition timing or a uniformly close setting of the tappet adjustments. The timing must never be set with a vacuum gauge; use a timing light for accuracy.

LATE VALVE TIMING. A steady but very low

Troubleshooting

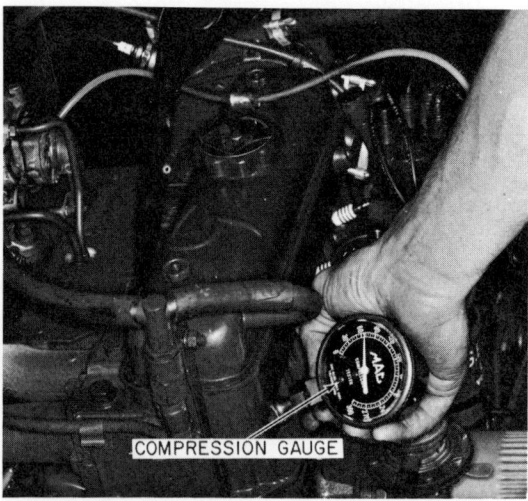

A compression gauge is important for checking the valve and ring condition. In practice, an equal number of pulses are recorded.

reading is generally caused by late ignition timing or late valve timing. If advancing the ignition timing does not increase the gauge reading to normal, then the valve timing is out of adjustment.

USING A COMPRESSION GAUGE

Another very important engine testing gauge is the compression tester. It measures the pressure within the cylinder in pounds per square inch (psi). As with the vacuum gauge, the theoretical numerical reading is not so important as the variation between cylinders. The cylinder pressures should not vary over 15 psi; otherwise, the engine cannot be tuned properly. Variations cause uneven idling and loss of power.

To use the gauge, remove all the spark plugs and insert the rubber tip into each spark plug hole in turn. With the throttle held wide open, crank the engine to obtain about 6 power impulses on the gauge; record the reading. Do this at each cylinder and compare the results. Generally, modern high-compression engines have a reading close to 175 psi. If one cylinder is low, insert a tablespoonful of heavy oil on top of the piston. Turn the engine over several times to work the oil around the piston rings, and then repeat the test. If the pressure shows a decided increase, there is a compression loss past the piston and rings. If the pressure does not increase, the valves are seating improperly. A defective cylinder head gasket will show a loss of compression in two adjacent cylinders.

LOW-COMPRESSION TROUBLESHOOTING CHART

TROUBLES & CAUSES

1. **Valves**
   1a. Insufficient tappet clearance
   1b. Sticking valves
   1c. Warped heads or bent stems
   1d. Burned, pitted, or distorted valve faces and seats
   1e. Weak or broken valve springs
   1f. Distortion of cylinder head and/or block caused by uneven tightening of the bolts
   1g. Incorrect valve timing
2. **Pistons and rings**
   2a. Excessive clearance between pistons and cylinder walls
   2b. Eccentric or tapered cylinder bores
   2c. Scored cylinder walls
   2d. Scored pistons
   2e. Broken pistons
   2f. Scuffed rings
   2g. Insufficient piston ring end gaps
   2h. Stuck piston rings
   2i. Binding of rings due to "set" caused by mechanic overstretching during installation
   2j. Insufficient piston ring-to-wall tension due to weak expanders
   2k. Ring lands worn unevenly
   2l. Ring grooves too deep for the expanders used
   2m. Standard rings installed in oversize bores
   2n. Top rings running dry because oil control rings are too severe
   2o. Top rings running dry because of gasoline dilution caused by stuck manifold heat control
   2p. Abrasive dust left in cylinder bores from honing or grinding valves
3. **Gaskets**
   3a. Warped head and/or block
   3b. Blown-out cylinder head gasket
   3c. Cylinder head bolts tightened unevenly
   3d. Incorrect type of gasket

TROUBLESHOOTING FOR EXCESSIVE OIL CONSUMPTION

Oil can be consumed in the combustion chamber or lost through leaks. If the engine is actually burning oil, a blue-gray smoke will emerge from the exhaust pipe whenever the engine is accelerated, especially after it has idled for a short period of time. Fouled spark plugs are a good indication that oil is being burned in the combustion chambers.

Oil can pass into the combustion areas in only 3 ways: it can go past the piston rings, past the valve guides, or it can pass through a defective crankcase ventilation system. Leaks can be caused by defective or improperly installed gaskets, by excessive crankcase pressures caused by blow-by, or by plugging of the crankcase ventilating system. Unless the vents are clean, blow-by pressures can force enough oil vapors from the crankcase to cause a noticeable increase in oil consumption.

OIL LEAKS

Fresh oil on any engine housing usually washes the dirt from that part and is an excellent indication that oil is leaking from that area. Washed

For Excessive Oil Consumption

Oil leaks can be pinpointed by mixing a special fluorescent powder with the oil, and then shining a blacklight under the pan to locate the source of the leak.

1. **Piston and ring defects**
   1a. Piston improperly fitted or finished
   1b. Snaky piston ring grooves
   1c. Ring grooves worn overwidth or flared
   1d. Insufficient number of drain holes in oil ring grooves
   1e. Drain holes in oil ring grooves too small
   1f. Piston and connecting rod assembly out of alignment
   1g. Excessive clearance between piston and cylinder bore
   1h. Badly worn or collapsed pistons
   1i. Scuffed rings
   1j. Improper seating of rings in grooves
   1k. Insufficient clearance at ring gap
   1l. Insufficient ring tension
   1m. Out-of-round rings from improper installation
   1n. Warped or twisted rings from improper installation
   1o. Not enough side clearance between rings and grooves
   1p. Compression rings installed upside down
   1q. Wrong size rings
   1r. Insufficient ventilation in oil rings
   1s. Slots in oil rings clogged
2. **Bearing defects**
   2a. Scored rod bearings
   2b. Spurt holes in rods with worn bearings adding to excessive bearing throw-off
   2c. Worn crankshaft throws
   2d. Worn main bearing oil seals
   2e. Excessive clearance
3. **Valve guide defects**
   3a. Worn valve guides
   3b. Intake valve guides installed upside down
   3c. Valve stem oil seals incorrectly installed or worn
4. **Cylinder bore defects**
   4a. Excessively worn, tapered, or out-of-round cylinder bores
   4b. Wavy cylinder bores caused by heat distortion or uneven tightening of head bolts
   4c. Ring ledge at top or bottom of cylinder bore
   4d. Scored cylinder bores

areas on the ventilator side of the chassis usually are caused by oil being blown or sucked out of the crankcase. It is surprising just how much oil can be lost through a small leak. One drop of oil every hundred feet causes an oil loss of a quart per thousand miles. Note how the center of each driving lane is covered with oil from external leaks, and you will realize the need for checking this loss. Note that these drippings are much heavier on an upgrade due to blow-by pressures forcing the oil through defective gaskets and bearings.

CRANKCASE VENTILATOR

On road-draft type crankcase ventilating systems, clogged inlet breather caps and plugged vents in the outlet tube increase the crankcase pressures and so contribute to oil leaks.

Where a positive-type crankcase ventilating system is used, clogging of the metering valve, located in the line between the crankcase and the intake manifold, will cause crankcase pressure to increase, which will force the oil out from around the pan gaskets and oil seals. If the valve sticks open, large quantities of oil vapors will be drawn into the combustion areas under high-vacuum operating conditions with resulting high oil consumption.

Since oil can be lost in any combination of the above ways, it is necessary for the mechanic to examine the engine carefully before it is disassembled. After disassembly has started, it is much more difficult to check many of these things.

EXCESSIVE OIL CONSUMPTION TROUBLE-SHOOTING CHART

TROUBLES & CAUSES

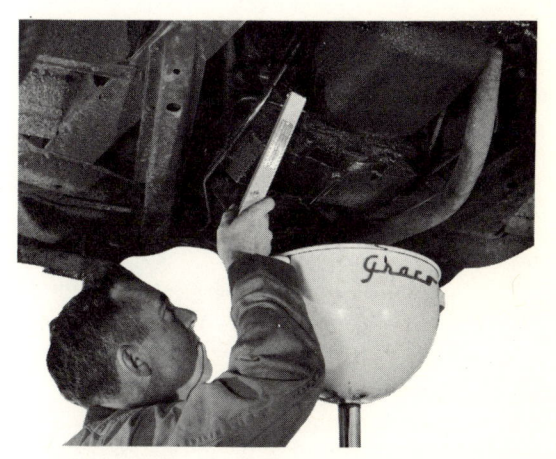

The blacklight is moved about until the source of the leak is located by a glow as the lamp causes the oil to fluoresce.

12 Troubleshooting

    4e. Rough finish on cylinder walls causing rapid ring wear
    4f. Cylinder block out of alignment with crankshaft
5. **Crankcase defects**
    5a. Main bearing oil return pipe clogged
    5b. Oil level too high
    5c. Broken pipe in oil line spraying oil into cylinder bores
    5d. Clogged breather pipe
    5e. Stuck valve in positive-type crankcase ventilating system
    5f. Excessive crankcase pressures caused by blow-by
    5g. Improper reading of dip stick (not pushed in fully)

TROUBLESHOOTING FOR ENGINE NOISES

One of the more difficult problems facing the mechanic is the locating of foreign noises. Engine noises vary in intensity and frequency, depending on their source. It is difficult to describe engine noises with mere words. Experience will have to be built up using the descriptions which follow as a guide.

The only tools which the mechanic has to help him locate the source of an engine noise are a screwdriver to short out spark plugs and a stethoscope or listening rod to carry the sound directly to his ear.

CRANKSHAFT KNOCKS

Noises classified as crankshaft knocks are usually dull, heavy metallic knocks which increase in frequency as the speed and load on the engine are increased. Or they may become more noticeable at extremely low speed when the engine is idling unevenly.

The most common crankshaft knock, due to excessive clearance, is usually apparent as an audible "bump" under the following conditions: when the engine is pulling hard, when an engine is started, during acceleration, or at speeds above 35 mph (56 km./h.). If excessive clearance exists at only one or two of the crankshaft journals, the "bump" will be less frequent and less pronounced. Usually, alternate short circuiting of each spark plug will determine the approximate location of a loose bearing.

Excessive crankshaft end-play causes a sharp rap to occur at irregular intervals, usually at idling speeds, and, in bad cases, can be detected by the alternate release and engagement of the clutch. To detect a loose flywheel, advance the engine idle to a road speed equivalent to 15 mph (24 km./h.). Turn off the ignition switch and, when the engine has almost stopped, turn the switch on again. If this operation is repeated several times and if, of course, the flywheel is loose, one distinct knock will be noted each time the switch is turned on.

CONNECTING ROD BEARING NOISES

Connecting rod bearing noises are usually a light rap or clatter of much less intensity than main bearing knocks. The noise is most audible when the engine is "floating" or running with a light load at approximately 25 mph (40 km./h.). The noise becomes louder as engine speed is increased. Connecting rod bearing knocks can be located best by grounding out each of the spark plugs, one at a time. Generally, the noise cannot be eliminated entirely by a short circuit, but ordinarily will be reduced considerably in intensity.

PISTON NOISES

The commonest piston noise is a slap due to the rocking of the piston from side to side in the cylinder. Although, in some engines, piston slap causes a clicking noise, usually it is a hollow, muffled, bell-like sound. Slight piston noises that occur when the engine is cold, and disappear after the engine is warm, do not ordinarily warrant correction. Piston ring noises generally cause a click, a snap, or a sharp rattle on acceleration.

Short circuit each spark plug in turn to locate piston and ring noises. As this test will affect other engine noises, sometimes the result is confusing. To detect piston slap more accurately, drive the car at low speeds under a load. The noise generally increases in intensity as the throttle is opened and additional load applied. On some engines, with very loose pistons, a piston rattle is encountered at speeds between 30–50 mph (48–80 km./h.) when the engine is not being accelerated.

To eliminate piston and ring noises momentarily, put 1–2 oz. (25–50 gr.) of very heavy engine oil into each cylinder through the spark plug hole. Crank the engine for several revolutions with the ignition switch turned off until the oil works itself down past the piston rings. Then install the spark plugs, start the engine, and determine whether or not the noise still exists.

A stethoscope or a listening rod is handy to locate the source of engine noises.

For Engine Noises

PISTON PIN NOISES

The commonest piston pin noise is the result of excessive piston pin clearance. This causes a sharp, metallic, double-knock, generally audible with the engine idling. On some engines, however, the noise is more noticeable at car speeds of 25–35 mph (40–56 km./h.). Interference between the upper end of the connecting rod and the pin boss (bossing) is difficult to diagnose and can be mistaken for a valve lifter noise.

To test for piston pin noises, allow the engine to run at idle speed. In most cases, a sharp metallic double-knock will become more evident when the spark plug, in the cylinder with the loose piston pin, is shorted out. Retarding the spark will generally reduce the intensity of the knock. If the pins in all pistons are loose, a metallic rattle, which is impossible to short out in any one cylinder, will be heard.

VALVE MECHANISM NOISES

Noisy valve mechanism has a characteristic clicking sound occurring at regular intervals. Inasmuch as the valves are operating at half crankshaft speed, the frequency of valve action noise is generally lower than that of other engine noises.

To determine whether the noise is due to excessive valve clearance, insert a feeler gauge between the valve stem and the rocker arm or tappet. If the noise stops, the clearance is probably excessive and the adjusting screw should be adjusted. Never reduce the clearance to below factory specification or the valve will burn.

A sticky valve will cause a clicking sound similar to a loose tappet adjustment which comes and goes according to driving conditions. A sticky valve can be detected by driving the car hard until the engine is well heated. Then quickly allow the engine to idle. If there is a sticky valve, the clicking will become quite pronounced but will lessen gradually and sometimes disappear as the engine returns to normal operating temperature. The noise is accompanied by a rhythmic jerk due to the misfiring cylinder. As the noise disappears, so does the jerk, and the engine will finally smooth out as the valve seats.

A loose timing gear generally can be detected by a sharp clatter at low engine speeds with an uneven idle. When testing for this condition, short circuit one or two spark plugs to produce the necessary rough idle.

SPARK KNOCK

Preignition, or spark knock, causes a metallic ringing sound, often described as a "ping." Usually, it is encountered when the engine is laboring, being accelerated rapidly, or is overheated. Preignition is caused by an incandescent particle of carbon or metal in the combustion chamber igniting the mixture prematurely while the piston is coming up on the compression stroke. This results in very heavy pressure being applied to the piston at the wrong time, causing the piston, the connecting rod, and the bearing to vibrate, and resulting in the sound known as "spark knock."

Detonation is caused most frequently by a fuel of too low an octane rating. It burns too rapidly, resulting in sudden and abnormal pressure against the piston.

ACCESSORY NOISES

Noises in the generator or water pump can be checked by removing the drive belt for a short operating period. If the noise remains, it is not in the generator or the water pump.

ENGINE NOISE TROUBLESHOOTING CHART

TROUBLES & CAUSES

1. **Crankshaft knocks**
   1a. Excessive bearing clearance
   1b. Excessive end-play
   1c. Eccentric or out-of-round journals
   1d. Sprung crankshaft
   1e. Bearing misalignment
   1f. Insufficient oil supply
   1g. Restricted oil supply to one main bearing
   1h. Low oil pressure
   1i. Badly diluted oil
   1j. Loose flywheel
   1k. Loose impulse neutralizer
   1l. Broken crankshaft web
2. **Connecting rod bearing knocks**
   2a. Excessive bearing clearance
   2b. Out-of-round crankpin journals
   2c. Misaligned connecting rods
   2d. Top of connecting rod bolt turned around and striking the camshaft
   2e. Insufficient oil supply
   2f. Low oil pressure
   2g. Badly diluted oil
3. **Piston noises**
   3a. Collapsed piston skirt
   3b. Excessive piston-to-cylinder bore clearance
   3c. Eccentric or tapered cylinder bores
   3d. Piston pin too tight
   3e. Connecting rod misalignment
   3f. Piston or rings hitting ridge at top of cylinder bore
   3g. Piston striking carbon accumulation at top of cylinder bore
   3h. Piston striking cylinder head gasket
   3i. Broken piston ring
   3j. Excessive side clearance between a ring and its groove
   3k. Piston pin hole out of square with the piston
   3l. Ring lands not properly relieved
4. **Piston pin noises**
   4a. Excessive piston pin clearance
   4b. Tight pin causing piston to slap

14 Troubleshooting

    4c. Piston pin rubbing against cylinder wall
    4d. Top end of connecting rod bossing
5. **Valve mechanism noises**
    5a. Excessive clearance between valve stem and tappet or rocker arm
    5b. Sticky valve
    5c. Excessive clearance between tappet and block
    5d. Lower end of lifter scored or broken
    5e. Tappet screw or rocker arm face pitted
    5f. Weak or broken valve spring
    5g. Inverted valve spring
    5h. Warped valve head
    5i. Valve seat not concentric with guide
    5j. Excessive stem-to-guide clearance
    5k. End of valve stem not faced square
    5l. Weak rocker arm spacer spring
    5m. Loose timing gear
6. **Spark knock**
    6a. Low octane fuel
    6b. Excessive carbon deposits
    6c. Ignition timed too early
    6d. Excessively lean air-fuel mixture
    6e. Weak automatic advance weight springs
    6f. Manifold heat control valve stuck in closed position
    6g. Spark plugs too hot
    6h. Burned spark plug porcelain
    6i. Sharp metallic edges in combustion chamber
    6j. Cylinder head gasket projecting into combustion chamber
    6k. Overheated valves
    6l. Excessive engine coolant temperatures
    6m. Loose fan belt
7. **Accessory noises**
    7a. Defective generator bearings
    7b. Loose generator drive pulley
    7c. Brushes not seating
    7d. Loose drive belt
    7e. Defective water pump bearings
    7f. Loose water pump drive pulley
    7g. Bent and out-of-balance fan

TROUBLESHOOTING FOR POOR PERFORMANCE DUE TO EXCESSIVE FRICTION

Excessive friction is a frequent contributing cause of power losses; tight rings are perhaps the greatest offender. In an attempt to stop oil pumping, severe expander springs are frequently used behind piston rings. These rings create such excessive cylinder wall friction that power and gas mileage drop amazingly. The best test of a tight engine is to hold the throttle open to an engine speed of approximately 1,000 rpm. Keep the accelerator pedal steady and shut off the ignition. Watch the fan blades to see whether or not the engine rocks as it comes to a stop. A tight engine will stop with a "jerk" while a normal engine will rock back and forth on compression.

EXCESSIVE-FRICTION TROUBLE-SHOOTING CHART

TROUBLES & CAUSES

1. **Engine conditions**
    1a. Piston ring expanders too severe
    1b. Piston expanders too severe
    1c. Piston slots not completed
    1d. Wrong cam grind on pistons
    1e. Insufficient piston-to-cylinder wall clearance
    1f. Insufficient piston ring end gap
    1g. Top ring lands not relieved
    1h. Too tight a bearing fit
2. **Miscellaneous conditions**
    2a. Dragging brakes
    2b. Tight wheel bearings
    2c. Misaligned wheels
    2d. Underinflated tires

TROUBLESHOOTING THE COOLING SYSTEM

The cooling system is thermostatically controlled in some engines to regulate the engine operating temperature to provide for a short warm-up period. Engine overheating and slow warm-up are the two engine troubles most commonly attributed to the cooling system.

OVERHEATING

Loss of coolant, the accumulation of rust and scale in the coolant chambers, and the passing of hot exhaust gases into the coolant through an internal leak are the main causes of overheating.

Loss of coolant can be checked visually by the red rust stains that often form around the leak area. Loss of coolant through an internal crack is often detected by noting the condition of the oil on the dip stick, where water bubbles will appear with the oil. A newly developed method of testing for coolant leaks is to pour a water-soluble dye into the radiator. The dye contains a fluorescent powder which turns green when exposed to a special test lamp's rays.

The source of water leaks can also be pinpointed by the use of a special fluorescent powder that can be added to the coolant. A blacklight is used to pick up the leak.

The Cooling System

By moving the special blacklight around, the exact point of the leak can be located.

TESTING FOR AN EXHAUST GAS LEAK

Start the test with a cold engine. Disconnect the fan belt so that the water pump does not operate. Disconnect the upper hose at the radiator. Drain the system until the water level is even with the top of the block. Remove the thermostat and replace the housing. Fill the radiator until the water reaches the top of the thermostat housing.

The object of this test is to place a load on the engine so that combustion chamber pressures approach maximum to force hot exhaust gases through any small leak that might exist.

To load the engine: jack up the rear wheels, start the engine, place the shift lever in high gear, open the accelerator wide with your right foot; at the same time apply the foot brakes with your left foot to hold the engine speed to about 20 mph (32 km./h.) road speed.

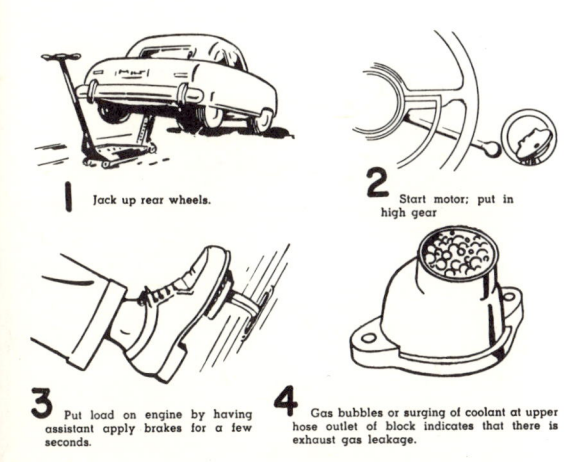

Gas bubbles or surging at the upper outlet indicate that exhaust gas is leaking into the cooling system. The test must be conducted quickly to prevent the coolant from boiling in the head.

Another method of testing the engine for leaks is to use a special radiator pressure pump. Drain some water until the level is about ½" (12 mm.) below the radiator neck. Attach the tester and apply 15 psi (1.0 kg./cm.^{2}) pressure. If the pressure drops, check all points for an exterior leak.

If you cannot locate an exterior leak after the gauge shows a drop in pressure, detach the tester and run the engine to normalize it. Reattach the tester and pump it to 7 psi (0.5 kg./cm.^{2}) while the engine is running. Race the engine and, if the dial fluctuates, it indicates a combustion leak. *CAUTION: Pressure builds up fast!* Never let the pressure exceed 15 psi (1.0 kg./cm.^{2}). Release excess pressure immediately!

COOLING SYSTEM TROUBLESHOOTING CHART

TROUBLES & CAUSES

1. **Overheating**
   - 1a. Insufficient coolant
   - 1b. Rust and scale formations in cooling system
   - 1c. Fan belt slipping
   - 1d. Defective water pump
   - 1e. Rusted-out distributor tube
   - 1f. Radiator or hoses clogged
   - 1g. Radiator air flow restricted
   - 1h. Thermostat stuck closed
2. **Engine fails to reach normal operating temperature**
   - 2a. Thermostat defective
   - 2b. Temperature sending unit defective
   - 2c. Temperature indicator defective
3. **Slow warm-up**
   - 3a. Thermostat defective
   - 3b. Manifold heat control stuck open
   - 3c. Automatic choke not closing properly

1. Jack up rear wheels.
2. Start motor; put in high gear
3. Put load on engine by having assistant apply brakes for a few seconds.
4. Gas bubbles or surging of coolant at upper hose outlet of block indicates that there is exhaust gas leakage.

To test for a crack in the block or head, which lets hot exhaust gases pass through the coolant, place a load on the engine and check for exhaust bubbles at the top water hose casting.

To check a cooling system for leaks, it can be pressurized by this special pump, and then the gauge can be checked to see whether the system holds the pressure.

16 Troubleshooting

4. Loss of coolant
  4a. Leaking radiator
  4b. Loose or damaged hose connections
  4c. Defective water pump
  4d. Cylinder head gasket defective or loose
  4e. Uneven tightening of cylinder head bolts
  4f. Cracked block or head
  4g. Pressure cap defective

TROUBLESHOOTING THE FUEL SYSTEM

The fuel system furnishes a combustible air-fuel mixture to each cylinder. Failure of the fuel system to function properly can result in various complaints: hard starting, poor performance, and excessive fuel consumption.

HARD STARTING

An engine may not start because of either too much or not enough fuel in the combustion chamber. Too much fuel can be caused by percolation or overchoking. Insufficient fuel may be the result of a defective fuel pump, a restricted line, a porous flexible line, a plugged gas tank vent, or an empty gas tank.

A quick test of the fuel system is to move the throttle back and forth while looking down into the carburetor bore. If fuel is present it will be squirted out into the throat of the carburetor. If overchoking is suspected, the accelerator pedal should be advanced to a wide-open position while the engine is cranked to admit more air. Do not pump the pedal or you will force more liquid fuel into the intake manifold and aggravate the condition.

POOR PERFORMANCE

Loss of power, resulting from defects in the fuel system, is due to an air-fuel mixture that is either too lean or too rich.

Lean Mixture. The most commonly experienced fuel system trouble is a pause or "flat spot" on acceleration. If such a condition exists, check the operation of the accelerating pump system in the carburetor. To check the carburetor, remove the air cleaner and move the throttle back and forth. A stream of fuel should flow from the accelerating jet if the system is functioning properly. If the fuel stream is missing completely, thin, deflected to one side, or merely dribbling out, the carburetor must be overhauled.

Another lean condition may result from too little fuel being supplied by the carburetor during the range period of operation. Such a condition gives a feeling of "mushiness" as the throttle is opened gradually; the engine doesn't seem to respond. In severe cases, the engine may backfire through the carburetor.

A lean condition can also result from a weak fuel pump or a restricted gas line. Generally, the engine seems to run out of fuel at a certain road speed when there are defects in the supply line.

Rich Mixture. A rich mixture will also cause a loss of power. Excessive quantities of fuel will not vaporize and burn completely. Liquid fuels wash the lubricant from the cylinder walls, allowing the rings to make metal-to-metal contact. Scuffed rings and excessive oil and fuel consumption result.

A rich mixture may result from high fuel pump pressure which forces the carburetor needle valve off its seat, causing flooding. It also can result from defects in the automatic choke.

A lean fuel mixture will cause excessively high combustion chamber temperatures, which generally result in spark plug and valve burning.

FUEL SYSTEM TROUBLESHOOTING CHART

TROUBLES & CAUSES

1. Mixture too lean
  1a. Manifold air leaks
  1b. Defective fuel pump
  1c. Defective carburetor
  1d. Clogged fuel line
  1e. Clogged fuel filter
  1f. Flexible gas line leaking
  1g. Plugged tank vent

2. Mixture too rich
  2a. Defective carburetor
  2b. Defective automatic choke
  2c. Carburetor percolating
  2d. Fuel pump pressure too high

3. No fuel in carburetor
  3a. Gas tank empty
  3b. Fuel pump defective
  3c. Clogged fuel filter
  3d. Vapor lock
  3e. Air leak at fuel pump inlet fitting or porous flexible hose
  3f. Fuel line kinked or plugged
  3g. Fuel vent closed
  3h. Carburetor needle valve stuck in seat by gum

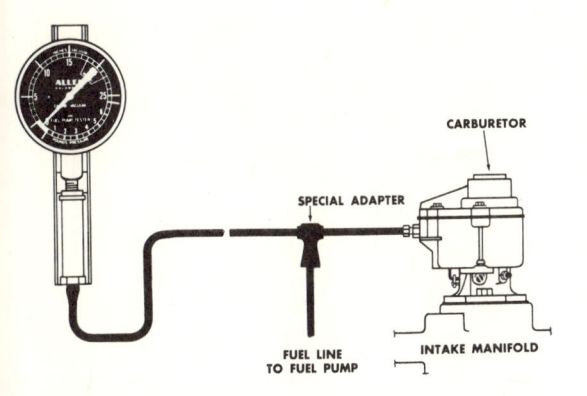

The Fuel System

A pressure gauge can be hooked into the fuel line with a "T" fitting to test the pump operating pressure.

By opening the valve in the "T" fitting, some of the fuel can be diverted into a measuring container. A good pump should deliver about 1 pint (0.5 liter) of fuel per minute.

TESTING THE FUEL PUMP

A fuel pump must be tested for both capacity and pressure. The pressure test is made to check for excessively low or high pressures. Low pressure indicates that the pump stroke is relatively short—an indication of worn linkage. High pressure can be caused only by installing the wrong pump or the wrong pump pressure spring during rebuilding. High pressure causes the float bowl level to rise, which enriches the mixture proportionately. In some cases, high pressure forces the needle valve off its seat and causes the carburetor to flood.

Pressure Test. To make the pressure test, disconnect the line leading into the carburetor. Use the proper fitting and a "T" adapter to connect the gauge into the line. Start the engine and let it idle. A good average pressure is from 3–5 psi (0.21–0.35 kg./cm.^{2}).

Capacity Test. The capacity test determines the ability of the pump to produce a specified quantity of fuel in a given time. To make this test, disconnect the rubber hose from the tester and insert it in a pint (0.5 liter) container. Start the engine and measure the time required to pump 1 pint (0.5 liter) of fuel. Most pumps will deliver 1 pint (0.5 liter) in 60 sec.

Road Test. A good quick road test of the efficiency of the fuel system is to run the car at high speed while keeping the shift lever in second gear. A good fuel pump will permit the car to attain speeds up to and above 50 mph (80 km./h.) in second gear. A defective fuel pump will permit the car to attain a high speed but then it will slow down rapidly.

The test results should not be confused with similar results obtained with a defective ignition system which will allow the car to attain a critical speed, and will maintain it regardless of additional throttle pressure, while a defective fuel pump will cause the car to slow down rapidly after the carburetor runs out of fuel.

FUEL PUMP TROUBLESHOOTING CHART

TROUBLES & CAUSES

1. **Insufficient fuel**
   1a. Worn diaphragm
   1b. Worn linkage
   1c. Valves not seating properly
   1d. Clogged fuel screen
   1e. Air leak at sediment bowl, at flexible line, or at inlet connection
   1f. Clogged fuel tank vent
   1g. Clogged fuel line
   1h. Vapor lock
2. **Excessive fuel**
   2a. Wrong diaphragm spring
   2b. Wrong linkage

A crack in the fuel pump diaphragm allows fuel to leak into the crankcase.

Troubleshooting

TROUBLESHOOTING THE CARBURETOR

The air-fuel mixture can be measured accurately by means of a combustion analyzer. Actual gas mileage or fuel consumption can be measured by use of a gas-mileage tester. However, there are times when a mechanic will want to make some simple tests to determine the carburetor condition without hooking up elaborate equipment. A rather simple test for the range condition is to advance the throttle to a road speed of about 30 mph (48 km./h.). Hold the palm of your hand partially over the choke bore to restrict some of the incoming air. At this speed, a normal carburetor mixture should be somewhat on the lean side. By restricting some of the air, you will enrich the mixture and the engine should speed up *slightly*. If it speeds up considerably, the mixture is too lean; if it doesn't speed up at all, the mixture is too rich. In either case, the carburetor needs to be overhauled.

CARBURETOR TROUBLESHOOTING CHART

TROUBLES & CAUSES

1. **Lean condition on range—surges**
   1a. Air leaks at manifold or carburetor flange
   1b. Clogged bowl vent
   1c. Needle valve seat orifice too small
   1d. Fuel level too low in bowl
   1e. Clogged air bleeds
   1f. Wrong main jet or metering rod installed
   1g. Clogged main jet
   1h. Worn throttle shaft
   1i. Insufficient fuel pump pressure or volume
   1j. Leaking heat riser
   1k. Manifold heat control stuck open
   1l. Leaking vacuum lines or defective vacuum booster pump
2. **Rich condition on range**
   2a. Fuel level too high in carburetor
   2b. Heavy float
   2c. Dirt under needle valve
   2d. Needle valve orifice too large
   2e. High fuel pump pressure
   2f. Restricted air cleaner
   2g. Wrong metering rod or main jet installed
   2h. Power jet leaking
3. **Excessive fuel consumption**
   3a. High float level
   3b. Heavy float
   3c. Worn or dirty float valve and seat
   3d. Worn metering rods and jets
   3e. Power jet not shutting off in the range
   3f. Idle mixture adjustment set too rich
   3g. Plugged idle vents
   3h. Carbonized throttle bore
   3i. Worn throttle shaft
   3j. Accelerating pump stroke too long
   3k. Worn linkage
   3l. Sticking choke valve
   3m. High fuel pump pressure
   3n. Clogged air cleaner
   3o. Fuel bleeding from accelerating pump discharge nozzle
4. **Poor acceleration**
   4a. Accelerating jet clogged
   4b. Defective accelerating pump plunger
   4c. Incorrect adjustment on pump stroke
   4d. Worn linkage
   4e. Leaking check valve in pump circuit
   4f. Fuel level too low
   4g. Too lean or too rich a range mixture
   4h. Manifold heat control stuck in open position
   4i. Air leaking into manifold
   4j. Carburetor throttle not opening fully
   4k. Choke valve stuck closed
   4l. Power jet not opening
5. **Poor idling**
   5a. Air leaking into intake manifold
   5b. Incorrect setting of idle mixture adjustment screw
   5c. Idle mixture adjustment screw grooved
   5d. Idle speed set too slow
   5e. Float level too high
   5f. Worn throttle shaft
   5g. Leaking vacuum power jet diaphragm
   5h. Carbon formation around the throttle plate
   5i. Dashpot adjustment incorrect
   5j. Automatic choke fast idle linkage not set correctly
6. **Poor low-speed performance**
   6a. Idle adjusting screws not balanced
   6b. Clogged idle transfer holes
   6c. Restricted idle air bleeds and passages
7. **Stalling when accelerator is released suddenly**
   7a. Improperly adjusted dashpot
   7b. Defective dashpot
   7c. Clogged air bleeds
   7d. Clogged idle passages
   7e. Leaking intake manifold and/or carburetor gaskets
   7f. Idle speed set too low
8. **Hard starting**
   8a. Automatic choke not closing properly
   8b. Binding linkage in the choke circuit
   8c. Restricted choke vacuum passages
   8d. Air leaking into the choke vacuum passages

TROUBLESHOOTING THE ELECTRICAL SYSTEM

The battery is the heart of the electrical system; it supplies the entire system with the current it needs to function. The generator charges the battery and develops the voltage or pressure on which the rest of the electrical system must work. The operation of all units is so interrelated that the improper functioning of any one will generally cause a malfunction in the others. For this reason, it is customary to make a series of tests to determine the condition of the entire electrical system to make sure that all troubles have been uncovered. All authorities recommend that the electrical system be tested in the following order: cranking circuit, charging circuit, and then the ignition circuit. In each case, the battery should be tested first because its condition determines the operating

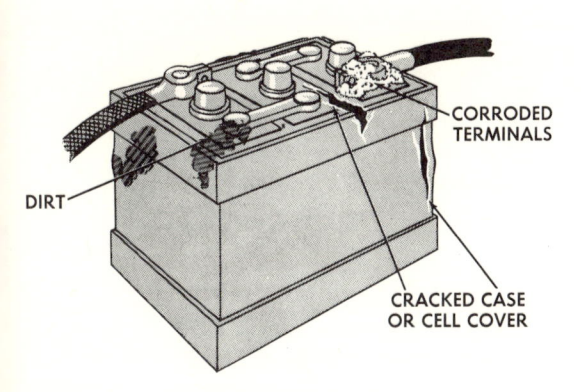

The Electrical System

A visual inspection is often helpful in discovering battery defects.

voltage of the entire electrical system of the car, and it is a functional part of each basic circuit.

TROUBLESHOOTING THE BATTERY

Two battery tests are generally performed; one has to do with the chemical condition of the electrolyte, and the second with the capacity of the battery to deliver the necessary quantities of electricity.

The electrolyte test is made with a hydrometer which measures the density of the fluid. As a battery becomes discharged, a chemical reaction takes place in which the heavy sulfuric acid combines with the lead of the plates. As the sulfuric acid leaves the electrolyte, the solution contains more water than acid. This lightens the density, which can be measured by a hydrometer; a reading of 1.270 indicates a fully charged battery, one of 1.175 a battery low in charge.

If the battery capacity test indicates low, but the cell voltage readings are even, but low, the state of the battery charge is low, and it should be recharged.

BATTERY TROUBLESHOOTING CHART

TROUBLES & CAUSES

1. **Low specific gravity readings**
   - 1a. Low state of charge
   - 1b. Loss of acid through leaks
   - 1c. Acid absorbed by spongy plates
   - 1d. Sulfated plates
   - 1e. Electrical drain due to acid resistance path on top of the case or to a short circuit in the car wiring
2. **Low individual cell voltage readings**
   - 2a. Low state of charge
   - 2b. Loss of acid through a leak
   - 2c. Shorted plates caused by a defective separator
3. **Low current capacity**
   - 3a. Low state of charge
   - 3b. Sulfated plates
   - 3c. Low fluid level
   - 3d. Acid absorbed by spongy plates
   - 3e. Powdered-out positive plates from overcharging
   - 3f. Replacement battery too small for vehicle demands

TROUBLESHOOTING THE CRANKING SYSTEM

The condition of the cranking system has a decided effect on the ease of starting the engine—or the lack of it. A good cranking system will spin the engine fast enough to draw in a full combustible

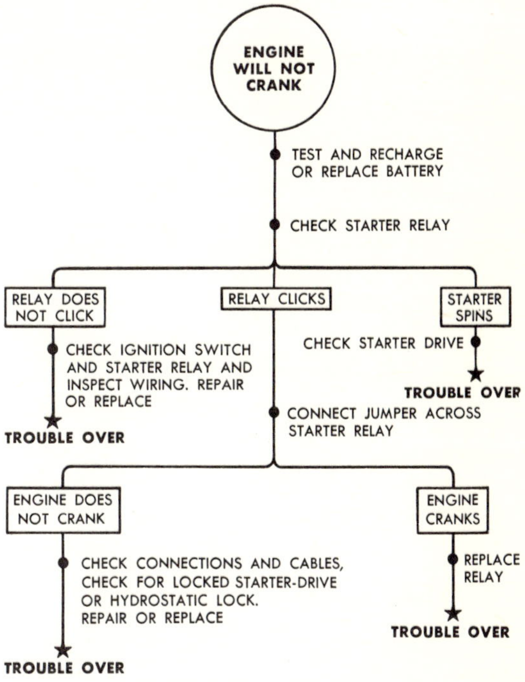

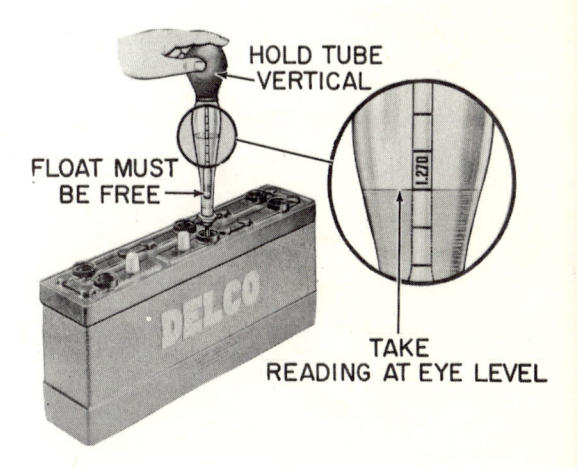

Roadmap for troubleshooting a starting motor that does not crank the engine.

A hydrometer is used to measure the specific gravity of the electrolyte.

20 Troubleshooting

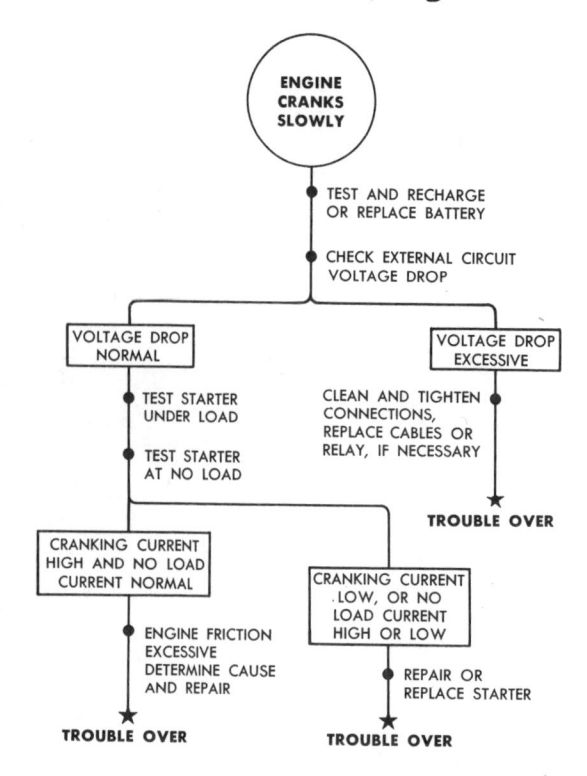

Roadmap for troubleshooting a starting motor that cranks the engine too slowly.

(Flowchart:)
- ENGINE CRANKS SLOWLY
- TEST AND RECHARGE OR REPLACE BATTERY
- CHECK EXTERNAL CIRCUIT VOLTAGE DROP
  - VOLTAGE DROP NORMAL
    - TEST STARTER UNDER LOAD
    - TEST STARTER AT NO LOAD
      - CRANKING CURRENT HIGH AND NO LOAD CURRENT NORMAL
        - ENGINE FRICTION EXCESSIVE DETERMINE CAUSE AND REPAIR
        - TROUBLE OVER
      - CRANKING CURRENT LOW, OR NO LOAD CURRENT HIGH OR LOW
        - REPAIR OR REPLACE STARTER
        - TROUBLE OVER
  - VOLTAGE DROP EXCESSIVE
    - CLEAN AND TIGHTEN CONNECTIONS, REPLACE CABLES OR RELAY, IF NECESSARY
    - TROUBLE OVER

charge, compress it high enough to develop sufficient heat to dry out most of the wet fuel particles, and maintain a sufficiently high battery voltage so that the ignition system can operate efficiently.

Any defect in the cranking circuit slows down the cranking speed. And, because the starting motor fields and armature are connected in series, a slower speed allows more time for the current to flow through each armature coil which increases the current drain on the system. In turn, this lowers the battery voltage available to the ignition system which then operates at less than maximum efficiency. Thus, a vicious cycle is set up which results in a hard starting complaint.

CRANKING SYSTEM TROUBLESHOOTING CHART

TROUBLES & CAUSES

1. **Cranks engine slowly**
   1a. Low state of battery charge
   1b. High resistance battery cable connection
   1c. High resistance starter switch
   1d. Bent armature shaft
   1e. Worn bushing in the drive end
   1f. Dirty or worn commutator
   1g. Worn brushes or weak brush springs
2. **Doesn't crank the engine at all**
   2a. Dead battery
   2b. Broken battery cable or high resistance connection
   2c. Open circuit in the ignition-to-solenoid circuit
   2d. Open circuit in the starting switch
   2e. Open circuit in the starting motor
   2f. Starting motor drive stuck to the flywheel gear
   2g. Hydrostatic lock
3. **Spins, but does not crank the engine**
   3a. Defective starter drive

TROUBLESHOOTING THE CHARGING SYSTEM

Modern automotive charging systems have a regulator to control the output of the generator or alternator. In practice, the charging rate increases when the battery is discharged and decreases when it is charged. The charging rate may be cut down to a very low rate with a fully charged battery.

To test the charging system, crank the engine with the ignition switch off in order to discharge the battery slightly. (On cars with an ignition key-type starter switch, it may be necessary to remove the coil high tension wire from the center of the distributor cap to prevent the engine from starting.) Now, start the engine and note the charging rate. (On a car without an ammeter, it is necessary to insert an ammeter in the charging circuit.) As the engine is run for a short period, the charging rate should decrease with a properly operating regulator. If the ammeter does not show any charge after the above test, it is an indication that either the generator or the regulator is at fault.

To isolate the trouble, disconnect the regulator from the circuit and energize the generator field. If the generator now charges, the trouble is in the regulator. If the generator does not charge with the regulator out of the circuit and the field energized, then the trouble is in the generator. In every case in which the generator is burned out, the regulator should be replaced too, as it obviously did not control the output of the generator. *CAUTION: Do not race the engine with the regulator out of the circuit, or the generator will burn up as it is operating without control.*

Because several manufacturers supply electrical equipment for European-built cars, the method of energizing the field is detailed according to the type of generator supplied as follows:

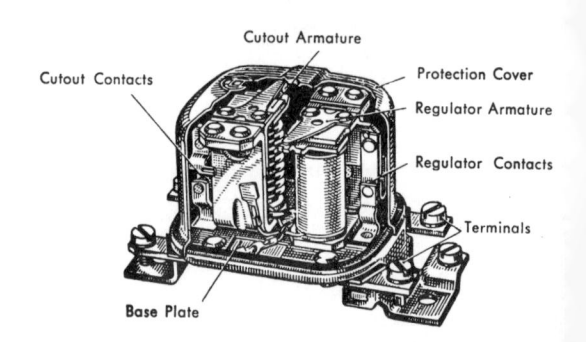

The Bosch, two-unit regulator, type TA and TB.

(Labels: Cutout Armature, Cutout Contacts, Protection Cover, Regulator Armature, Regulator Contacts, Terminals, Base Plate)

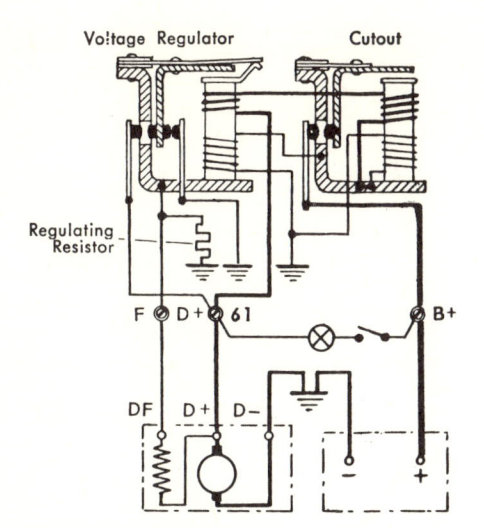

The Charging System

Internal wiring of the Bosch, two-unit regulator.

BOSCH: Connect a jumper wire from the field terminal on the generator or the regulator to ground.

DUCELLIER: Connect a jumper wire from the EXC terminal on the regulator to the DYN terminal.

FIAT: Connect a jumper wire from No. 15 to No. 67 terminals on the regulator.

LUCAS: Connect a jumper from the D terminal to the F terminal on the regulator.

MARELLI: On 2-unit regulators, connect a jumper from the DF terminal on the regulator to ground. On the 3-unit regulators, connect a jumper between the DF-1 terminal and the D+ 61 terminal.

PARIS-RHONE: Connect a jumper wire from the EXC terminal on the regulator to the DYN terminal.

If the generator output is excessive, the trouble can be caused by the regulator points being welded together or by a short circuit in a field wire. In either case, there is no regulation, and the generator is running wide open. To test for this type of trouble, it must be remembered that there are two basic types of field circuits: one grounded at the regulator and one supplied with current at the regulator. By removing the field wire from the regulator, the generator can be isolated. If the generator still charges with the field wire removed, then the ground or short is in the generator itself.

Another generator check can be made by removing the cover band. If the inner surface of the band is covered with a layer of solder, the generator was overloaded until the solder from the armature commutator slots melted. Obviously, this leads to open circuited coils in the armature. The wires can be resoldered and the commutator turned, provided that the coils have not grounded out; otherwise, the armature should be replaced.

Voltage losses, due to poor connections, cause an increase of operating voltage because the generator tries to overcome the added resistance of the circuit by forcing current through at a higher voltage. When the voltage increases, the regulator senses it and returns it to normal by regulating the field. Thus, even though the battery is low in charge, the generator output remains low, and another vicious cycle is set up.

CHARGING SYSTEM TROUBLESHOOTING CHART

TROUBLES & CAUSES

1. **Battery requires water too frequently**
   1a. Voltage regulator set too high
   1b. Current regulator set too high
   1c. Cracked battery case
2. **Battery will not remain charged**
   2a. Voltage regulator set too low
   2b. Current regulator set too low
   2c. Short circuit in car wiring
   2d. High-resistance connection in charging circuit
   2e. Excessive low-speed driving while operating accessories
   2f. Defective battery
   2g. Defective generator
   2h. Defective regulator
3. **Battery will not accept a charge**
   3a. Sulfated battery
   3b. Open circuit between cells
4. **Generator has no output**
   4a. Defective generator
   4b. Defective regulator
   4c. Grounded or open lead from armature terminal of generator or regulator
   4d. Ground or open circuit in the field lead
   4e. Field or ground wires reversed on generator
5. **Generator output low**
   5a. Slipping fan belt
   5b. Voltage regulator set too low
   5c. Current regulator set too low

A rough commutator surface is a sure indication of trouble in the making.

Troubleshooting

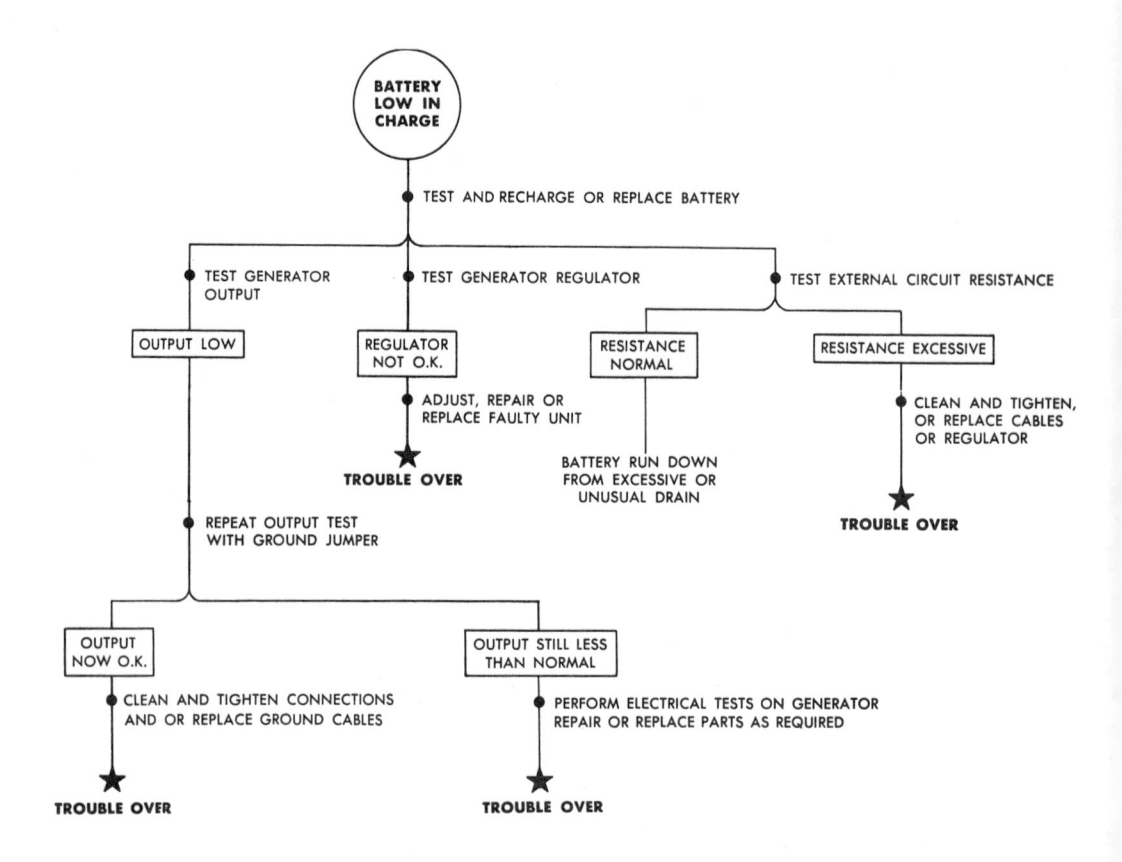

Roadmap for troubleshooting the charging circuit.

5d. High resistance in field circuit
5e. Defective generator
6. **Generator output too high**
   6a. Voltage regulator set too high
   6b. Current regulator set too high
   6c. Defective regulator
   6d. Ground or short in field lead
7. **Voltage or current regulator points badly burned**
   7a. Shorted generator field windings
   7b. Radio condenser connected to field terminal
8. **Cutout points chatter**
   8a. Generator polarity reversed
   8b. Battery installed in reverse
   8c. Cutout relay closing voltage set too low
9. **Noises**
   9a. Bad bearings
   9b. Loose generator drive pulley
   9c. Brushes not seating
   9d. Loose fan belt

TROUBLESHOOTING THE IGNITION SYSTEM

The efficient operation of the ignition system probably has a great deal more to do with the smooth operation of an internal combustion engine than any other mechanical or electrical part. The importance of the ignition system can be realized from the fact that every minute 20,000 sparks are developed and delivered to the spark plugs of an 8-cylinder engine running at high speed. And, that these sparks must be distributed to each of the cylinders when they have been charged with an explosive air-fuel mixture that has been compressed to the point of maximum efficiency. Naturally, any slipup in the chain of events needed to create and time the sparks will result in poor engine performance.

The spark needed to fire the compressed air-fuel mixture is close to 20,000 volts. To step up the battery's 12 volts to the high voltage needed to jump the gaps of the spark plugs is the duty of the ignition coil. This transformer contains a primary and a secondary winding. The primary circuit, operating on the battery voltage, consists of the battery, ignition switch, ignition contact points, condenser, primary winding of the ignition coil, and ballast resistor. The secondary circuit develops the high voltage needed to fire the spark plugs, and it consists of the ignition coil, rotor, distributor cap, high tension wiring, and spark plugs.

The primary circuit contains a set of contact points which interrupts the circuit. The action of interrupting the primary circuit develops the high-tension spark in the secondary circuit. At the same time, the contact-point interruption is precisely

The Ignition System

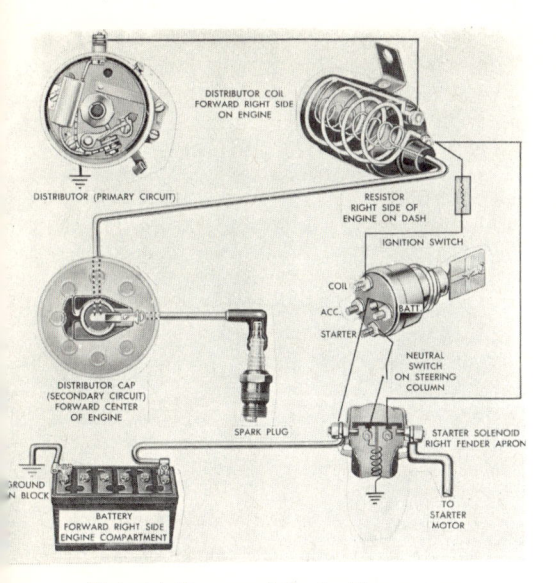

Pictorial diagram of the ignition system.

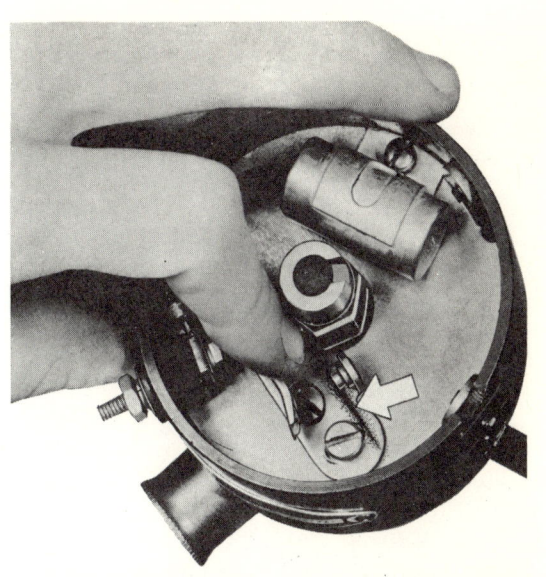

Oil on the contact point faces is a frequent offender of burned points. Its presence can often be detected by the smudge line under the contact points.

timed so as to send the spark to the cylinder at the instant the air-fuel charge has been compressed to the point of maximum efficiency. Naturally, the contact point set must open and close once for each spark delivered, or 20,000 times per minute at top speed. It is no wonder, then, that the contact points require periodic servicing. Without it, they soon deteriorate and cause such troubles as hard starting, misfiring, poor performance, and low fuel mileage.

There is no way to test the performance of the ignition system with accuracy except with precision test equipment. Any other way is subject to error. However, a rough check can be made of the ignition system by road testing the car while placing the engine under a heavy load. Drive the car in high gear at about 6 mph (10 km./h.) on a smooth road; place your left foot lightly on the brake pedal to put a load on the engine. Open the accelerator fully with your right foot. As the engine picks up speed, apply the foot brake to keep the car speed constant at about 25 mph (40 km./h.). Ignition troubles will cause the car to jerk sharply. Defective spark plugs are especially sensitive to such a test.

If the car can be driven wide open in second gear, a good ignition system will allow the car to attain a maximum speed. A defective ignition system will cause it to "float" long before it reaches maximum.

TESTING THE IGNITION SYSTEM FOR CONDITIONS CAUSING POWER LOSSES

Two common ignition system troubles, with regard to power losses, are late ignition timing and misfiring cylinders.

Late ignition timing causes overheating and loss of power. It can be detected by too smooth an idle, a deep-sounding exhaust, a low vacuum gauge reading, and a lack of "ping" on acceleration. Misfiring cylinders are characterized by a rough idle, a stuttering exhaust on acceleration, and a jerky vacuum gauge needle.

CHECKING IGNITION TIMING

A timing light should be used to check the ignition timing. One of the test instrument leads is connected to the distributor primary terminal and the other to ground. With the ignition switch turned on, the engine should be rotated by hand until the lamp lights, which indicates the moment of point opening.

Generally, the crankshaft pulley has a notch to indicate TDC (top dead center), and it is necessary to measure along the edge of the pulley to locate the exact point that ignition must occur. In many cases, no timing or degree scale is provided. The ignition timing specification can be found in the Commonly Used Specifications table according to car model.

To set the timing, turn the engine by hand until the pointer is at the exact point on the flywheel specified in the table. Loosen the distributor clamp bolt, and then turn the distributor in a direction opposite that of normal rotation until the points just separate (timing lamp lights). Lock the distributor in this position.

TESTING FOR A MISS

An engine is composed of several cylinders arranged to fire successively in order to develop a smooth flow of power. If one of these cylinders does not fire, it causes the engine to jerk, lose

Troubleshooting

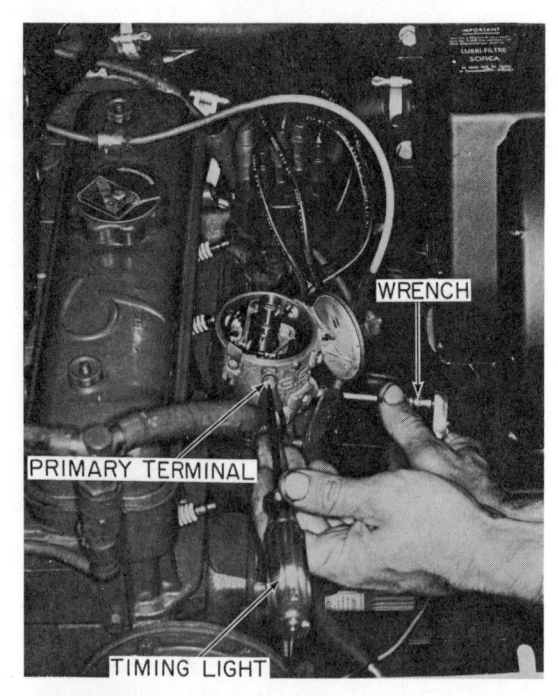

A timing light is used to check the moment of point opening. With the engine positioned at the specified point, adjust the position of the distributor until the lamp lights.

power, and waste fuel. A misfiring cylinder can be caused by a lack of spark, fuel, or compression.

The best test for a misfiring cylinder is to short out all the cylinders with the exception of one, and thereafter have the engine operate on each cylinder in turn. Any variation in power, or a cylinder which is not firing, will show up, because the engine will not run at all when the defective cylinder has to carry the load alone.

To make this test, loosen each high tension wire from its spark plug terminal before starting the engine, but do not disconnect any until needed. With the engine running fast enough to prevent stalling, short out each cylinder, except number 1, by removing its spark plug wire and laying it on the engine block. This is done so that the spark does not reach the spark plug and the cylinder cannot fire. To minimize the chances of getting an electrical shock when handling high tension wires, keep your fingers at least an inch from the metallic tip.

After all the cylinders, except one, have been shorted out, adjust the engine speed so that the engine runs as slowly as possible without stalling. Change the wires, one at a time. In this way, you can run the engine on each cylinder in turn. If a vacuum gauge is connected during this test, a very accurate comparative measurement can be made between the relative efficiency of each cylinder.

To Find the Cause of the Miss. Remove the defective cylinder spark plug wire; hold it ¼" (6 mm.) from the spark plug terminal, then start the engine. If a steady spark jumps to the spark plug terminal, the trouble must be fuel, compression, or a defective spark plug. If no spark jumps to the spark plug terminal, the trouble is in the ignition system.

To make a compression test, use a compression gauge or hold your thumb over the spark plug hole while cranking the engine.

If the engine misses on adjacent cylinders, the trouble may be a blown cylinder head gasket or a leaky intake manifold gasket. A blown cylinder head gasket will lack compression in either of the two affected cylinders. To test for a leaking intake manifold gasket, squirt water around the suspected surfaces. A sucking noise will indicate the entrance of the water into the manifold.

IGNITION SYSTEM TROUBLESHOOTING CHART

TROUBLES & CAUSES

1. **Primary circuit troubles causing misfiring or hard starting**
   1a. Defective contact points
   1b. Point dwell not set correctly
   1c. Defective condenser
   1d. Defective coil
   1e. Defective primary wire in distributor
   1f. Resistance contacts in ignition switch
   1g. Discharged battery
   1h. Low voltage due to resistance connections
   1i. Worn distributor shaft bushings
2. **Secondary circuit troubles causing misfiring or hard starting**
   2a. Defective spark plugs
   2b. Spark plug gaps set too wide
   2c. Defective high tension wiring
   2d. Cracked distributor cap
   2e. Defective rotor
   2f. Defective coil
   2g. Moisture on the ignition wires, cap, or spark plugs
3. **Ignition troubles causing poor acceleration**
   3a. Ignition timing incorrect
   3b. Centrifugal advance incorrect
   3c. Vacuum advance unit incorrect
   3d. Defective vacuum advance diaphragm
   3e. Preignition due to wrong heat-range spark plugs, or to overheated engine
   3f. Spark plug gaps set too wide
   3g. Defective spark plugs
   3h. Cracked distributor cap
   3i. Weak coil
4. **Ignition troubles causing erratic engine operation**
   4a. Defective contact points
   4b. Sticking point pivot bushing
   4c. Worn distributor shaft bushings
   4d. Worn advance plate bearing
   4e. Defective ignition coil
   4f. Spark plug gaps set too wide
   4g. High resistance spark plugs
   4h. Defective high tension wiring

The Clutch

TROUBLESHOOTING THE CLUTCH

To test a clutch for slipping, set the hand brake tightly, open the throttle until the engine is running at about 30 mph (48 km./h.) road speed, depress the clutch pedal, and shift into high gear. Now, release the clutch; the engine should stall if the clutch is good. If the clutch is slipping, the engine will continue to run.

Check to see that the slipping is not due to a tight adjustment of the clutch pedal linkage. There must be ¾" (20 mm.) free play at the pedal, before the clutch thrust bearing contacts the clutch pressure plate levers.

The only other clutch trouble is chattering when starting in first or reverse gear. Loose engine mounts and uneven clutch finger adjustments contribute to this trouble.

CLUTCH TROUBLESHOOTING CHART

TROUBLES & CAUSES

1. Slipping
  1a. Worn facings
  1b. Weak pressure plate springs
  1c. Pedal linkage out of adjustment
  1d. Sticking release levers
  1e. Pressure plate binding against the drive lugs

2. Dragging
  2a. Pedal linkage adjustment too loose
  2b. Warped clutch disc
  2c. Splined hub sticking on clutch shaft
  2d. Torn disc facings
  2e. Release fingers adjusted unevenly
  2f. Sticking pilot bearing
  2g. Sticking release sleeve
  2h. Warped pressure plate
  2i. Misalignment of clutch housing

3. Noise
  3a. Clutch release bearing requires lubrication
  3b. Pilot bearing requires lubrication
  3c. Loose hub in clutch disc
  3d. Worn release bearing
  3e. Worn driving pins in pressure plate
  3f. Uneven release lever adjustment
  3g. Release levers require lubrication

4. Chattering
  4a. Oil or grease on clutch disc facings
  4b. Glazed linings
  4c. Warped clutch disc
  4d. Warped pressure plate
  4e. Sticking release levers
  4f. Unequal adjustment of release levers
  4g. Uneven pressure plate spring tension
  4h. Loose engine mounts
  4i. Loose splines on clutch hub
  4j. Loose universal joints or torque mountings
  4k. Misalignment of clutch housing

TROUBLESHOOTING A TRANSMISSION

Transmission noises can be heard much better with the engine shut off and the car coasting. By moving the shift lever from neutral into the various gearing positions, different gears can be meshed for testing purposes.

TRANSMISSION TROUBLESHOOTING CHART

TROUBLES & CAUSES

1. Noisy with car in motion, any gear
  1a. Insufficient lubrication
  1b. Worn clutch gear
  1c. Worn clutch gear bearing
  1d. Worn countergear
  1e. Worn countershaft bearings
  1f. Worn mainshaft rear bearing
  1g. Worn mainshaft front bearing
  1h. Worn sliding gears
  1i. Excessive mainshaft end play
  1j. Speedometer gears worn
  1k. Misalignment between transmission and clutch housing

2. Noisy in neutral
  2a. Insufficient lubrication
  2b. Worn clutch gear
  2c. Worn clutch gear bearing
  2d. Worn countergear drive gear
  2e. Worn countershaft bearings

3. Slips out of high gear
  3a. Misalignment between transmission and clutch housings
  3b. Worn shift detent parts
  3c. Worn clutch shaft bearing
  3d. Worn teeth on dog clutch
  3e. Improper adjustment of shift linkage

4. Slips out of second gear
  4a. Misalignment between transmission and clutch housings
  4b. Weak shift lever interlock detent springs
  4c. Worn mainshaft bearings
  4d. Worn clutch shaft bearing
  4e. Worn countergear thrust washers allowing too much end play
  4f. Improper adjustment of shift linkage

5. Slips out of first/reverse gear
  5a. Worn detent parts
  5b. Improper adjustment of shift linkage
  5c. Worn mainshaft bearings
  5d. Worn clutch shaft bearing
  5e. Excessive mainshaft end play
  5f. Worn countergear
  5g. Worn countergear bearings
  5h. Worn first/reverse sliding gear

6. Difficult to shift
  6a. Clutch not releasing
  6b. Improper adjustment of shift linkage

7. Clashing when shifting
  7a. Worn synchronizing cones
  7b. Excessive mainshaft end play

8. Backlash
  8a. Excessive mainshaft end play
  8b. Excessive countergear end play
  8c. Broken mainshaft bearing retainer
  8d. Worn mainshaft bearing

Troubleshooting

TROUBLESHOOTING THE REAR AXLE

A rear axle should not be disassembled until a thorough diagnosis is made of the trouble and symptoms observed during the operation of the car. The most common rear axle complaint is noise. Care must be taken to be sure that the noise is not caused by the engine, tires, transmission, wheel bearings, or some other part of the car.

Before road testing the car, make sure that sufficient lubricant is in the axle housing and inflate the tires to the correct pressure. Drive the car far enough to warm the lubricant to its normal operating temperature before making the tests.

Engine noise or exhaust noise can be detected by parking the car and running the engine at various speeds with the transmission in neutral. A portable tachometer will assist in duplicating road speeds at which the noises occurred.

Tire noise can be detected by driving the car over various road surfaces. Tire noise is minimized on smooth asphalt or black-top roads. Switching tires can help to detect or eliminate tire noises.

Wheel bearing noise can sometimes be detected by jacking up each wheel in turn and feeling for roughness as the wheel is rotated. Wheel bearing noise is most obvious on a low-speed coast. Applying the brakes lightly while the car is moving will often reduce or eliminate the noise caused by a defective wheel bearing.

A car should be tested for axle and driveline noise by operating it under four driving conditions:

1. Drive: Higher than normal road-load power, where the speed gradually increases on level road acceleration.
2. Cruise: Constant speed operation at normal road speeds.
3. Float: Using only enough throttle to keep the car from driving the engine. Car will slow down (very little load on rear axle gears).
4. Coast: Throttle closed—engine is braking the car (load is on the coast side of the gear set).

Backlash or play in the running gear can be checked by driving the car on a smooth road at 25 mph (40 km./h.) and lightly pressing and releasing the accelerator pedal. Backlash is indicated by a slapping noise with each movement of the accelerator pedal. Raising the car on a lubrication rack will permit you to make a more detailed examination.

REAR AXLE TROUBLESHOOTING CHART

TROUBLES & CAUSES

1. **Noise on acceleration**
   1a. Heavy heel contact on ring gear
2. **Noise on coast**
   2a. Heavy toe contact on ring gear
3. **Noise on both coast and acceleration**
   3a. Differential gears worn
   3b. Pinion and ring gears worn
   3c. Defective bearings
4. **Noise only when rounding a curve**
   4a. Damaged differential case gears
5. **Backlash**
   5a. Worn axle shaft splines
   5b. Loose axle shaft nut
   5c. Worn universal joints
   5d. Excessive play between pinion and ring gear
   5e. Worn differential bearings
   5f. Worn differential side gear thrust washers and/or case
6. **Vibration**
   6a. Worn universal joints
   6b. Universal spline not assembled according to matching arrows
   6c. Undercoating applied to drive shaft
   6d. Drive line center bearing out of alignment
   6e. Drive line angle incorrect

TROUBLESHOOTING THE FRONT END

Drive the car on a smooth road at about 30 mph (48 km./h.), and then take your hands off the steering wheel. The car should maintain a straight course. If the road is crowned, it may cause the car to wander toward the low side of the road and, therefore, it may be necessary to make this test evenly straddled over the center line. Choose a road with no traffic to make this test. On a windy day, the test should be duplicated by going back and forth over the same road. Uneven front-end angles will cause the car to wander to one side.

Hold your hand lightly on the steering wheel at about 30 mph (48 km./h.) to check whether any shocks are being transmitted back to the steering wheel. A constantly jiggling wheel indicates that the front wheels are out of balance. This constant movement is very tiring to a driver on long trips and is hard on every moving part of the front end.

Turn into a deserted side street at about 25 mph (40 km./h.), and then release the steering wheel; it should come back to a straight-ahead position without any assistance from the driver; otherwise there is binding in the linkage, insufficient caster or insufficient steering axis inclination.

To check for misalignment, stop the car and inspect the front tires for uneven tread wear. Pass your hand over the surface of each tire tread. Sharp edges felt going one way are called feather edges and are developed from sideward scuffing. Be especially critical of the right-front tire wear as this wheel is most frequently knocked out of alignment by bumping the curb. When the right front wheel tire is worn more unevenly than the left, it is an indication of a bent steering arm.

FRONT-END TROUBLESHOOTING CHART

TROUBLES & CAUSES

1. **Excessive looseness**
   1a. Improper adjustment of the steering gear
   1b. Worn steering linkage
   1c. Loose wheel bearing adjustment on worn bearings
   1d. Worn king pins or ball joints

The Front End

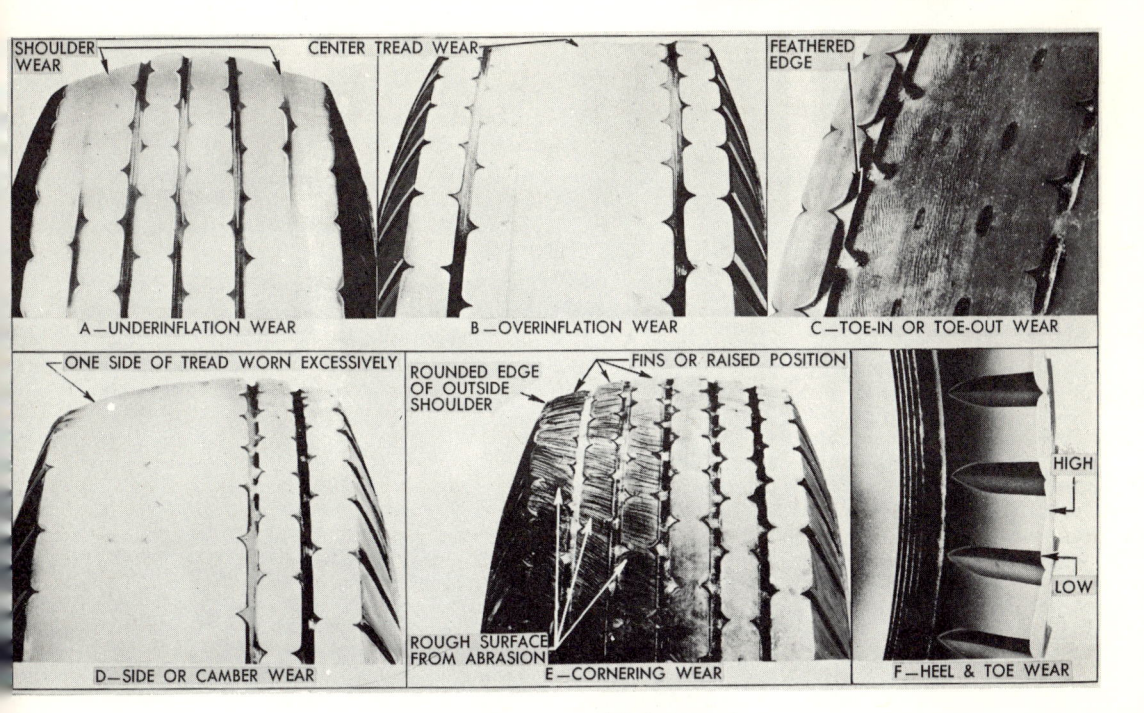

Types of tire wear and their causes.

- A—UNDERINFLATION WEAR
- B—OVERINFLATION WEAR
- C—TOE-IN OR TOE-OUT WEAR
- D—SIDE OR CAMBER WEAR
- E—CORNERING WEAR
- F—HEEL & TOE WEAR

   1e. Loose steering gear mounting
2. **Hard steering**
   2a. Tight adjustment of the steering gear
   2b. Lubrication needed
   2c. Low tire pressure
   2d. Wheels out of alignment
   2e. Excessive caster
3. **Wanders**
   3a. Loose front wheel bearings
   3b. Loose steering linkage
   3c. Loose front end supports
   3d. Uneven tire pressure
   3e. Low pressure in both rear tires
   3f. Incorrect caster
   3g. Bent spindle arm
   3h. Sagging spring
4. **Pulls to one side**
   4a. Uneven caster
   4b. Uneven camber
   4c. Uneven tire pressure
   4d. Frame out of alignment
   4e. Tire sizes not uniform
   4f. Bent spindle arm
   4g. Sagging spring
5. **Shimmy, low speed**
   5a. Loose support arms
   5b. Loose linkage
   5c. Loose wheel bearings
   5d. Soft springs
   5e. Static unbalance of front wheels
   5f. Incorrect tire pressure
6. **Shimmy, high speed**
   6a. Dynamic unbalance of front wheels
   6b. Too much caster
   6c. Soft springs
7. **Squeals on turns**
   7a. Low tire pressure
   7b. Incorrect camber
   7c. Bent spindle arm
   7d. Frame out of alignment
8. **Excessive tire wear**
   8a. Improper toe-in
   8b. Improper turning radius
   8c. Underinflation
   8d. Overinflation
   8e. Grabbing
   8f. Excessive camber

TROUBLESHOOTING A HYDRAULIC BRAKE SYSTEM

Perhaps the most common complaint about brakes is that the car cannot be brought to a satisfactory stop. As the lining wears, the brake pedal must be pushed down farther and farther in order to move the brake shoes into contact with the drums. Eventually, it reaches the floorboard, and an emergency application does not stop the car. When this happens, it is necessary to adjust the position of the brake shoes so that they are closer to the drums. This restores the pedal to its former position.

Generally, a soft pedal, or one that goes slowly to the floorboard under continued pressure, is caused by air trapped in the hydraulic lines or by a leak in the system. The system must be bled to get rid of the air. To repair the leak, the defective unit must be removed. However, it is considered good practice to overhaul the entire hydraulic system in the event of a leak in any one part, because all of the units are in the same condition; unless repaired at the same time, they too will soon leak.

Troubleshooting

Another frequent complaint has to do with noise. Actually, the squeals and squeaks that are heard are due to loose parts, which cause high-frequency vibration.

HYDRAULIC BRAKE SYSTEM TROUBLESHOOTING CHART

TROUBLES & CAUSES

1. **Pedal goes to floorboard**
   1a. Brake shoes out of adjustment
   1b. Brake fluid level low
   1c. Leaking lines or cylinders
   1d. Air in brake lines
   1e. Defective master cylinder
2. **One brake drags**
   2a. Incorrect shoe adjustment
   2b. Clogged brake line
   2c. Sluggish wheel cylinder piston
   2d. Weak brake shoe return spring
   2e. Loose wheel bearing
   2f. Brake shoe binding on backing plate
   2g. Out-of-round drum
3. **All brakes drag**
   3a. Insufficient play in master cylinder push rod
   3b. Master cylinder relief port plugged
   3c. Lubricating oil in system instead of hydraulic fluid
   3d. Master cylinder piston sticking
4. **Car pulls to one side**
   4a. Brake fluid or grease on lining
   4b. Sluggish wheel cylinder piston
   4c. Weak retracting spring
   4d. Loose wheel bearing
   4e. Wrong brake lining
   4f. Drum out-of-round
5. **Soft pedal**
   5a. Air in system
   5b. Improper anchor adjustment
   5c. Improper linings
   5d. Thin drums
   5e. Warped brake shoes
6. **Hard pedal**
   6a. Wrong brake lining
   6b. Glazed brake lining
   6c. Mechanical resistance at pedal or shoes
7. **One or more wheels grab**
   7a. Grease or hydraulic fluid on lining
   7b. Loose wheel bearings
   7c. Loose front end supports
   7d. Loose backing plate
   7e. Distorted brake shoe
   7f. Improper brake lining
   7g. Primary and secondary shoes reversed
8. **Erratic braking action**
   8a. Loose brake support
   8b. Loose front end suspension parts
   8c. Grease or hydraulic fluid on lining
   8d. Binding of the shoes in the guides
   8e. Sticking hydraulic wheel cylinder piston
9. **Noisy brakes**
   9a. Loose backing plate
   9b. Loose wheel bearing adjustment
   9c. Loose front end supports
   9d. Warped brake shoes
   9e. Linings loose on shoes
   9f. Improperly installed brake shoes
   9g. Improper anchor adjustment
   9h. Loose brake shoe guides
   9i. Weak brake return springs
   9j. Dust in rivet holes
   9k. Grease or hydraulic fluid on brake lining

TROUBLESHOOTING THE CALIPER DISC BRAKE SYSTEM

Disc brakes are generally mounted on the front wheels, and non-servo, drum-type brakes are mounted on the rear. On other installations, all four wheels have disc brakes. The brakes are frequently actuated by a power unit on the larger cars.

The usual hydraulic brake troubleshooting procedures apply with the following Troubleshooting Chart showing specific complaints:

CALIPER DISC BRAKE TROUBLESHOOTING CHART

TROUBLES & CAUSES

1. **Brake pedal meets no resistance; brake pedal has soft or spongy feel**
   1a. Insufficient brake fluid in reservoir
   1b. Air in brake system
2. **Brake pedal can be depressed without braking effect, after bleeding**
   2a. Leaky brake lines
3. **Brake pedal can be depressed after extensive downhill driving (soft and spongy)**
   3a. Inferior or low boiling point fluid, with overheated brake system
   3b. Air in system
4. **Brakes heat up during driving and fail to release**
   4a. Compensating port in master brake cylinder blocked
   4b. Power unit push rod incorrectly adjusted so that master cylinder piston is not released.
   4c. Piston of wheel cylinder sticking
5. **Poor braking effect in spite of high pedal pressure**
   5a. Oil or grease on friction pads
   5b. Glazed friction pads
6. **Brakes pull to one side**
   6a. Brake fluid, oil, or grease on friction pads of one wheel
   6b. Excessive wear of one brake caliper friction pad
   6c. Calipers not parallel to brake disc
7. **Brakes chatter**
   7a. Excessive lateral runout of brake disc
   7b. Bad contact pattern of friction pads
   7c. Rough surface on brake disc
8. **Frequent replenishing of brake fluid in reservoir needed**
   8a. Brake line system leaks
   8b. Master cylinder leaks
   8c. Wheel cylinder leaks
9. **Leaky wheel cylinder**
   9a. Leaking piston seal
   9b. Cylinder walls scored or pitted
   9c. Rust formation on cylinder wall

2

Tuning and Identification

MODEL IDENTIFICATION

Renault 4CV, through 1957.

Renault Caravelle, 1960–62 and Caravelle "S," 1963–64.

Renault Dauphine, 1958–61, and Gordini 1961–62. Note the rectangular turn signal lights.

Renault R-8, 1963–64.

Renault Dauphine, 1962–64. Note the round turn signal lights.

GENERAL INFORMATION—4CV, DAUPHINE, GORDINI, AND CARAVELLE

The Dauphine is powered by a 4-cylinder, rear-mounted powerplant of 32 hp, consisting of an engine and trans-axle combination with three-forward speeds. The 4CV, an earlier version, had a 28 hp engine. The Gordini, a deluxe model produced in 1961–62, was equipped with a 40 hp engine and a four-forward speed transmission. In 1963, the 40 hp engine and four-forward speed transmission were offered as optional equipment on the Dauphine. The Caravelle, a sports model produced in 1960–62, came equipped with the 40 hp engine and either a three- or a four-forward speed transmission. Early models were optionally

29

30 Tuning

equipped with a Ferlec clutch. This electrically operated clutch simplified the shifting procedure somewhat, but the shift lever had to be moved manually. An automatic transmission was introduced as optional equipment for the Dauphine in 1963.

The Dauphine powerplant is one of the smallest liquid-cooled, 4-cylinder engines in the import field, having only 51.5 cu. in. (845 cc.) displacement. The engine has push rod operated overhead valves and wet-type replaceable cylinder sleeves. Carburetion is by Solex. Electrical equipment is supplied by Bosch, Ducellier, Paris-Rhone, and S.E.V.

The trans-axle can be either the standard three-forward speed unit or the optional four-forward speed box, sychronized in all but the lowest gear. In 1962, first speed gear was synchronized in the three-speed unit. The four-forward speed unit is standard equipment on the Gordini, R-8, and Caravelle "S." In 1963, an automatic transmission was offered on the Dauphine. The unit consists of an electro-magnetic clutch and an electric-motor-actuated shift mechanism attached to the standard three-forward speed transmission.

GENERAL INFORMATION—R-8 AND CARAVELLE "S"

In 1963, the R-8 and Caravelle "S" were introduced. Both cars have many similarly designed units and share a larger engine (956 c.c.), differing only in power output. Both cars have 4-wheel disc brakes.

IGNITION SERVICE NOTES

DISTRIBUTOR DRIVE GEAR

The gear is splined to the oil pump extention shaft, and an offset coupling drives the distributor shaft.

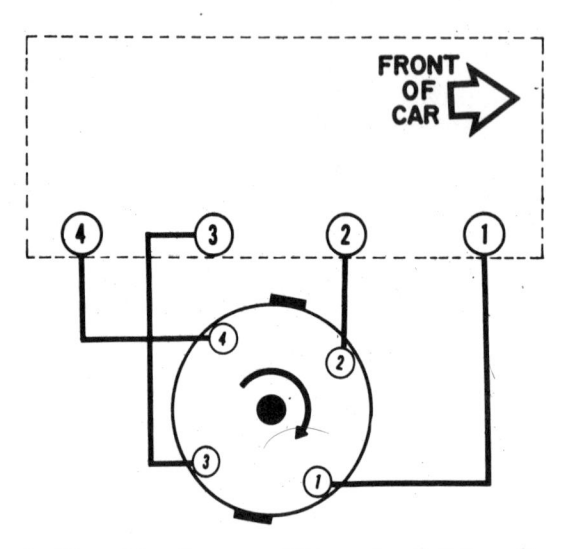

Ignition wiring diagram and firing order of all Renaults.

IGNITION TIMING—4CV, DAUPHINE, GORDINI, AND CARAVELLE

The notch in the crankshaft pulley lines up with the pin in the timing gear cover at TDC. The correct static setting is 0.118″ (3.0 mm.) ahead of the notch in the pulley, except for distributor types XD and XC, in which case the ignition timing is TDC.

To adjust the ignition timing, connect a test lamp between the primary terminal of the distributor and ground, and then turn on the ignition switch. The lamp will light when the points open as you turn the distributor in a counterclockwise direction. The use of a strobe light is not recommended.

IGNITION TIMING—R-8 AND CARAVELLE "S'"

The static timing is TDC for both models. The crankshaft pulley is marked with a notch, which will be in alignment with the top pointer (the one with the hole in it) when cylinder No. 1 is at TDC.

ROAD TESTS

The road tests that are part of this chapter are made by trained drivers of the *Road & Track* magazine staff. Their stated policy in accumulating this data is to tell the reader how the car performs and how well it will fulfill the function for which it is intended.

The speedometer is the first instrument checked because much of the resulting data depends on an accurate speedometer. The speedometer error is determined by making several timed runs over a

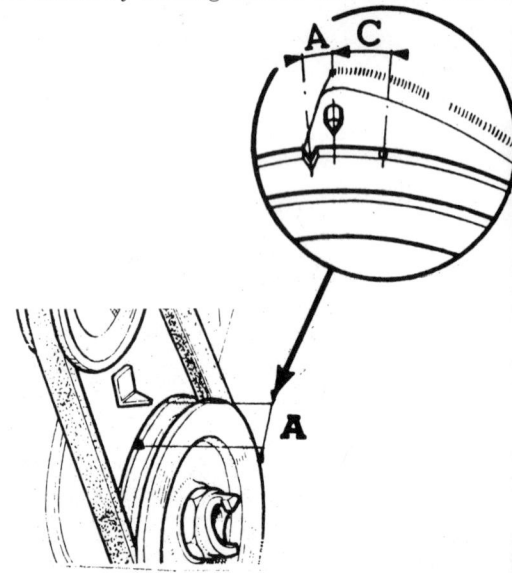

Ignition timing marks for the Renault are located on the front pulley. The notch is TDC, and the ignition timing must be set a measured distance in front of the notch (A) as specified according to model. (Courtesy of Renault, Inc.)

For Performance 31

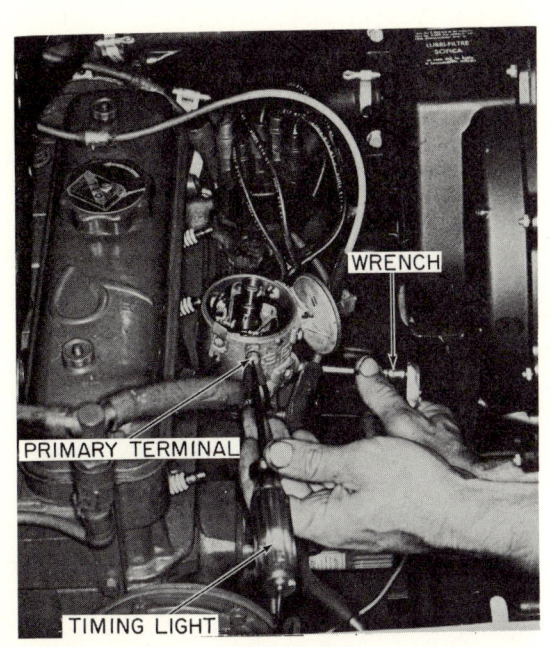

When setting the ignition timing, use a test lamp to determine the exact instant of point opening.

For a smooth-running engine, check and adjust the rocker arm clearance to the dimension given in this chapter. The valve clearance must be adjusted before the carburetor is adjusted.

Because the engine is so small, it is important to use a torque wrench to avoid distorting the block by uneven tightening of the cylinder head studs.

32 Tuning

IDLE SPEED ADJUSTMENT

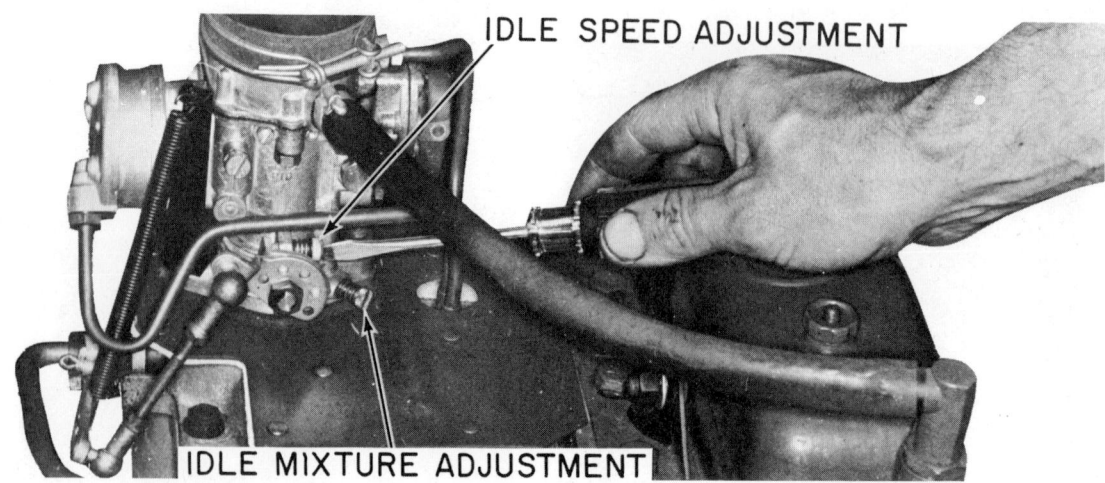

IDLE MIXTURE ADJUSTMENT

To adjust the idle speed, turn the adjusting screw in until the engine runs smoothly.

measured quarter mile course at increments of 10 mph speeds.

The gear ratios are shown in two columns; the figures on the right being those at the rear wheels, and those at the left are the actual box ratios.

The brake test data is gathered by running the car at 80 mph, and then applying the brakes as firmly as possible without locking the wheels. The measurement is made on a decelerometer.

The grade climbing ability of the car is measured with a Tapley meter. The figure shown is the maximum percentage grade that the car can climb in each gear. It is necessary to bear in mind that a 100% grade rises one foot for every foot forward, or is a 45° slope. The Tapley meter can also be used to measure drag, and the procedure is to accelerate to 80 mph on level ground and then coast back down to 60 mph. To ensure accuracy, several runs are made in each direction to compensate for slight changes in grade and wind variations.

The calculated data panel contains useful information not obtainable from the usual measured sources. *The pounds/horsepower* unit is the power-to-weight ratio. The *cubic feet per ton/mile* represents the volume of air pumped by the engine per ton of weight and per mile in high gear. When compared with the same item for other cars, it gives an excellent indication of the performance to be expected in high gear. It is calculated by dividing the displacement in half (because every second down stroke is a working stroke); and then multiplying by the engine revolutions per mile. Then the result is divided by the weight of the car to include the weight factor. *Mph per 1,000 rpm* is closely related to *piston travel in feet per mile*, which shows the number of feet traveled by the piston for each mile. These two figures are an indication of the longevity of the engine because they show the amount of activity in the engine compartment required to propel the car over a given distance.

The R&T wear index is useful in determining the amount of engine wear that can be expected. It is calculated by multiplying the engine rpms/mile by the piston travel, and then dividing by 100,000 to obtain a reasonable figure. While this figure does not take into account differences in engine design or the quality of materials used, the results do seem to be surprisingly accurate as a wear index.

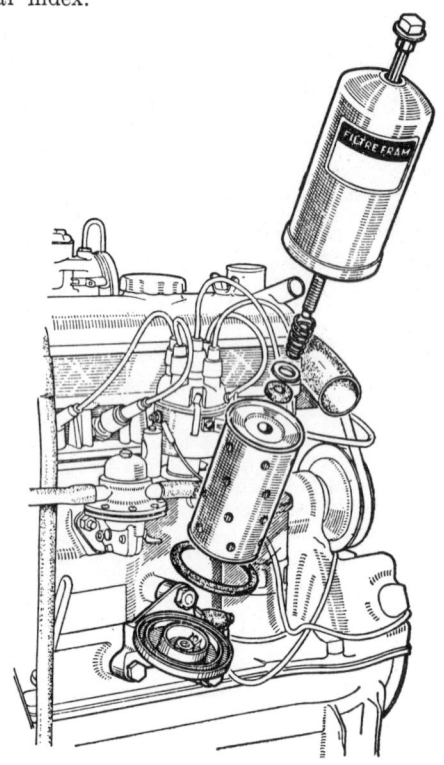

The Fram oil filter was installed on vehicles imported into North America after 1961. The element should be replaced every 6,000 miles (10,000 km). (Courtesy of Renault, Inc.)

COMMONLY USED SPECIFICATIONS—RENAULT

MODEL	SPARK PLUGS Make and Type	Gap In.	Gap Mm.	DISTRIBUTOR Point Gap In.	DISTRIBUTOR Point Gap Mm.	TIMING (Degrees)	VALVE CLEARANCE Intake C—Cold H—Hot In.	VALVE CLEARANCE Intake Mm.	VALVE CLEARANCE Exhaust C—Cold H—Hot In.	VALVE CLEARANCE Exhaust Mm.	ENGINE IDLING SPEED IN NEUTRAL (RPM)	FRONT END ALIGNMENT Caster (Degrees)	FRONT END ALIGNMENT Camber (Degrees)	Toe-in In.	Toe-in Mm.
4CV	ChI10	.024-.028	.6-.7	.016	.4	①	.006C	.15C	.008C	.20C	600 ②	P10	Nil	1/8-3/16	3.1-4.7
Dauphine	AC44F	.024-.028	.6-.7	.016-.020	.40-.50		.008C		.008C	.20C		P10	Nil	1/8-3/16	3.1-4.7
Gordini, Caravelle	AC44F	.024-.028	.6-.7	.016-.020	.40-.50	TDC	.005C	.12C	.008C	.20C	600	P10	Nil	1/8-3/16	3.1-4.7
R-8	AC44F	.024-.028	.6-.7	.016-.020	.40-.50	TDC	.005C	.12C	.008C	.20C	600	P9	P1½	1/4	6
Caravelle "S"	AC43F	.024-.028	.6-.7	.016-.020	.40-.50	TDC	.005C	.12C	.008C	.20C	600	P9	P1½	1/4	6

① Ignition should occur 0.118" (3.0 mm.) before the notch in the pulley reaches the pointer, except with distributor XC and XD, in which case the ignition timing should be set to TDC.
② Dauphine and 4CV:550 rpm with Ferlec clutch.

CAPACITIES—RENAULT

MODEL	FUEL TANK Gallons U.S.	FUEL TANK Gallons Imp.	FUEL TANK Ltr.	RADIATOR Pints U.S.	RADIATOR Pints Imp.	RADIATOR Ltr.	CRANKCASE Pints U.S.	CRANKCASE Pints Imp.	CRANKCASE Ltr.	TRANSMISSION-DIFFERENTIAL Pints U.S.	TRANSMISSION-DIFFERENTIAL Pints Imp.	TRANSMISSION-DIFFERENTIAL Ltr.	TIRE PRESSURE Front Psi	TIRE PRESSURE Front Kg./cm.²	TIRE PRESSURE Rear Psi	TIRE PRESSURE Rear Kg./cm.²
4CV	7	5.9	26.5	10	8.3	4.8	4	3.3	1.9	2.7	2.3	1.25	16	1.1	23	1.6
Dauphine	8.5	7	32	9.6	8.0	4.6	5.3②	4.5	2.5	2.7	2.3	1.25	14	1.0	23	1.6
Gordini, Caravelle																
R-8	7.5	6.4	28.4	14.6	12.0	6.9①	5.3②	4.5	2.5	3.2	2.8	1.6	14	1.0	26	1.8
Caravelle "S"				12.0	10.0	5.7①										

① Plus 1.5 U.S. pints, 1.25 Imp. pints, or 0.7 liter for the expansion tank.
② With oil filter, 6.0 U.S. pints, 5.0 Imp. pints, or 2.85 liters.

34 Tuning

GENERAL ENGINE SPECIFICATIONS—RENAULT

MODEL	CYL.	BORE In.	BORE Mm.	STROKE In.	STROKE Mm.	DISPLACEMENT Cu. In.	DISPLACEMENT CC.	COMPRESSION RATIO	PERFORMANCE SAE (Hp @ Rpm)	TORQUE SAE (Ft.-Lbs. @ Rpm)	TORQUE DIN (Kg./m. @ Rpm)
4CV R-1062	4	2.145	54.5	3.150	80	45.58	747	7.75/1.0	28 @ 4,500	43 @ 1,800	5.9 @ 1,800
Dauphine R-1090	4							8.0/1.0	32 @ 4,350	50 @ 2,000	6.9 @ 2,000
Gordini R-1091	4	2.283	58	3.15	80	51.56	845				
Caravelle R-1092	4							8.0/1.0	40 @ 5,200	47.7 @ 3,300	6.6 @ 3,300
Caravelle "S" R-1131	4	2.5991	65	2.835	72	58.28	955	9.5/1.0	51 @ 5,500	54 @ 3,500	7.5 @ 3,500
R-8 R-1130	4	2.5991	65	2.835	72	58.28	955	8.5/1.0	48 @ 5,500	55 @ 2,500	7.65 @ 2,500

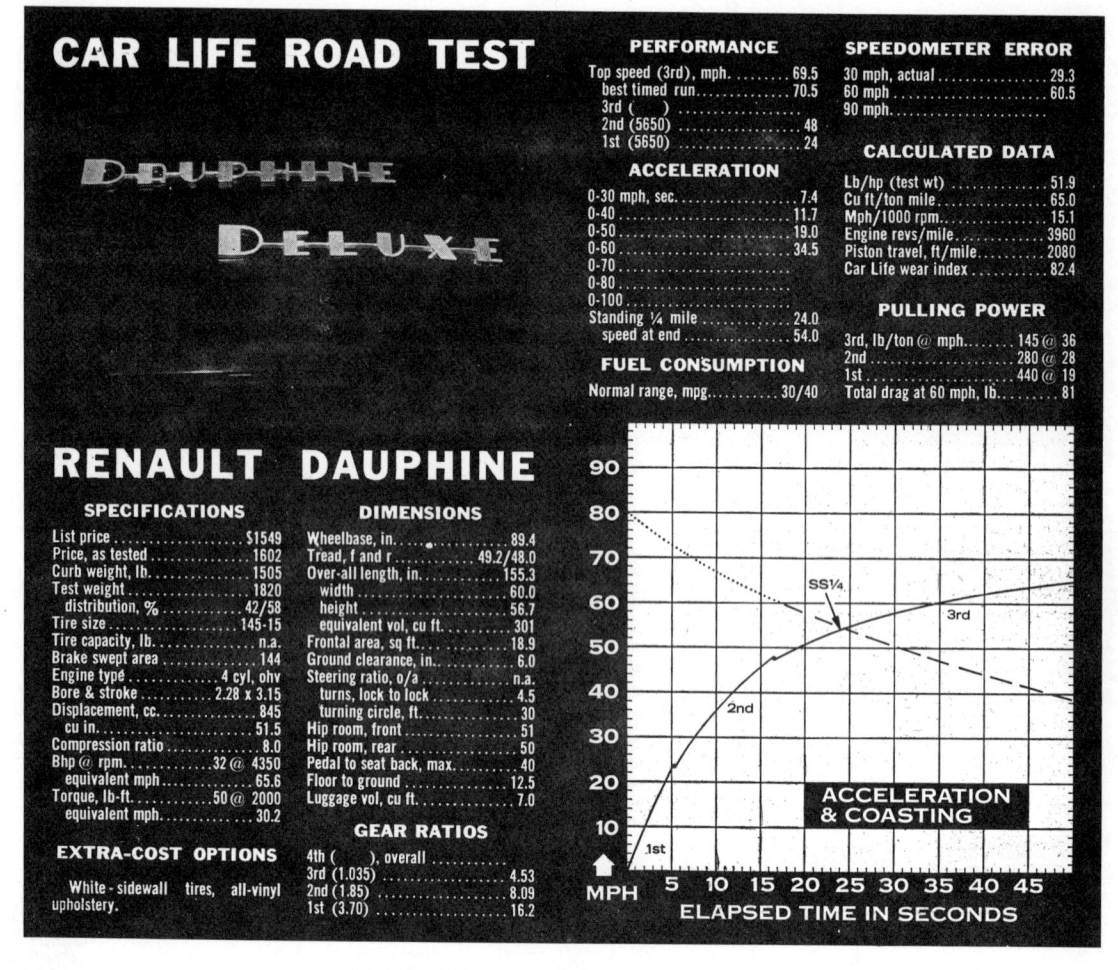

CAR LIFE ROAD TEST

Dauphine Deluxe

PERFORMANCE
- Top speed (3rd), mph ... 69.5
- best timed run ... 70.5
- 3rd ( ) ...
- 2nd (5650) ... 48
- 1st (5650) ... 24

ACCELERATION
- 0-30 mph, sec. ... 7.4
- 0-40 ... 11.7
- 0-50 ... 19.0
- 0-60 ... 34.5
- 0-70 ...
- 0-80 ...
- 0-100 ...
- Standing ¼ mile ... 24.0
- speed at end ... 54.0

FUEL CONSUMPTION
- Normal range, mpg ... 30/40

SPEEDOMETER ERROR
- 30 mph, actual ... 29.3
- 60 mph ... 60.5
- 90 mph ...

CALCULATED DATA
- Lb/hp (test wt) ... 51.9
- Cu ft/ton mile ... 65.0
- Mph/1000 rpm ... 15.1
- Engine revs/mile ... 3960
- Piston travel, ft/mile ... 2080
- Car Life wear index ... 82.4

PULLING POWER
- 3rd, lb/ton @ mph ... 145 @ 36
- 2nd ... 280 @ 28
- 1st ... 440 @ 19
- Total drag at 60 mph, lb. ... 81

RENAULT DAUPHINE

SPECIFICATIONS
- List price ... $1549
- Price, as tested ... 1602
- Curb weight, lb. ... 1505
- Test weight ... 1820
- distribution, % ... 42/58
- Tire size ... 145-15
- Tire capacity, lb. ... n.a.
- Brake swept area ... 144
- Engine type ... 4 cyl, ohv
- Bore & stroke ... 2.28 x 3.15
- Displacement, cc. ... 845
- cu in. ... 51.5
- Compression ratio ... 8.0
- Bhp @ rpm. ... 32 @ 4350
- equivalent mph ... 65.6
- Torque, lb-ft. ... 50 @ 2000
- equivalent mph. ... 30.2

EXTRA-COST OPTIONS
White - sidewall tires, all-vinyl upholstery.

DIMENSIONS
- Wheelbase, in. ... 89.4
- Tread, f and r ... 49.2/48.0
- Over-all length, in. ... 155.3
- width ... 60.0
- height ... 56.7
- equivalent vol, cu ft. ... 301
- Frontal area, sq ft. ... 18.9
- Ground clearance, in. ... 6.0
- Steering ratio, o/a ... n.a.
- turns, lock to lock ... 4.5
- turning circle, ft. ... 30
- Hip room, front ... 51
- Hip room, rear ... 50
- Pedal to seat back, max. ... 40
- Floor to ground ... 12.5
- Luggage vol, cu ft. ... 7.0

GEAR RATIOS
- 4th ( ), overall ...
- 3rd (1.035) ... 4.53
- 2nd (1.85) ... 8.09
- 1st (3.70) ... 16.2

ACCELERATION & COASTING

Road and Track road tests for the Renault.

Road Tests

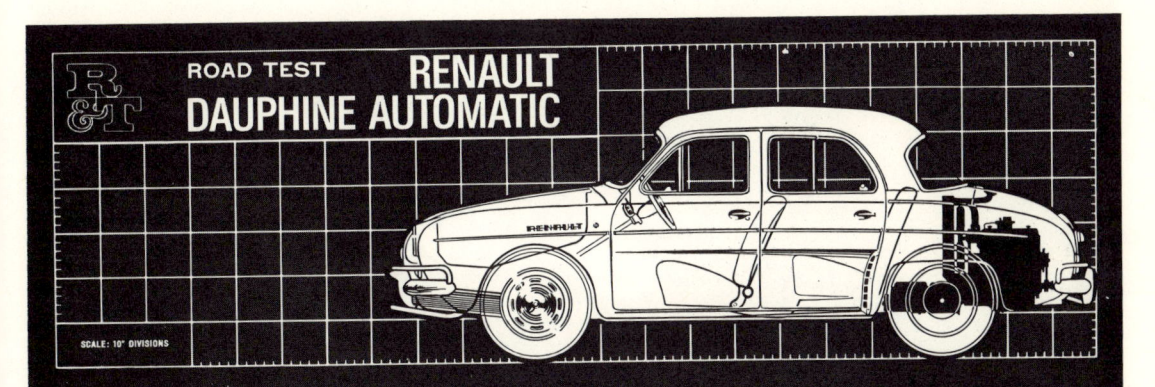

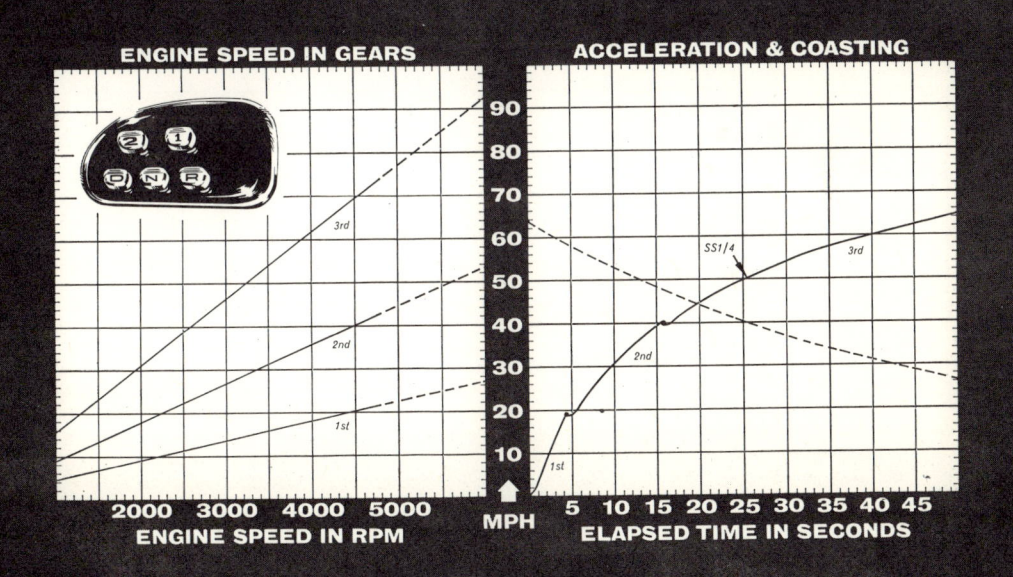

ROAD TEST RENAULT DAUPHINE AUTOMATIC

SCALE: 10" DIVISIONS

DIMENSIONS

Wheelbase, in 89.0
Tread, f and r 49/48
Over-all length, in 157.0
    width 60.0
    height 57.0
    equivalent vol, cu ft . 301
Frontal area, sq ft 18.9
Ground clearance, in 6.0
Steering ratio, o/a 24:1
    turns, lock to lock ... 4.2
    turning circle, ft 30.0
Hip room, front .... 2 x 20
Hip room, rear 48
Pedal to seat back, max . 40.0
Floor to ground 12.5

CALCULATED DATA

Lb/hp (test wt) 59.6
Cu ft/ton mile 60.9
Mph/1000 rpm (3rd) 15.4
Engine revs/mile 3888
Piston travel, ft/mile 2041
Rpm @ 2500 ft/min 4761
    equivalent mph 74.9
R&T wear index 79.4

SPECIFICATIONS

List price $1699
Curb weight, lb 1495
Test weight 1845
    distribution, % 42/58
Tire size .... 135 x 380
Brake swept area 342
Engine type .... 4 cyl, ohv
Bore & stroke .... 2.283 x 3.15
Displacement, cc 845
    cu in 51.5
Compression ratio 8.1
Bhp @ rpm .... 32 @ 4200
    equivalent mph 64.7
Torque, lb-ft .... 50 @ 2000
    equivalent mph 30.8

GEAR RATIOS

4th ( ) ....
3rd (1.03) 4.50
2nd (1.81) 7.92
1st (3.54) 15.62

SPEEDOMETER ERROR

30 mph .... actual, 27.5
60 mph 54.4

PERFORMANCE

Top speed (3rd), mph ... 72.2
    Shifts, rpm-mph
    2nd (4800) 42.0
    1st (4800) 21.3

FUEL CONSUMPTION

Normal range, mpg 32-36

ACCELERATION

0-30 mph, sec 10.0
0-40 .... 15.0
0-50 .... 26.4
0-60 .... 39.9
0-70 .... 76.0
0-80 ....
0-100 ....
Standing ¼ mile 26.0
    speed at end 49.9

TAPLEY DATA

3rd, maximum gradient, % .. 5
2nd 12
1st 19
Total drag at 60 mph, lb . 115

ENGINE SPEED IN GEARS

ACCELERATION & COASTING

Road and Track road tests for the Renault Dauphine with an automatic transmission.

Tuning

ROAD TEST: RENAULT GORDINI

DIMENSIONS
Wheelbase, in............89.4
Tread, f and r.......49.2/48.0
Over-all length, in......155.3
  width..................60.0
  height.................56.7
  equivalent vol, cu ft...301
Frontal area, sq ft......18.9
Ground clearance, in......6.0
Steering ratio, o/a......n.a.
  turns, lock to lock.....4.5
  turning circle, ft......30
Hip room, front...........51
Hip room, rear............50
Pedal to seat back, max...40
Floor to ground..........12.5

CALCULATED DATA
Lb/hp (test wt)..........47.5
Cu ft/ton mile...........62.2
Mph/1000 rpm (4th).......15.1
Engine revs/mile.........3960
Piston travel, ft/mile...2080
Rpm @ 2500 ft/min........4760
  equivalent mph.........72.1
R&T wear index...........82.4

SPECIFICATIONS
List price.............$1596
Curb weight, lb.........1550
Test weight.............1900
  distribution, %...41.5/58.5
Tire size.............145-15
Brake swept area........133
Engine type.......4 cyl, ohv
Bore & stroke....2.28 x 3.15
Displacement, cc........845
  cu in................51.5
Compression ratio.......8.0
Bhp @ rpm......40 @ 5000
  equivalent mph.......75.7
Torque, lb-ft.....48 @ 3300
  equivalent mph.......50.0

GEAR RATIOS
4th (1.035)............4.53
3rd (1.458)............6.38
2nd (2.105)............9.21
1st (3.700)...........16.2

SPEEDOMETER ERROR
30 mph..........actual, 30.2
60 mph..................60.8

PERFORMANCE
Top speed (4th), mph....80.0
  best timed run........80.5
3rd (5800)..............62
2nd (5800)..............43
1st (5850)..............25

FUEL CONSUMPTION
Normal range, mpg.....32/40

ACCELERATION
0-30 mph, sec............6.0
0-40.....................9.4
0-50....................15.0
0-60....................22.3
0-70....................39.1
0-80.....................
0-100....................
Standing ¼ mile.........22.4
  speed at end..........60.1

TAPLEY DATA
4th, lb/ton @ mph..150 @ 45
3rd..............210 @ 40
2nd..............315 @ 28
Total drag at 60 mph, lb...65

Road and Track road tests for the Renault Gordini.

ROAD TEST
RENAULT R-8

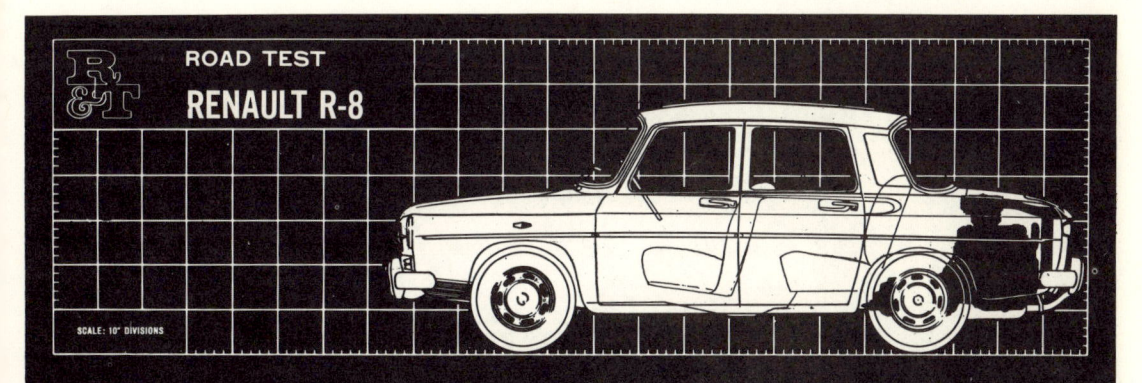

SCALE: 10" divisions

DIMENSIONS
Wheelbase, in........89.37
Tread, f and r.....49.4/48.3
Over-all length, in....157.5
   width............58.7
   height...........55.5
   equivalent vol, cu ft...297
Frontal area, sq ft......18.2
Ground clearance, in....5.7
Steering ratio, o/a....20.0
   turns, lock to lock....3.6
   turning circle, ft.....30.4
Hip room, front......2 x 22
Hip room, rear........52.7
Pedal to seat back....40.0
Floor to ground.......12.0

CALCULATED DATA
Lb/hp (test wt).........39.6
Cu ft/ton mile.........70.2
Mph/1000 rpm (4th)....15.2
Engine revs/mile......3950
Piston travel, ft/mile...1865
Rpm @ 2500 ft/min....5290
   equivalent mph......80.4
R&T wear index.......73.6

SPECIFICATIONS
List price...........$1795
Curb weight, lb.......1600
Test weight..........1900
   distribution, %......42/58
Tire size...........155-15
Brake swept area......342
Engine type......4-cyl, ohv
Bore & stroke....2.56 x 2.83
Displacement, cc.......956
   cu in.............58.3
Compression ratio.....8.50
Bhp @ rpm......48 @ 5200
   equivalent mph......79.0
Torque, lb-ft....55 @ 2500
   equivalent mph......37.9

GEAR RATIOS
4th (1.03)............4.53
3rd (1.52)............6.65
2nd (2.28)............9.98
1st (3.70)............16.2

SPEEDOMETER ERROR
30 mph..........actual, 27.0
60 mph..............55.0

PERFORMANCE
Top speed (5200), mph....79
   best timed run......n.a.
3rd (5800).............60
2nd (5800).............40
1st (5900).............25

FUEL CONSUMPTION
Normal range, mpg.....27/35

ACCELERATION
0-30 mph, sec..........5.0
0-40..................9.7
0-50.................15.0
0-60.................21.4
0-70.................37.0
0-80..................
0-100.................
Standing ¼ mile......22.5
   speed at end.........61

TAPLEY DATA
4th, lb/ton @ mph....155 @ 42
3rd..............220 @ 31
2nd..............340 @ 17
Total drag at 60 mph, lb....90

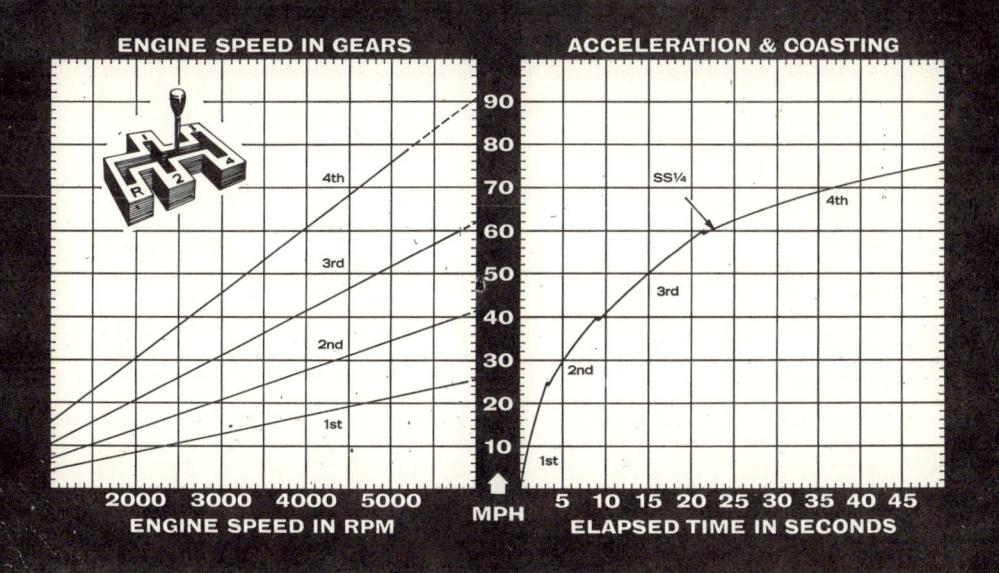

ENGINE SPEED IN GEARS

ACCELERATION & COASTING

Road and Track road tests for the Renault R-8.

38 Tuning

ROAD TEST
RENAULT CARAVELLE S

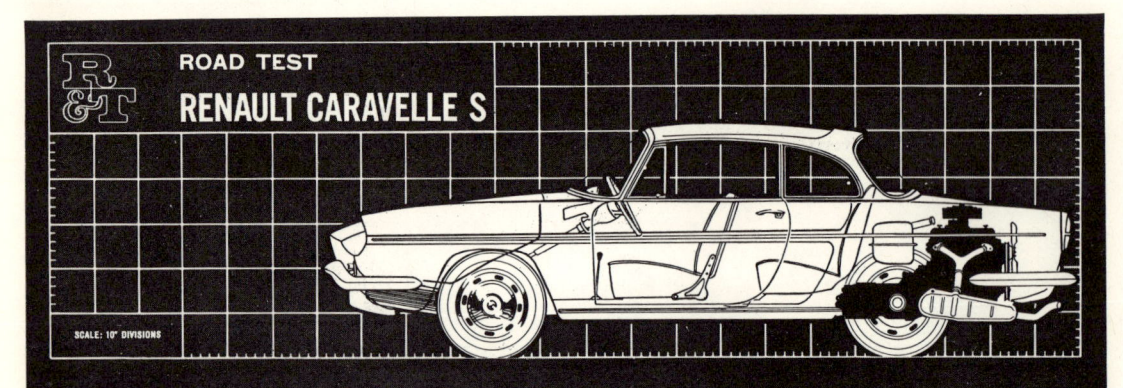

SCALE: 10" DIVISIONS

DIMENSIONS

Wheelbase, in............89.4
Tread, f and r......49.3/48.0
Over-all length, in......167.9
   width................62.0
   height................52.8
   equivalent vol, cu ft....318
Frontal area, sq ft.......18.7
Ground clearance, in.....5.75
Steering ratio, o/a........n.a.
   turns, lock to lock......3.7
   turning circle, ft.......31.5
Hip room, front.......2 x 20
Hip room, rear..........47.5
Pedal to seat back, max..43.5
Floor to ground..........11.2

CALCULATED DATA

Lb/hp (test wt).........40.8
Cu ft/ton mile...........61.7
Mph/1000 rpm (4th)....15.3
Engine revs/mile........3920
Piston travel, ft/mile....1855
Rpm @ 2500 ft/min....5280
   equivalent mph........81
R&T wear index.........72.7

SPECIFICATIONS

List price............$2456
Curb weight, lb.......1715
Test weight...........2080
   distribution, %.....39/61
Tire size............145-15
Brake swept area......342
Engine type......4-cyl, ohv
Bore & stroke....2.56 x 2.84
Displacement, cc......956
   cu in...............58.3
Compression ratio......9.5
Bhp @ rpm......51 @ 5500
   equivalent mph........84
Torque, lb-ft....54 @ 3500
   equivalent mph........54

GEAR RATIOS

4th (1.03)............4.51
3rd (1.52)............6.65
2nd (2.28)............9.98
1st (3.70)............16.2

SPEEDOMETER ERROR

30 mph........actual, 28.1
60 mph................56.7

PERFORMANCE

Top speed (5550), mph....85
   best timed run........n.a.
   3rd (6100).............63
   2nd (6050).............42
   1st (6100).............26

FUEL CONSUMPTION

Normal range, mpg....26/32

ACCELERATION

0-30 mph, sec..........5.7
0-40..................8.8
0-50.................13.5
0-60.................19.4
0-70.................30.8
0-80.................57.0
0-100..................
Standing ¼ mile......21.5
   speed at end..........62

TAPLEY DATA

4th, lb/ton @ mph..130 @ 54
3rd................215 @ 47
2nd................330 @ 35
Total drag at 60 mph, lb....70

ENGINE SPEED IN GEARS

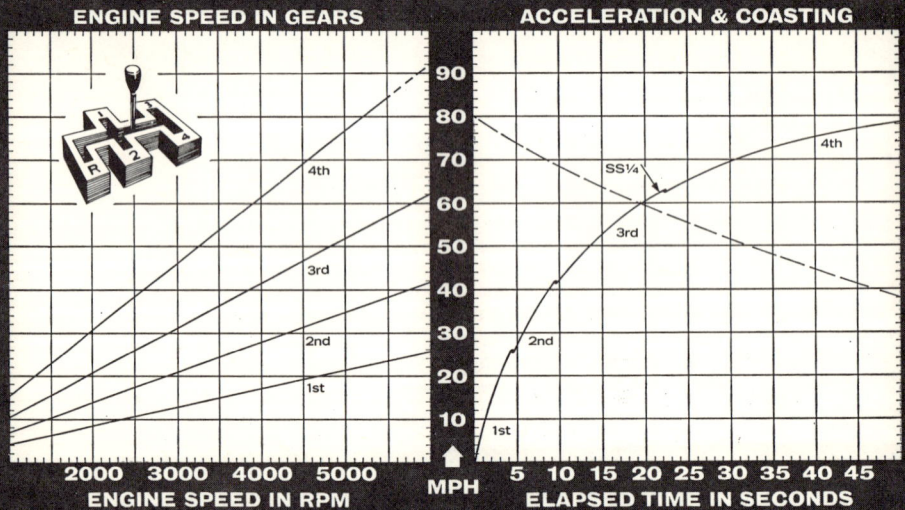

ACCELERATION & COASTING

Road and Track road tests for the Caravelle "S."

3

The Fuel System

All Renault models use Solex carburetors, which differ only in minor degree. The jet sizes can be found in the Solex Carburetor Specification table. A series of illustrated step-by-step instructions show how to overhaul the Solex 28 IBT model, used on the Renault, and exploded views are provided as a guide for the other models.

OVERHAULING A SOLEX MODEL 28 IBT CARBURETOR

Disassembling

① Remove the three float chamber cover screws and lift off the cover. Remove the pilot jet (g) (called the idle jet in the United States), the plug, and the main jet (Gg) from the side of the carburetor. Remove the idle adjusting screw.

② Lift out the float and hinge pin. Remove the three screws holding the automatic choke cover in place, and then remove the cover.

③ Remove the two screws holding the starter body, and then lift off the assembly. Slide the starter valve from the thermostatic spring. Remove the air corrector jet (a) with the emulsion tube (s) attached.

④ Remove the screw which holds the auto starter piston assembly in place. Keep your hand over the top to prevent the piston from popping out. Lift out the piston and spring. Remove the starter petrol jet (Gs).

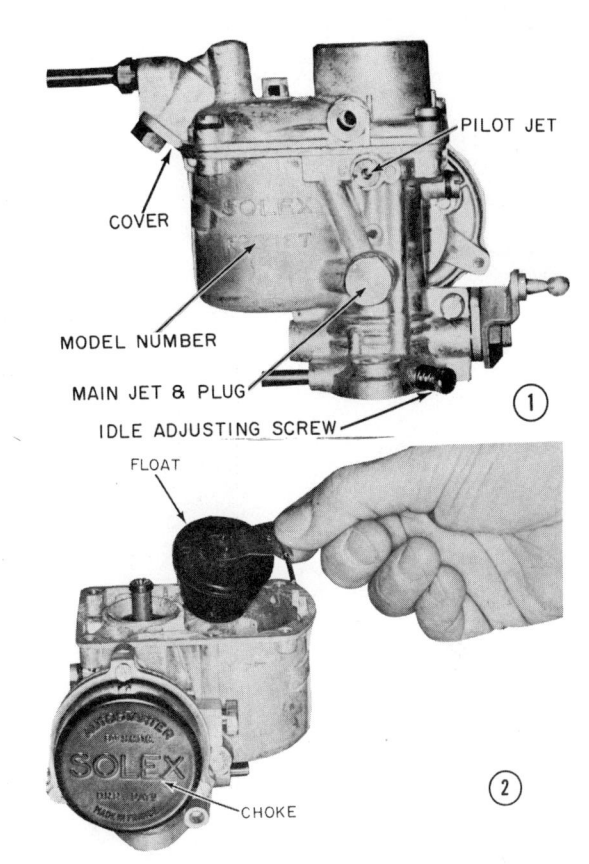

SOLEX CARBURETOR SPECIFICATIONS—RENAULT

CAR MODEL	CARBURETOR MODEL	CHOKE TUBE (Venturi) K	MAIN JET Gg	AIR CORRECTOR JET a	PILOT JET g	EMULSION TUBE s	NEEDLE VALVE P	FLOAT (gr.) F	ACCELERATING PUMP Pump Jet Gp	No.	STARTER Air Jet Ga	Petrol Jet Gs
4CV	22BIC	18	100	165	40		1.5	12.5				95
	22ICBT	18	100	165	40		1.5	12.5				95
5CV Dauphine	281BT	19	92	155 K	45		1.5	5.7				95
5CV Dauphine Since 1961	28IBT	20.8	90	165 X	37		1.6	5.7				95
Caravelle	32PIBT	22	97	200	40	60	1.2	5.7	40	73		115
	32PIBT ①	22	110	175	40	19	1.5	5.7	40	72		110
Gordini	32PIBT	22	112	175	40	19	1.2	5.7	40	52		115
R-8 & Caravelle "S"	32PDIST	26	125	100	50		1.5	5.7				

① Since May 1960. Earlier models can be so modified provided the acceleration enricher is plugged.

39

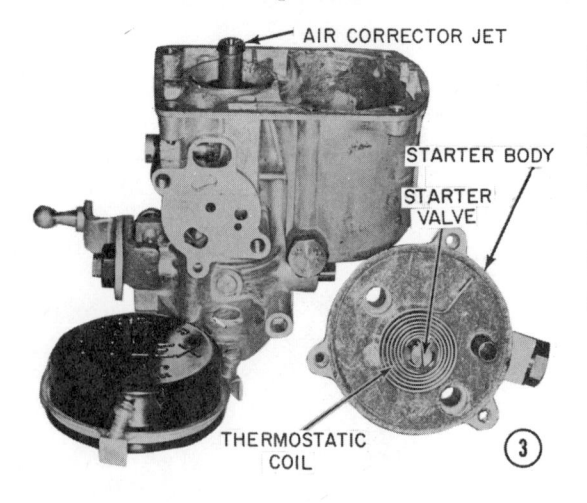

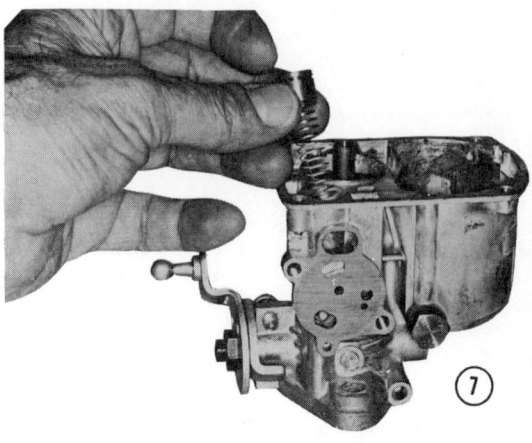

Fuel System

(Figure 3: AIR CORRECTOR JET, STARTER BODY, STARTER VALVE, THERMOSTATIC COIL)

(Figure 4: STARTER PETROL JET)

(Figure 5: NEEDLE VALVE & SEAT, FUEL STRAINER)

(Figure 6)

(Figure 7)

⑤ From the cover, remove the needle valve and seat assembly. Take out the fuel strainer.

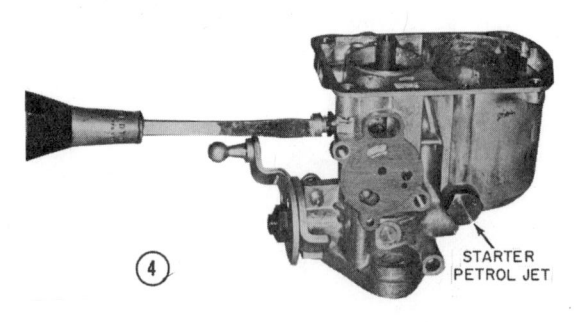

Cleaning and Inspecting

Clean all parts in carburetor cleaner. Follow with a solvent bath and blow dry. The diaphragms should be cleaned only in solvent—never in carburetor cleaner. Blow compressed air through all passageways and jets to make sure that they are open.

Check the throttle shaft for wear. If it appears to be excessively loose, replace the shaft. Service parts are available.

Shake the float to check for leaks. Replace the float assembly if it contains liquid. Check the float arm needle contacting surface and replace the float assembly if it is grooved.

Always replace any diaphragms as they deteriorate on exposure to air.

A carburetor kit is generally purchased for each carburetor overhaul. It contains new parts to replace those which wear the most, plus a complete set of gaskets. Each kit contains a matched fuel inlet needle and seat assembly, which should be replaced each time the carburetor is taken apart; otherwise, leaking will result.

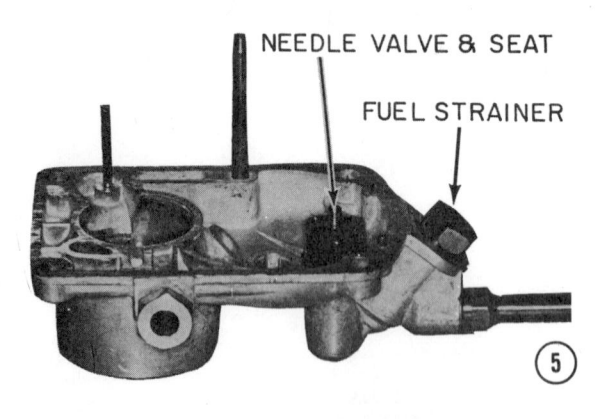

Assembling

⑥ Replace the starter petrol jet (Gs).
⑦ Replace the auto starter piston and spring assembly. Retain it with the screw-type pin from the front of the carburetor. Make sure that the piston moves freely in its bore by pressing on it with a thin screwdriver.

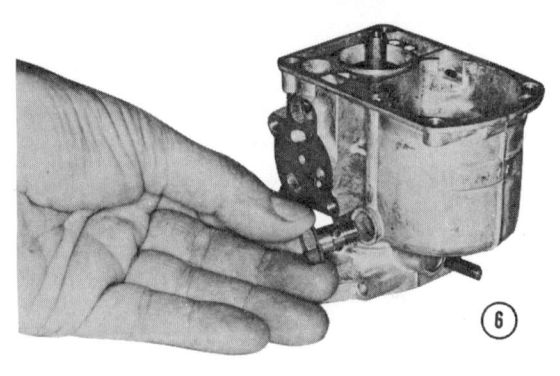

(Figure 8)

Service 41

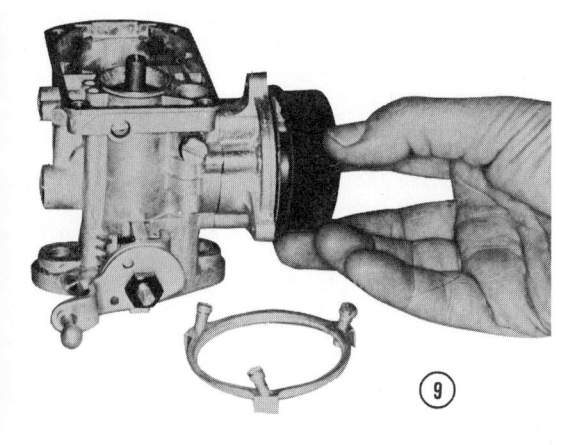

⑧ Replace the starting valve by sliding it through the thermostatic spring and hooking the spring over the slot in the end of the shaft. Fasten the assembly to the carburetor with the two retaining screws. *CAUTION: Make sure that the hole in the starter valve indexes with the hole in the carburetor body.*

⑨ Replace the choke cover; the slot in the cover must pick up the thermostatic coil end. Adjust its position so that the ridge on the cover indexes with the mark on the starting valve body. Install the ring and tighten the three retaining screws evenly.

⑩ Replace the main jet (Gg), and then install the cover.

⑪ Install the idle jet (g).

⑫ Replace the idle mixture adjusting screw. Turn it in gently until it just contacts the seat, and then back it out one turn for a preliminary adjustment. *CAUTION: Be careful not to force*

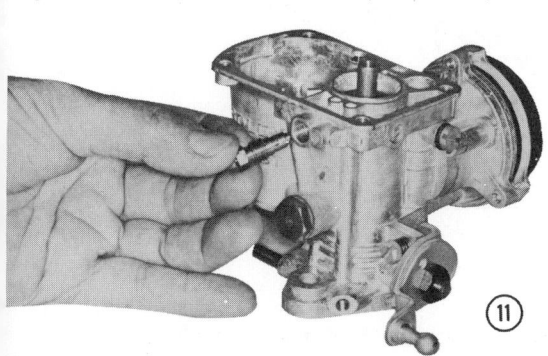

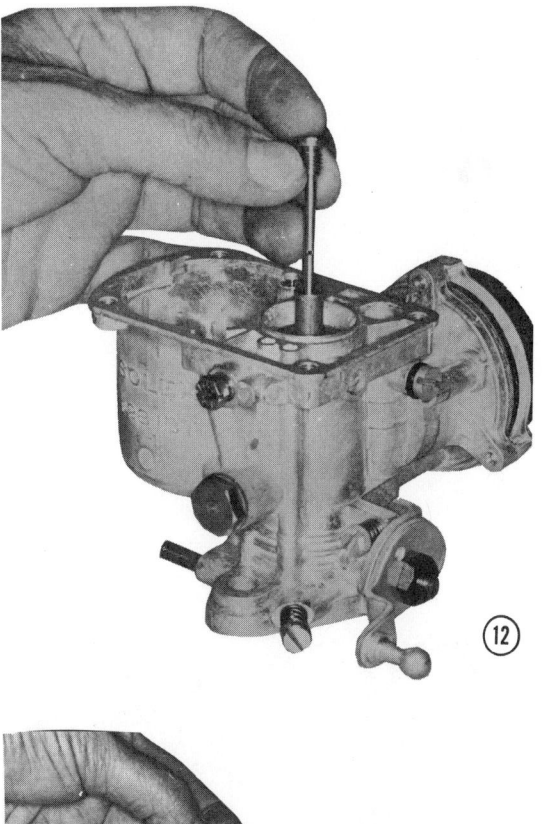

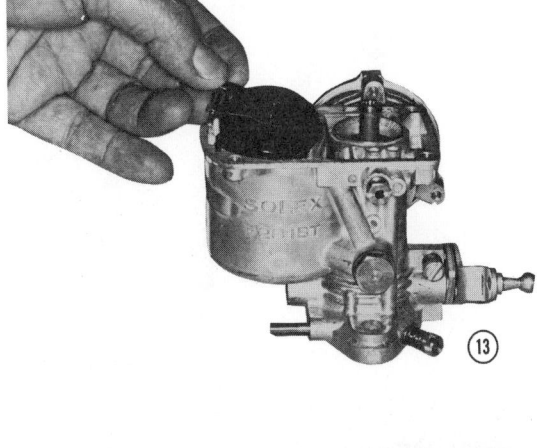

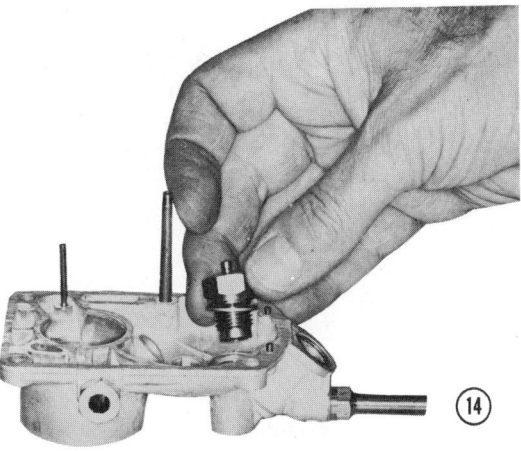

42　Fuel System

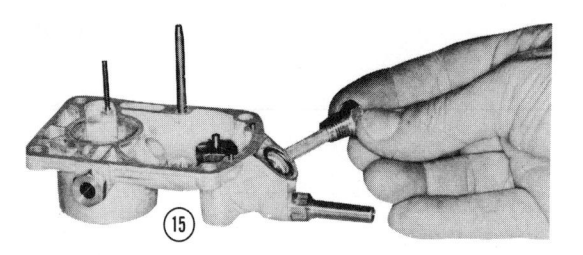

the needle into contact with the seat. Excessive pressure will groove it, making it difficult to obtain the correct idle mixture adjustment. Install the emulsion tube, with the air corrector jet attached.

⑬ Replace the float and hinge pin assembly.
⑭ Install a new needle and seat assembly.
⑮ Replace the screen and plug assembly.
⑯ Position a new gasket over the cover, and then place the cover on the body. Replace the cover attaching screws, tightening them securely.

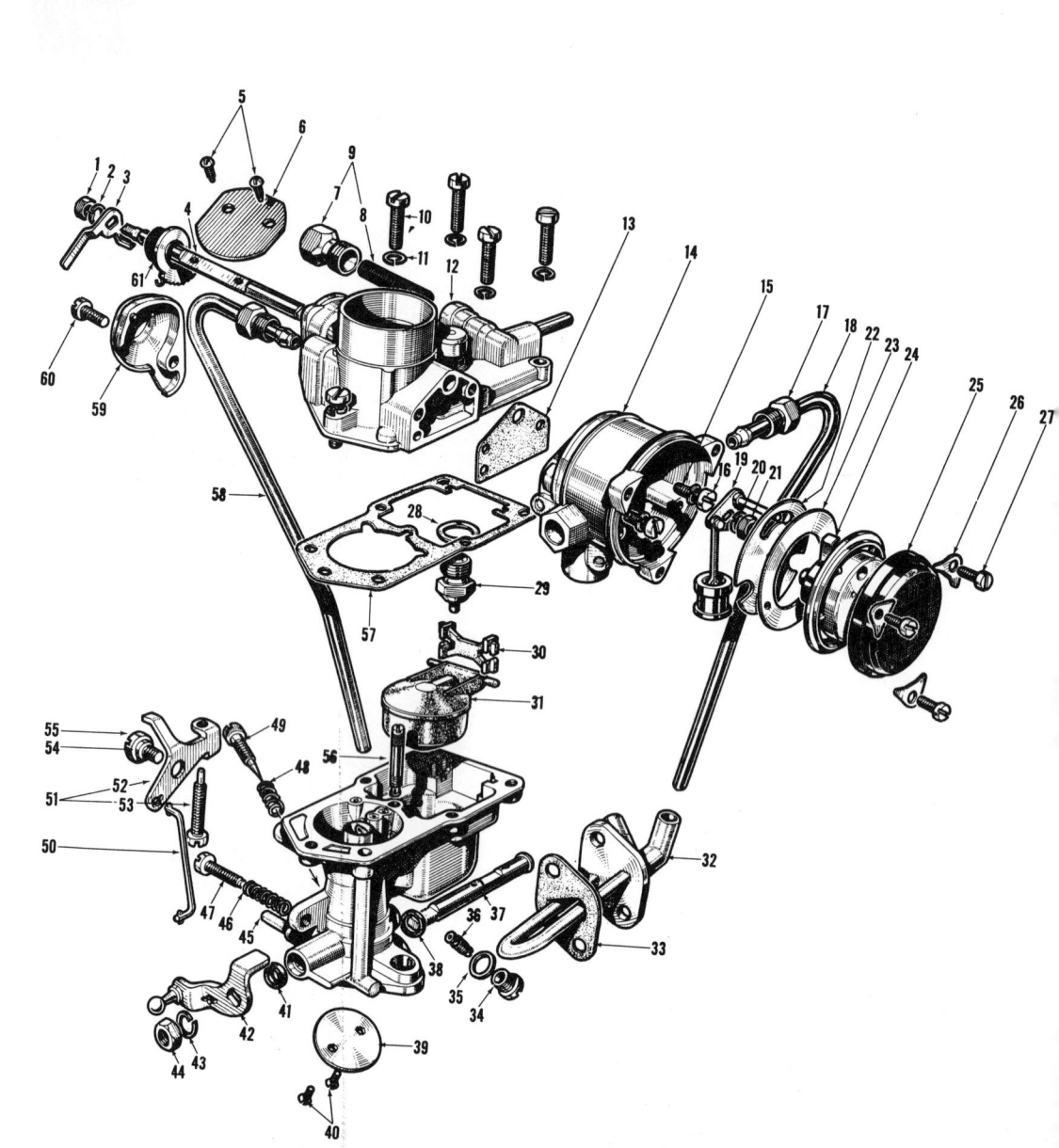

Exploded view of the Zenith 28 IFT carburetor used on the Renault, 1963-64.

Service 43

Exploded view of the Solex 22 ICBT carburetor used on the Renault 4CV.

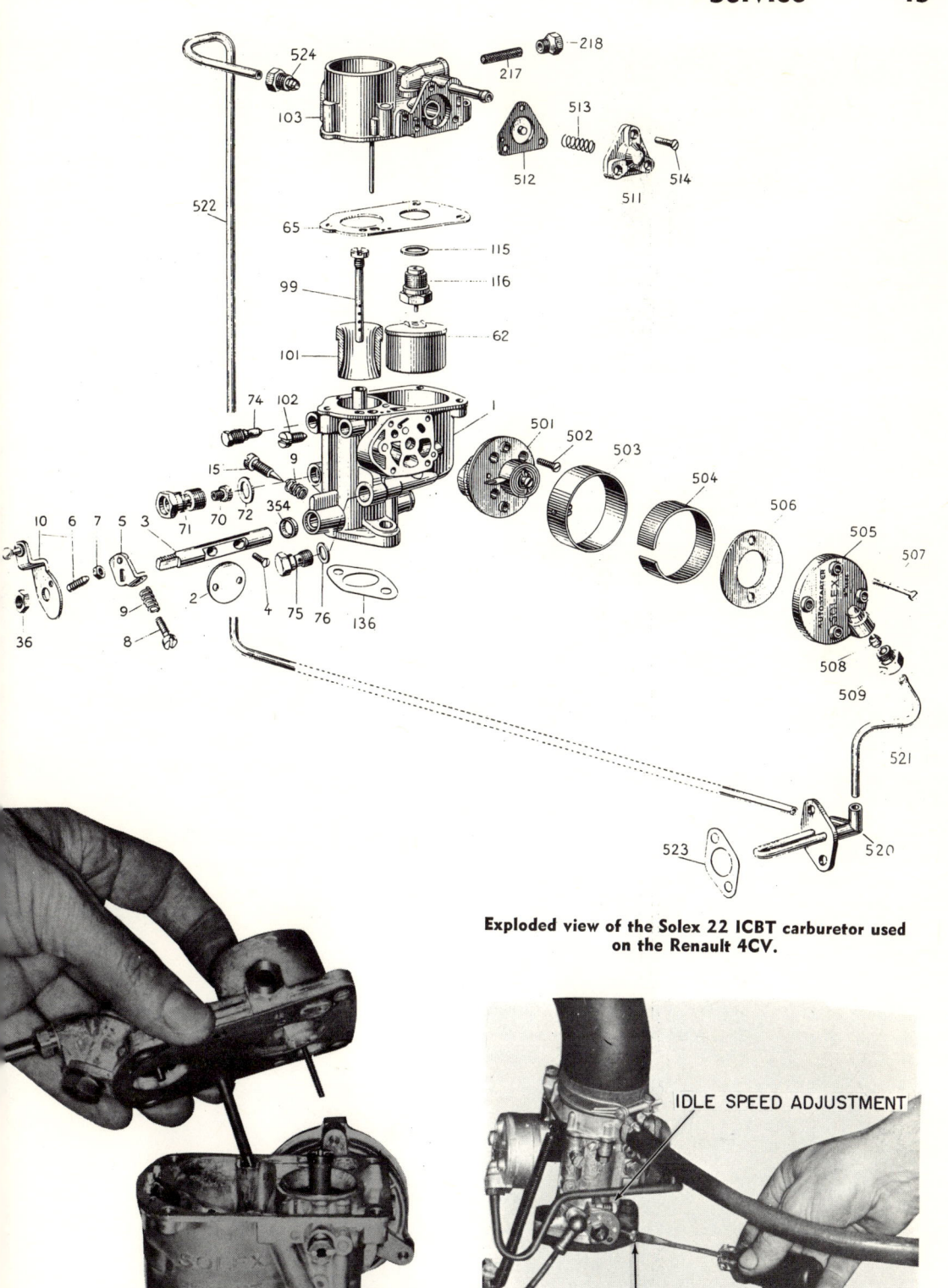

The final tuning adjustment is idle speed and mixture. Turn the mixture adjusting screw in until the engine rocks, and then back it out until it runs smoothly.

44 Fuel System

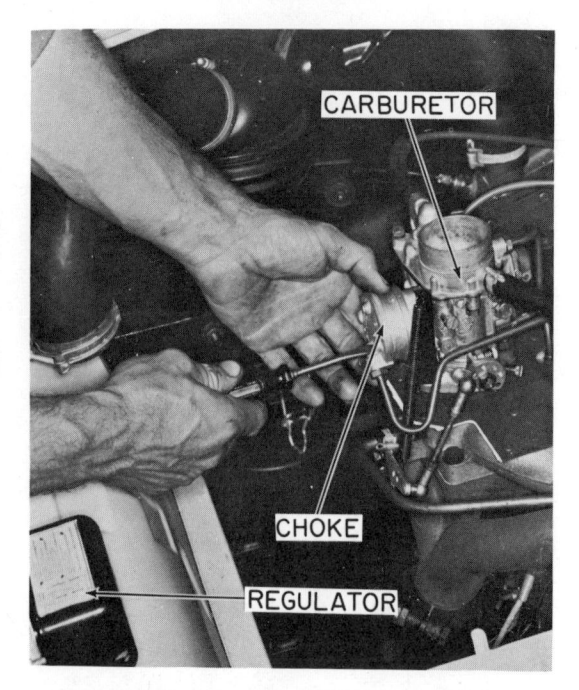

To adjust the automatic choke, loosen the three retaining screws, and then turn the cover clockwise to enrich the mixture.

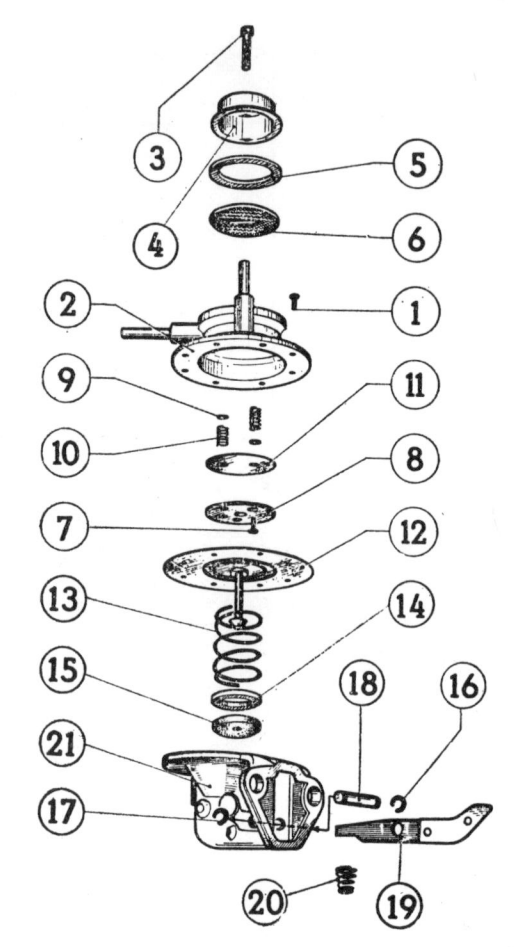

Exploded view of the S.E.V. fuel pump. (Courtesy of Renault, Inc.)

Service 45

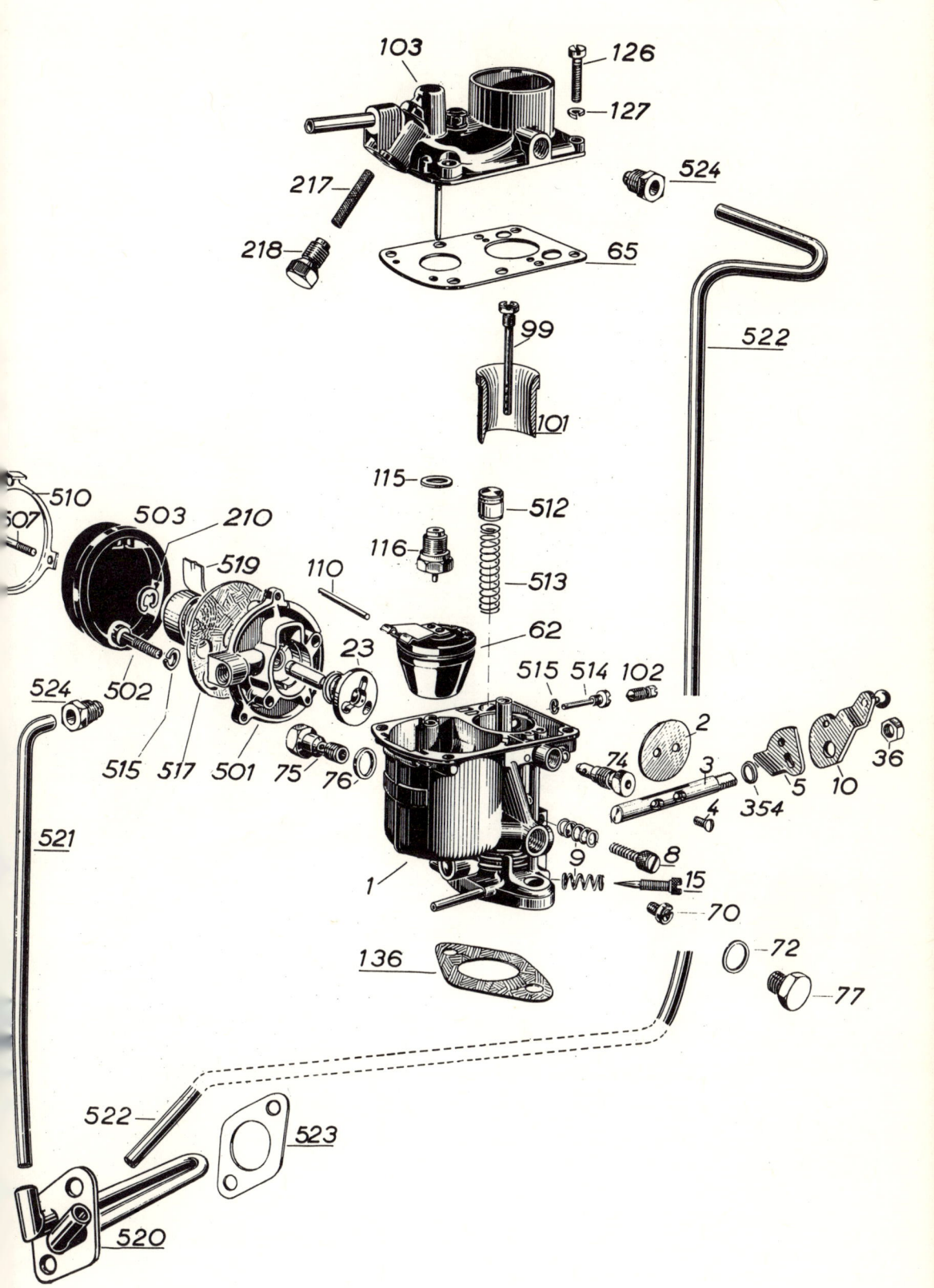

Exploded view of the Solex 28 IBT carburetor used on the Dauphine through 1960.

46 Fuel System

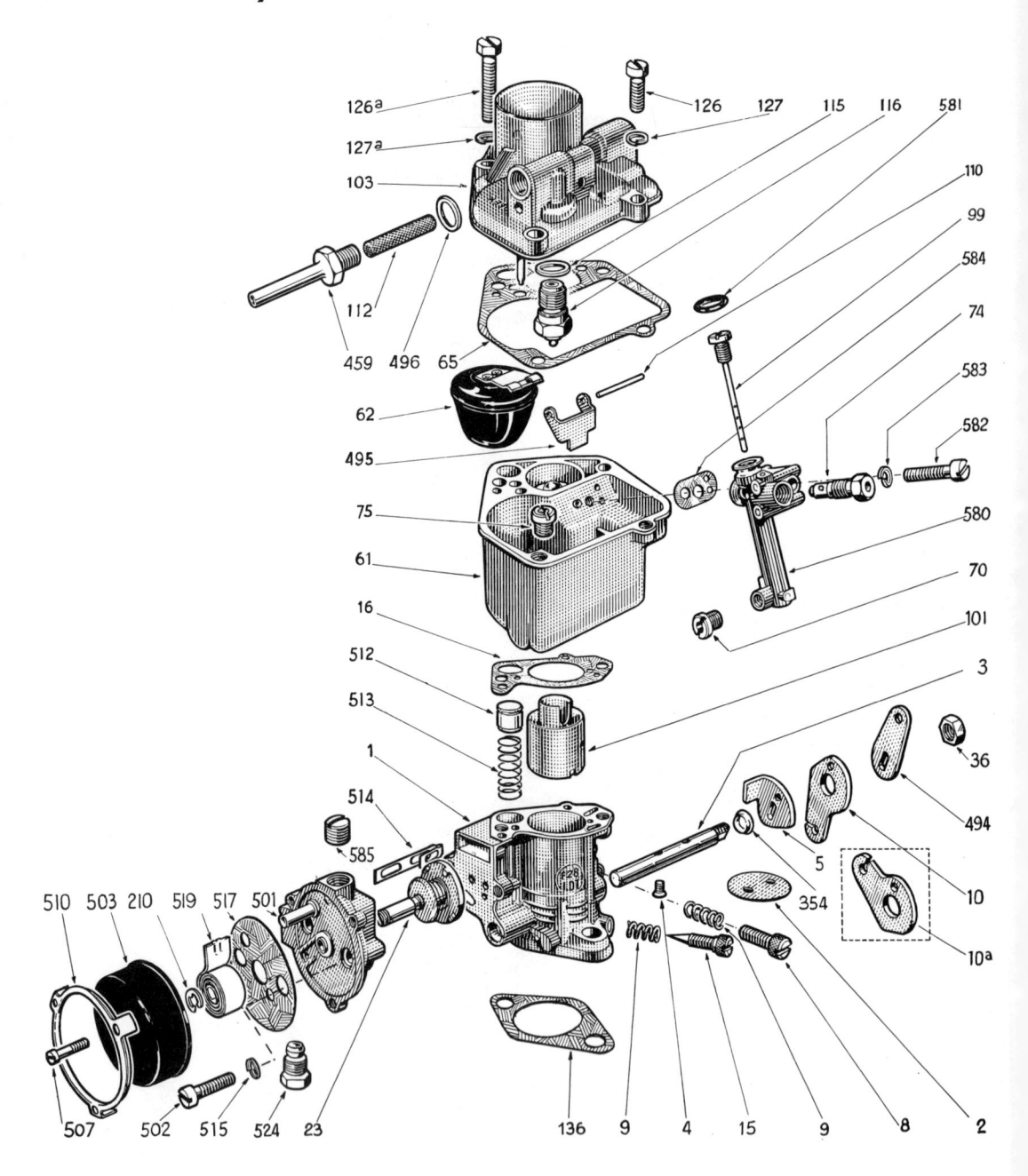

Exploded view of the Solex 28 IDT carburetor used on the Renault, 1961–62.

Service 47

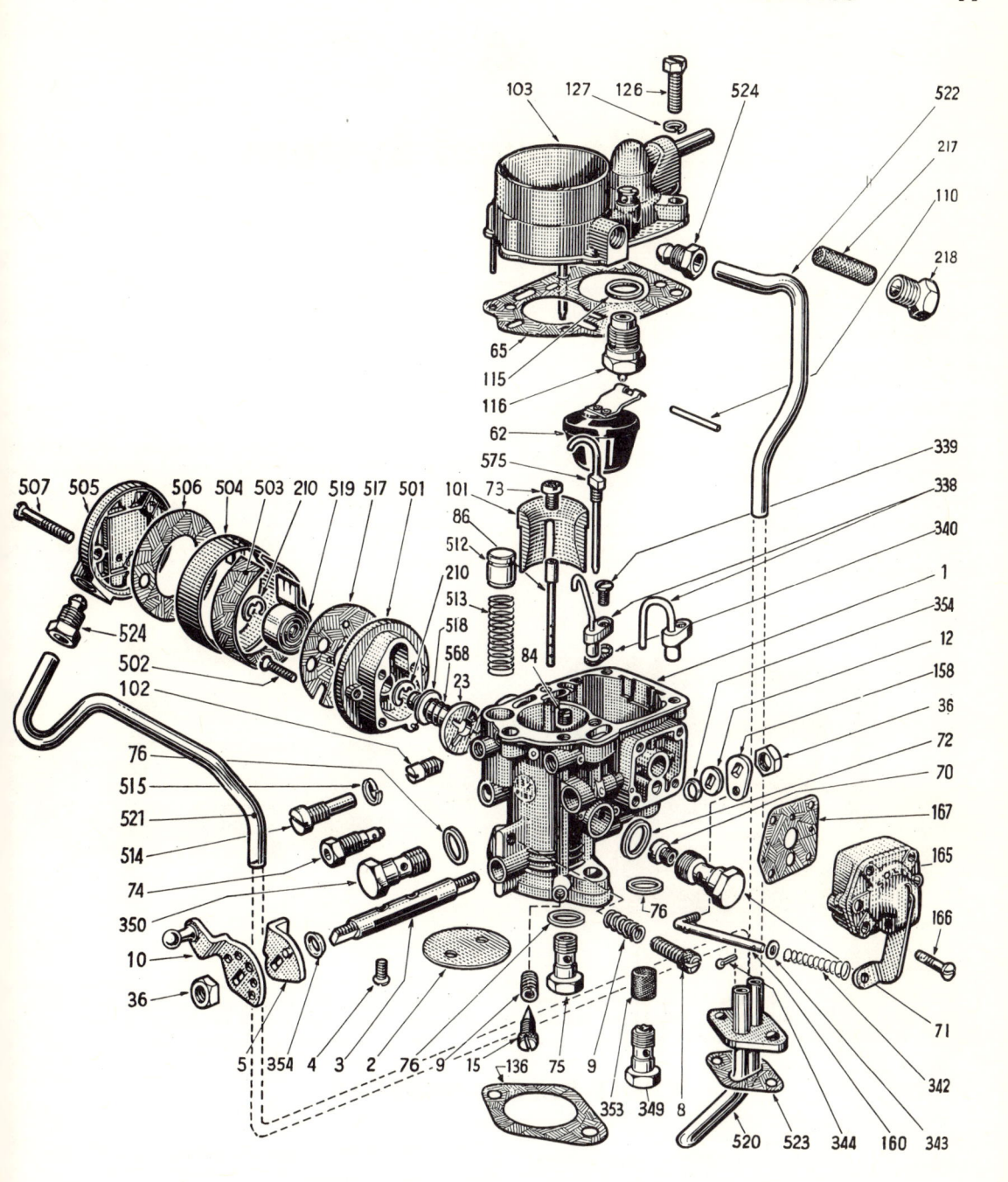

Exploded view of the Renault Caravelle carburetor.

4

The Electrical System

The 4CV and the Dauphine used a 6-volt electrical system through 1960, up to vehicle number 1178371. From 1961 on, a 12-volt system was installed in all models, including the Caravelle "S" and the R-8. The negative post of the battery is grounded in all models.

The Dauphine comes equipped with an S.E.V. ignition system; the generator is made by Paris-Rhone or Ducellier for the 6-volt systems and by Bosch for the 12-volt units. The regulators used with the Paris-Rhone generators are manufactured by Cibié.

Generator and regulator testing is covered in the Troubleshooting chapter and ignition service is covered in Chapter 2.

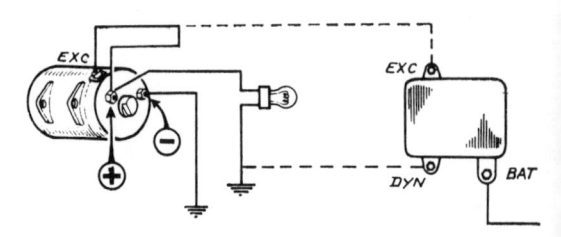

To check the generator, remove the EXC wire at the generator and connect a jumper wire between the EXC terminal and the DYN terminal on the generator. This test is valid for all 6-volt generators. *CAUTION: It must not be used on the 12-volt units.* Run the engine at not over 1,000 rpm to test. (Courtesy of Renault, Inc.)

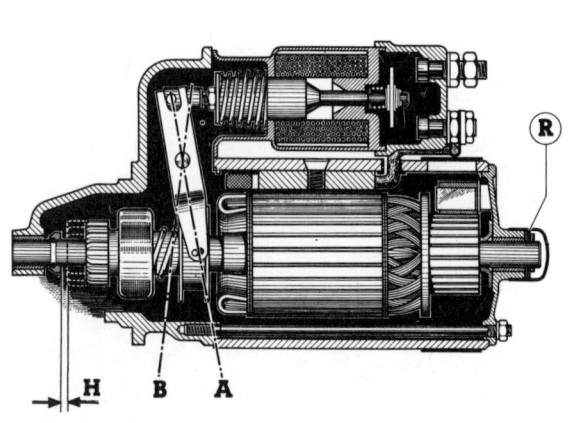

Sectioned view of the Paris-Rhone starting motor, Type D8E 15. Dimension "H" should be 0.020"–0.100" (0.5–2.5 mm.). (Courtesy of Renault, Inc.)

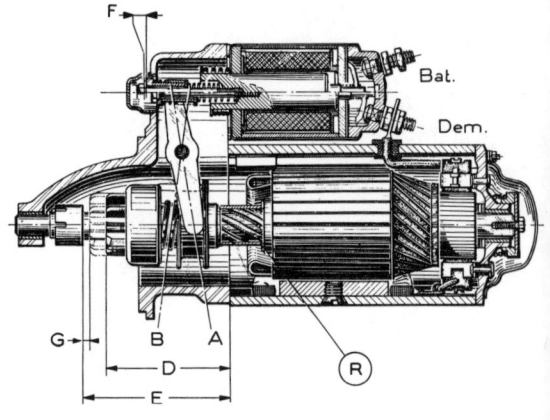

Sectioned view of the Ducellier starting motor, Type 6010 D. "F" should be 0.004"–0.020" (0.1–0.5 mm.) and "G" should be 0.004"–0.060" (0.1–1.5 mm.). (Courtesy of Renault, Inc.)

LIGHT BULBS—RENAULT

MODEL	HEAD LAMPS Outer	HEAD LAMPS Indicator	PARKING	TAIL	STOP	DIRECTION SIGNALS Front	DIRECTION SIGNALS Rear	DIRECTION SIGNALS Indicator	LICENSE PLATE	INSTRUMENT	IGNITION	BACK-UP
4CV, 1950-54	6006	44	55	63	81	81	81	44	81	44	44	
4CV, 1956-58	6006	44	1154	63	81	1154	81	44	81	44	44	
4CV, 1959-61	6006	44	1154	1154	1154	1154	1154	44	81	44	44	
Dauphine 6-Volt	6006	44	1154	1154	1154	1154	1154	44	81	44	44	
Dauphine, Caravelle, & Gordini 12-Volt	6012	53	1034	1034	1034	1034	1034	53	89	53	53	

Specifications

GENERATOR AND REGULATOR SPECIFICATIONS—RENAULT

GENERATOR

Part Number	Brush Spring Tension Ounces	Brush Spring Tension Grams	Field Amperes 6 Volts	Field Amperes 12 Volts	Resistance
DUCELLIER 6-VOLT—					
7138 / 7181 / 7188	16-21	450-600			
PARIS-RHONE 6-VOLT—					
G11R79	16-21	450-600			
G11R90	16-21	450-600			
BOSCH 12-VOLT—					
LJ/GG240/12/2400R14	16-21	450-600			

REGULATOR

Part Number	Air Gap In.	Air Gap Mm.	Cutout Relay Point Gap In.	Cutout Relay Point Gap Mm.	Cut-in Voltage	Cut-out Voltage	Current Regulator (Amps.)	Voltage Regulator (Volt. @ 69°F.)
Ducellier-1331 8212	.004-.010 ①	.10-.25			6.0-6.5	4.8 min.	30-32	7.7-8.1
Cibié-H.26							24	6.4-6.8
H.27							30	6.4-6.8
RS/UA240/12/42					12.7-13.4	5-9 ②	27-31	14.5-15.3

① With points closed.
② Reverse current.

STARTER AND BATTERY SPECIFICATIONS—RENAULT

STARTER

Mfg. Part Number (Ducellier)	Brush Spring Tension Ounces	Brush Spring Tension Grams	Free Running Test Max. Amps.	Free Running Test Min. Volts	Free Running Test Min. Rpm	Resistance Test Max. Amps.	Resistance Test Min. Volts	Resistance Test Torque Ft.-Lbs.	Resistance Test Torque M.Kg.	Rpm	Lock Test Max. Amps.	Lock Test Min. Volts	Lock Test Torque Ft.-Lbs.	Lock Test Torque M.Kg.
6010B, 6060			65	6							400		5.4	.75
6077A			50	12							330		7.0	.95

BATTERY

Volts	Terminal Grounded	Capacity (Ampere hour @ 20 hour rate)	Group Number TEM	Group Number S.A.E.	Group Number A.A.B.M.
6	N	75/90	M3AS	7L1	18M
12	N	40/50	M10AS	2SM	24S

50 Electrical System

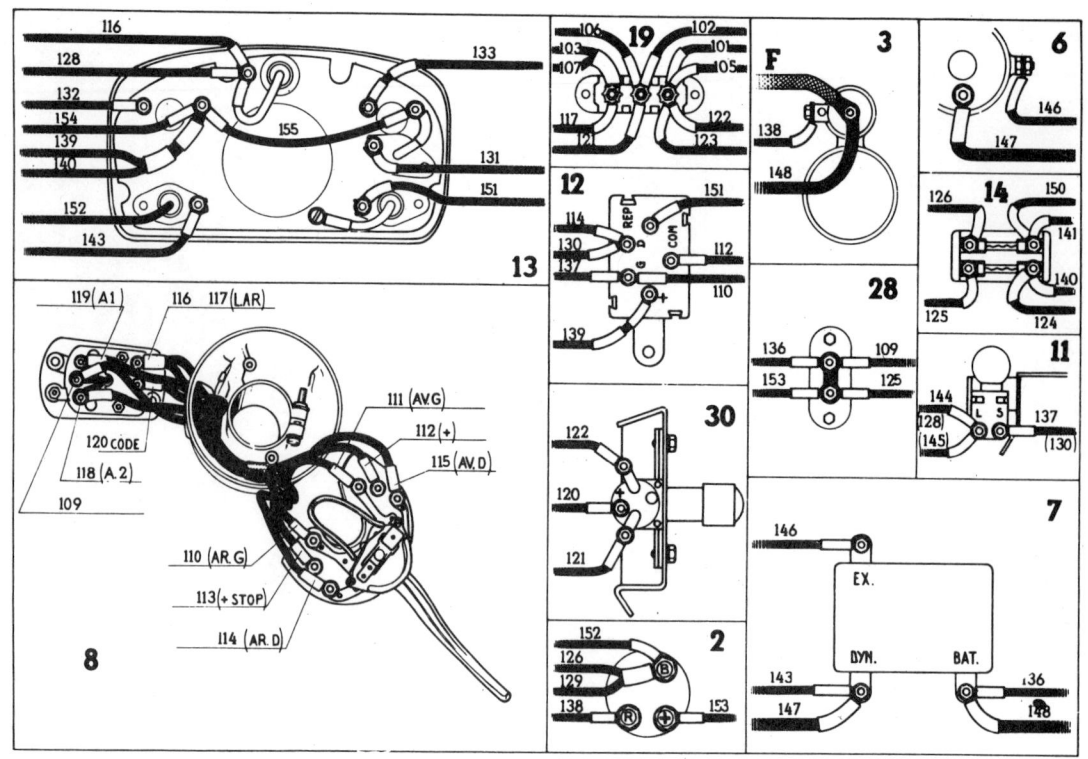

Wiring connection details for the Renault 4CV below. (Courtesy of Renault, Inc.)

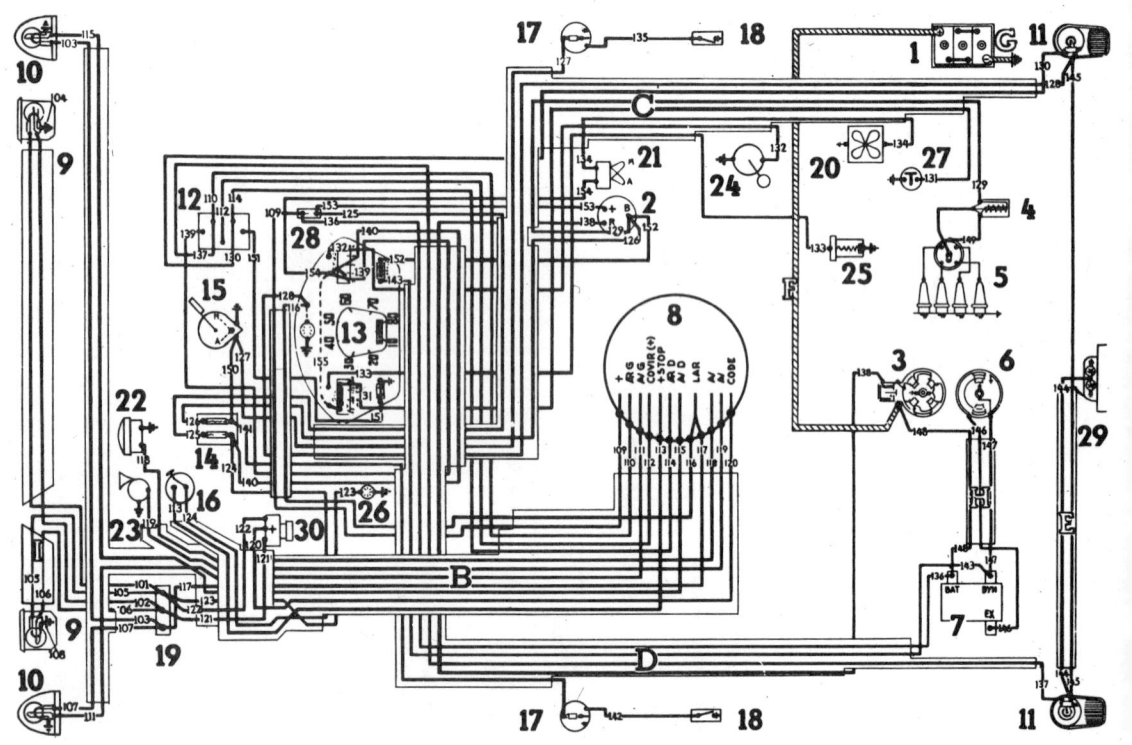

Chassis wiring diagram for the Renault 4 CV. (Courtesy of Renault, Inc.)

Wiring Diagrams

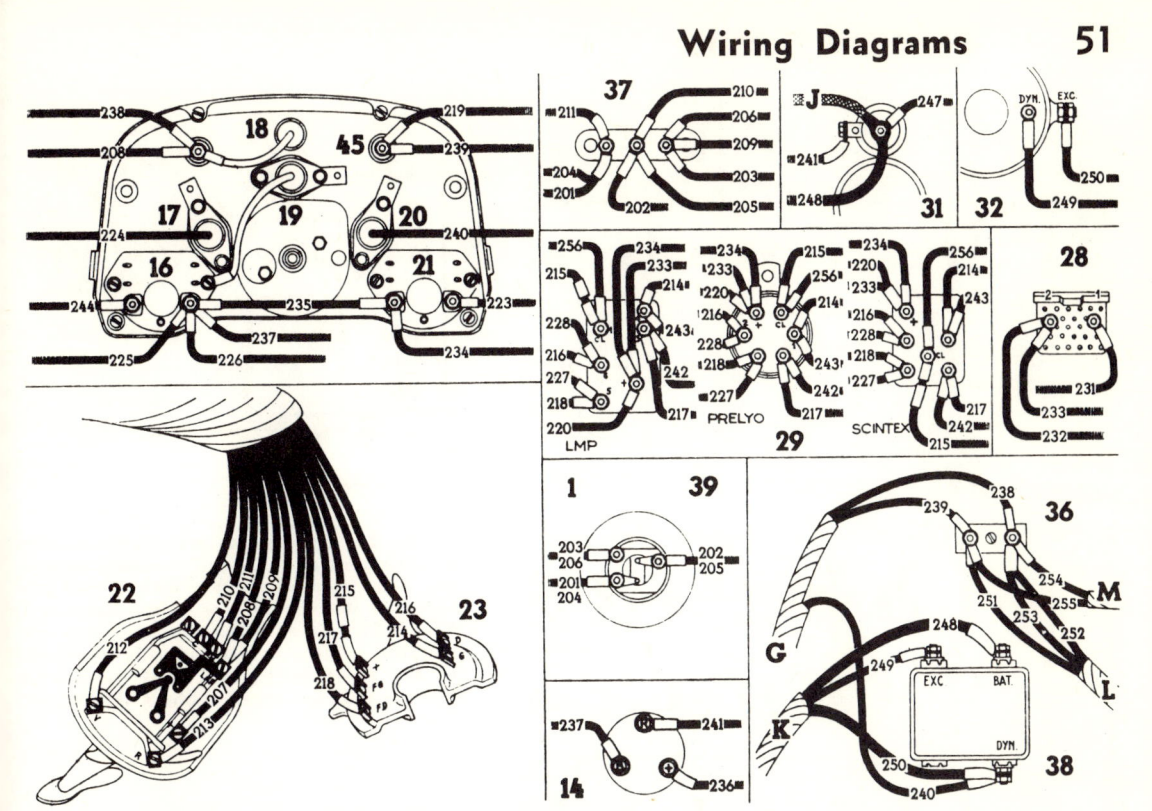

51

Wiring connections and details for the 6-volt Dauphine chassis wiring diagram below. (Courtesy of Renault, Inc.)

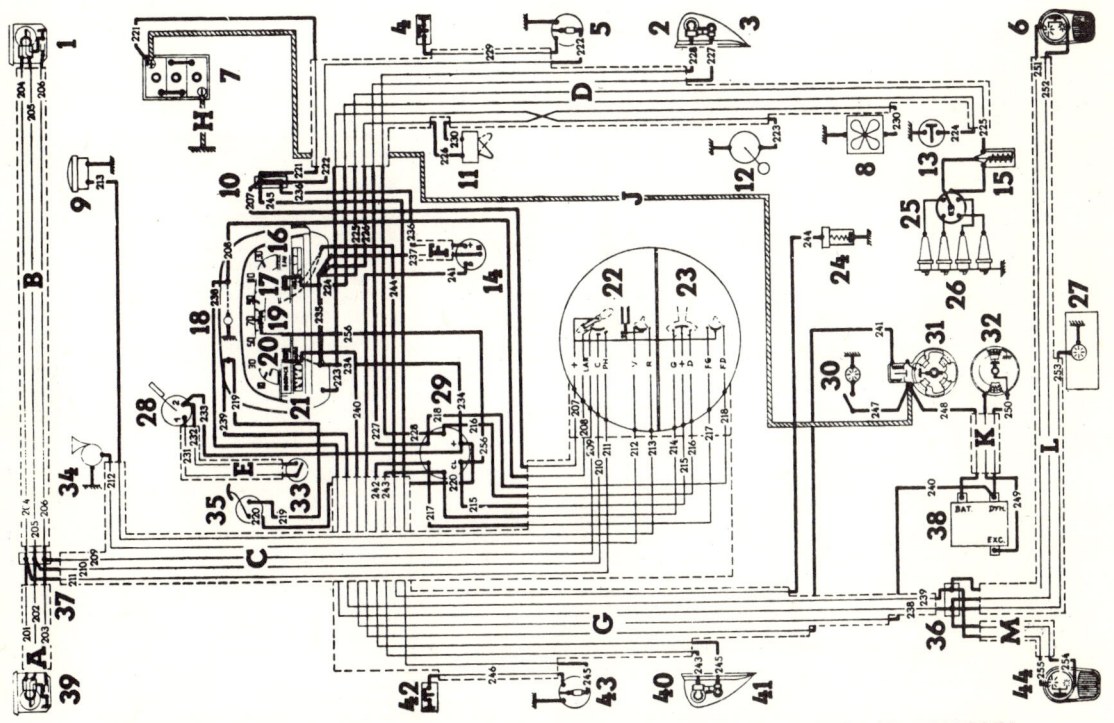

Chassis wiring diagram, Dauphine 6-volt system through 1960, vehicle No. 1178371.
1. headlight, 2. direction indicator, 3. parking light, 4. door pillar switch, 5. interior light, 6. rear light, 7. battery, 8. heater, 9. road horn, 10. connection plate behind instrument panel, 11. heater switch, 12. gas gauge, 13. oil pressure gauge, 14. ignition starting switch, 15. coil, 16. temperature indicator, 17. oil pressure warning light, 18. instrument panel light, 19. direction indicator warning light, 20. charge warning light, 21. gas level indicator, 22. directional signal switch, 23. Covir change-over switch, 24. thermal switch on water pump, 25. distributor, 26. spark plugs, 27. license plate light, 28. windshield wiper, 29. direction indicator control center, 30. engine compartment light, 31. starter, 32. generator, 33. windshield wiper switch, 34. town horn, 35. stoplight switch, 36. terminal rear connection plate, 37. terminal front connection plate, 38. voltage regulator, 39. parking headlight, 40. front flash direction indicator, 41. parking light, 42. door switch, 43. interior light, 44. rear light, 45. connection terminal on panel. (Courtesy of Renault, Inc.)

Electrical System

DISTRIBUTOR SPECIFICATIONS—RENAULT

MANUF. PART NUMBER S.E.V.	ROTATION	BREAKER POINT GAP (In.)	BREAKER POINT GAP (Mm.)	CAM ANGLE (Degrees)	BREAKER ARM SPRING TENSION (Ozs.)	BREAKER ARM SPRING TENSION (Gr.)	CONDENSER CAPACITY (Mfds.)	CENTRIFUGAL ADVANCE Start	CENTRIFUGAL ADVANCE Intermediate	CENTRIFUGAL ADVANCE Maximum	Code No.	VACUUM ADVANCE Start (Inches)	VACUUM ADVANCE Maximum (Inches)	VACUUM ADVANCE Maximum (Degrees)
LH, MU								750	5 @ 1200	17½ @ 1800		—	—	—
RK								475	5 @ 1100	12½ @ 2100		—	—	—
WW	C	.016-.020	.40-.50	56	15-19	425-530		500	5 @ 1600	9 @ 2500	RO	6	15	11.0
XC								750	6 @ 1300	13½ @ 1950	XD	6	16	13.0
R-8	C	.016-.020	.40-.50	56	15-19	425-530		700	13½ @ 1,275	17½ @ 2,250	—	4	16	10.0
Caravelle "S"	C	.016-.020	.40-.50	56	15-19	425-530		525	11 @ 1,150	14 @ 2,250	—	4	18	5.5

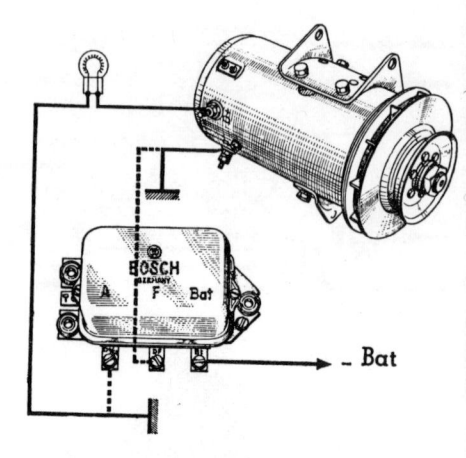

The 12-volt systems are equipped with a Bosch generator. To test this unit, ground the field terminal (DF) with a jumper, either at the regulator or at the generator. *CAUTION: Be sure that the engine is not running when you ground this terminal, or the points will burn.* Start the engine and run it at low speed to check the system.

1. Headlights.
2. Parking and turn indicator lights.
3. Road horn.
4. City horn.
5. Battery.
6. Windshield wiper motor.
7. Windshield wiper switch.
8. Stoplight switch.
9. Headlight foot dimmer switch.
10. Junction block behind cluster.
11. Water temperature gauge, dash unit.
12. Fuel gauge, dash unit.
13. Battery charge warning light.
14. Oil pressure warning light.
15. High beam indicator light.
16. Turn indicator signal.
17. Instrument cluster light.
18. Flasher unit.
19. 2-fuse block.
20. Ignition switch.
21. Dome light door switch.
22. Dome lights.
23. Fuel gauge, tank unit.
24. Temperature gauge, engine unit.
25. Oil pressure gauge, engine unit.
26. Ignition coil.
27. Distributor.
28. Spark plugs.
29. Engine compartment light.
30. Starter motor and solenoid.
31. Generator.
32. License plate lights.
33. Voltage regulator.
34. 1-terminal rear junction block.
35. 2-terminal rear junction block.
36. Stop and directional tail lights.
37. Front junction plate.
38. "Avercovir"—Main lighting switch.
39. Heater blower motor.
40. Heater blower switch.
41. Heater circuit resistance.

Explanation of the parts of the chassis wiring diagram for the 12-volt system used on the Dauphine and Gordini since 1961.

Wiring Diagrams 53

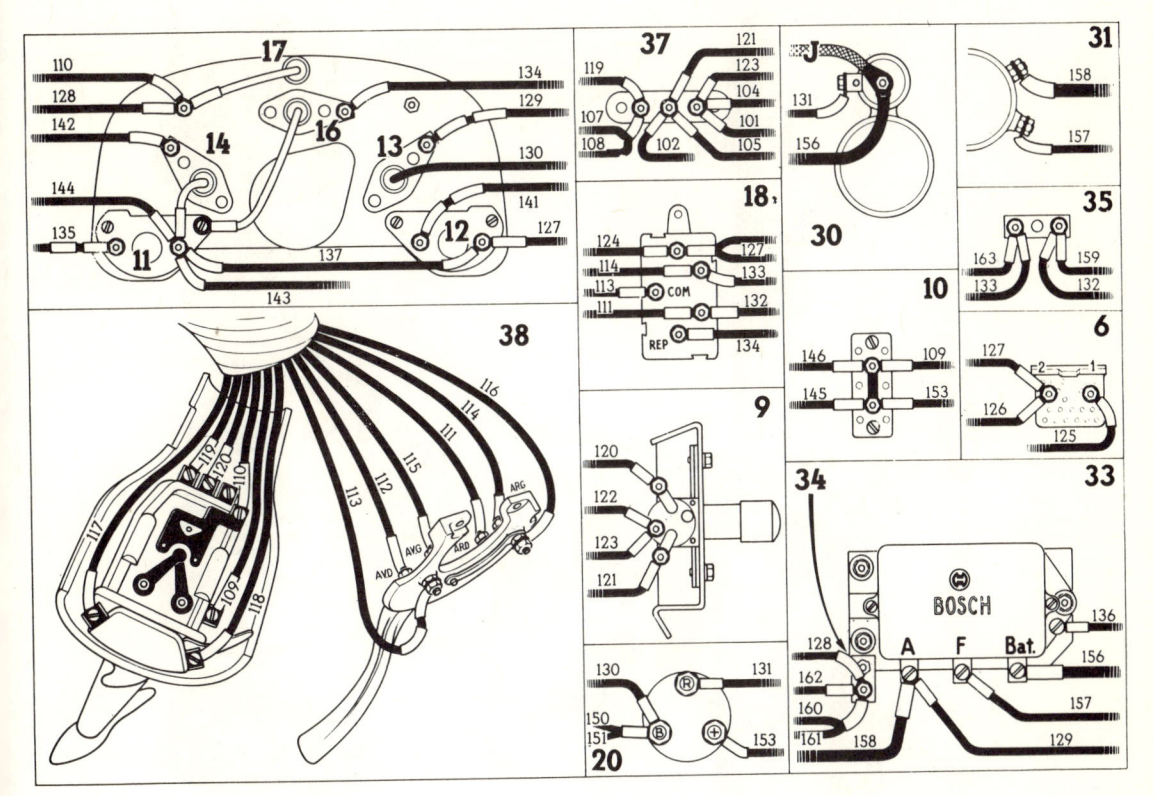

Wiring connection details for the Dauphine and Gordini. (Courtesy of Renault, Inc.)

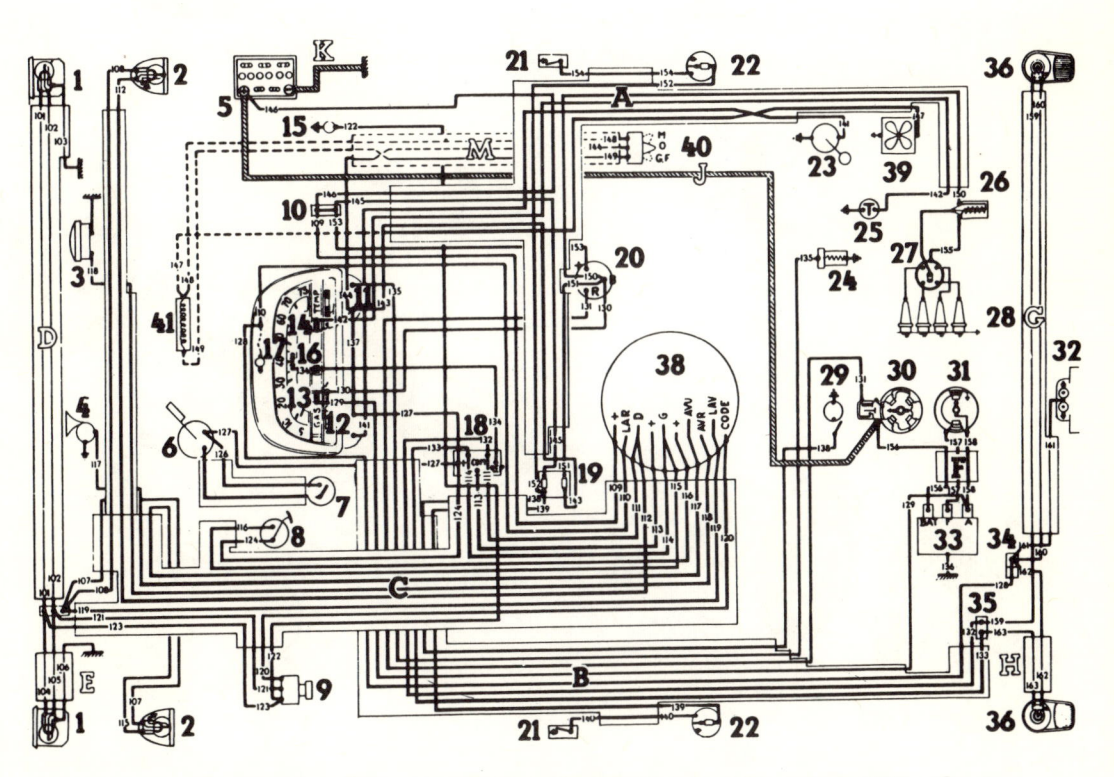

Chassis wiring diagram for the Dauphine and Gordini, 12-volt systems since 1961. (Courtesy of Renault, Inc.)

54 Electrical System

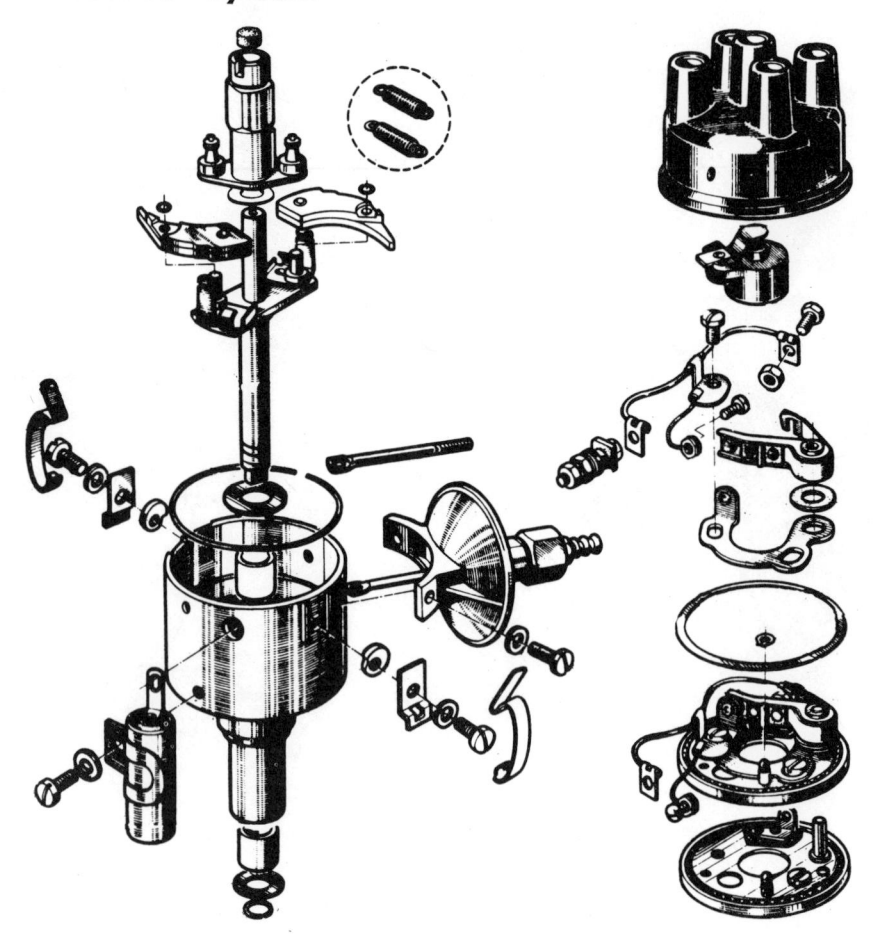

Exploded view of the Renault S.E.V. distributor. (Courtesy of Renault, Inc.)

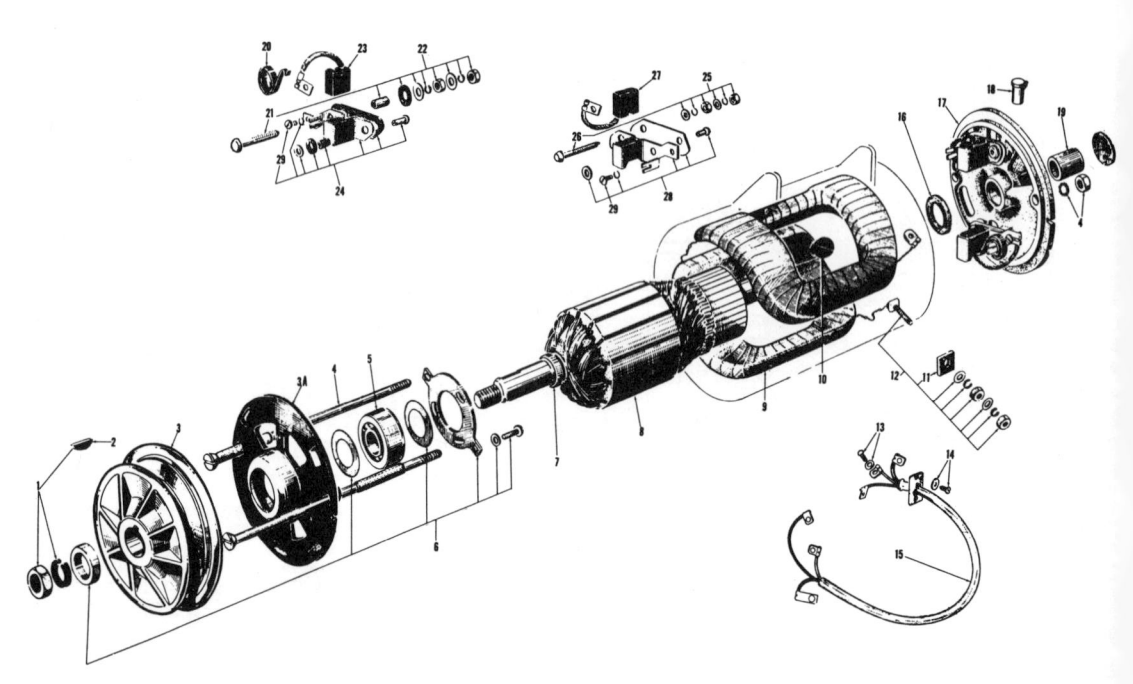

Exploded view of the Paris-Rhone generator. (Courtesy of Renault, Inc.)

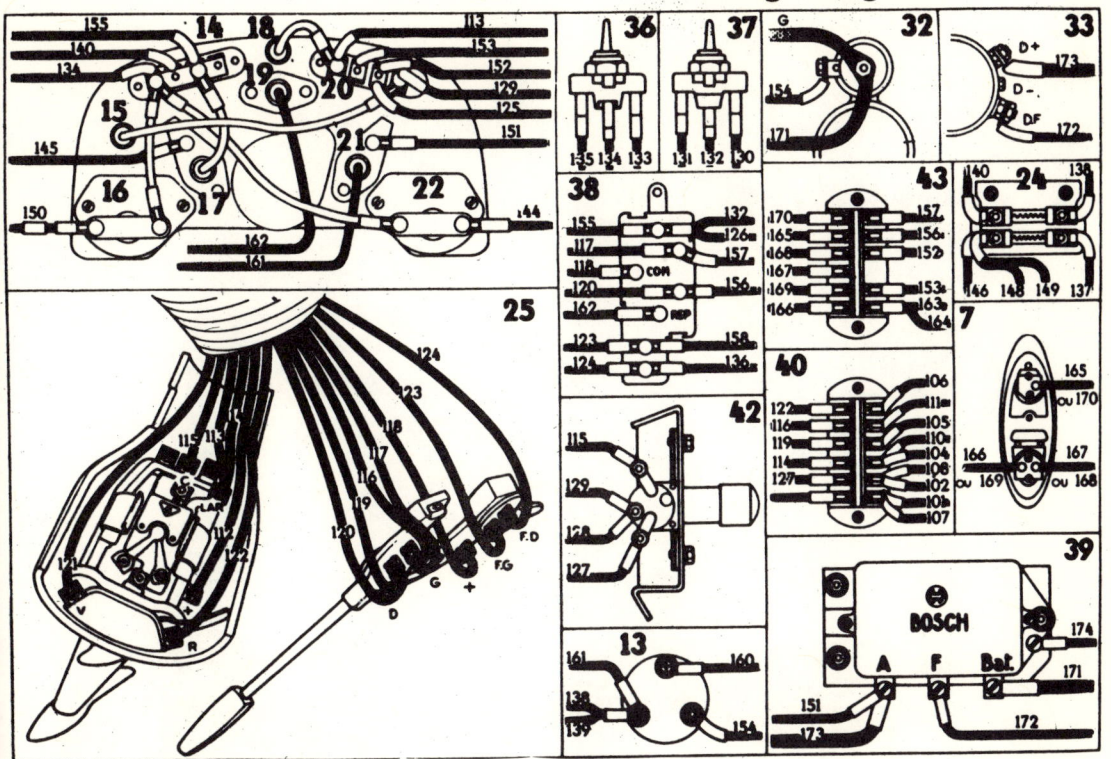

Wiring Diagrams

Wiring connection details for the Caravelle diagram below. (Courtesy of Renault, Inc.)

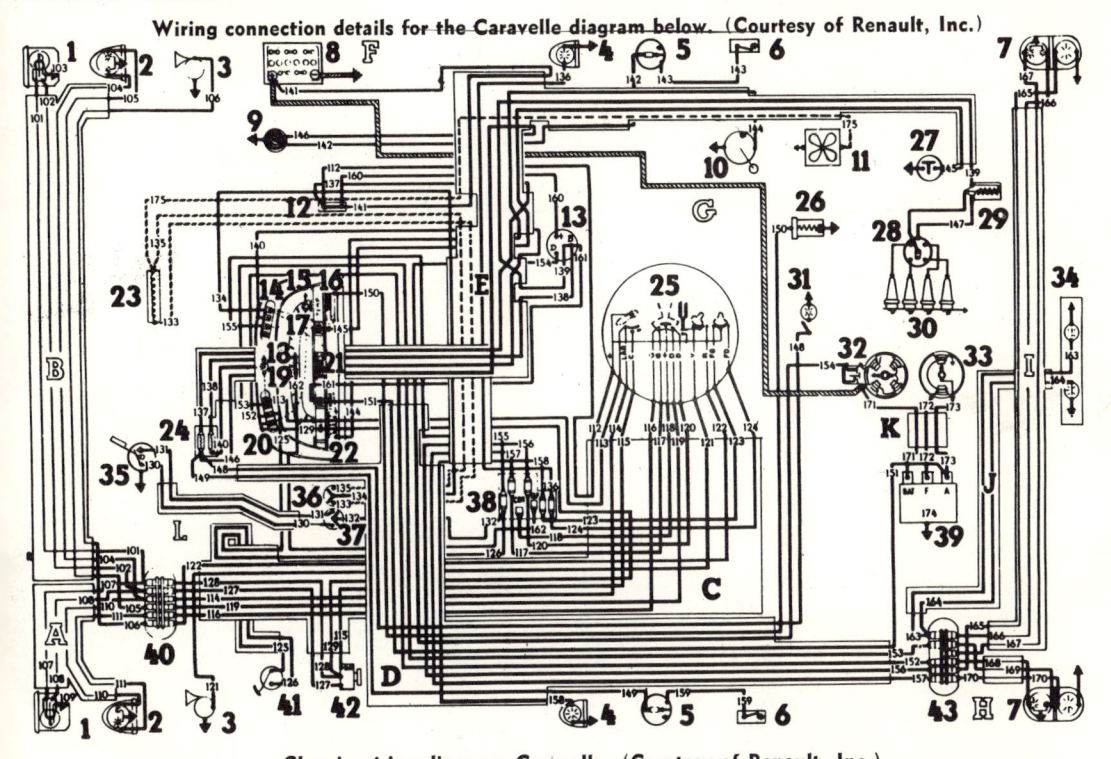

Chassis wiring diagram, Caravelle. (Courtesy of Renault, Inc.)

1. headlight, 2. direction indicator light, 3. horns, 4. parking lights, 5. inside lights, 6. door switches, 7. tail lights, indicator lights, and stop lights, 8. battery, 9. cigar lighter, 10. gas gauge, 11. heater, 12. connection plate behind dashboard, 13. ignition starting switch, 14. instrument panel connection plate, 15. headlight warning light, 16. water temperature indicator, 17. oil pressure warning light, 18. instrument panel light, 19. direction indicator warning light, 20. instrument panel connection plate, 21. battery charge warning light, 22. gas level indicator, 23. resistance in heating circuit, 24. fuses, 25. signaling switch, 26. thermistor on radiator, 27. oil pressure indicator switch, 28. distributor, 29. coil, 30. spark plugs, 31. engine compartment light, 32. starter, 33. generator, 34. license plate light, 35. windshield wiper, 36. heater switch, 37. windshield wiper switch, 38. direction indicator control center, 39. voltage regulator, 40. front connection plate, 41. stop light switch, 42. tilt-ray switch, 43. rear connection plate.

56 Electrical System

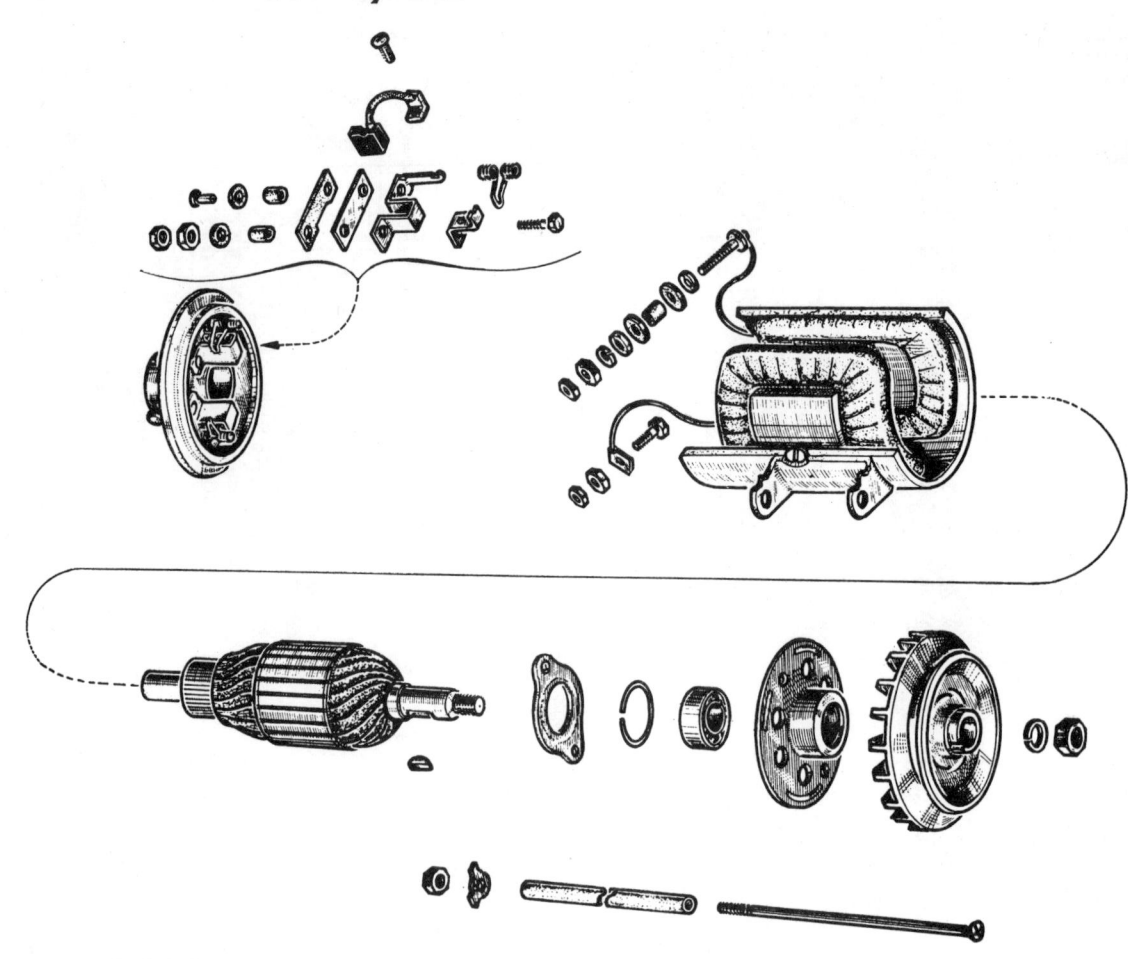

Exploded view of the Ducellier generator used with the 6-volt system. (Courtesy of Renault, Inc.)

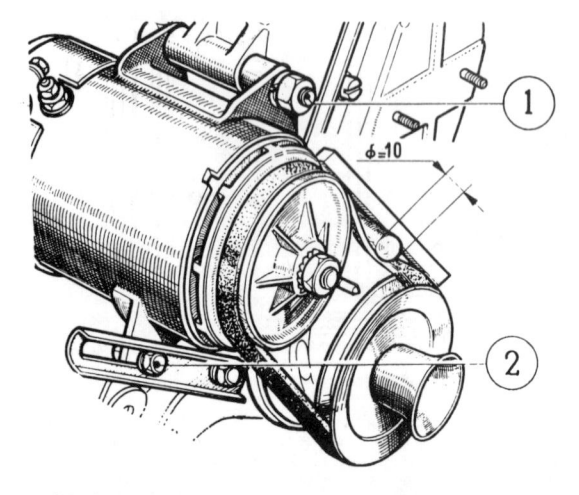

Method of adjusting the generator drive belt. (1) Pivot bolt, (2) clamp bolt. The deflection at midpoint should be 3/8" (10 mm.). (Courtesy of Renault, Inc.)

Wire No.	Wire and Sleeve Colors	Wire Connected From	To
1	Blue	24	18
2	Yellow	24	16
3	Yellow	24	7 b
4	Pink	24	40
4 a	Pink	40	7 b
5	Green	40	7 b
6	Green	40	16
7	Violet	40	24
8	Violet	24	20
9	Blue	24	20
10	Brown	24	7 a
11	Brown	24	20
12	Violet	24	7 a
13	White	24	7 a
14	Violet	24	19
15	Brown	24	22
16	Red	20	13
17	Pink	16	13

Explanation for the Caravelle "S" wiring diagram. (Courtesy of Renault, Inc.)

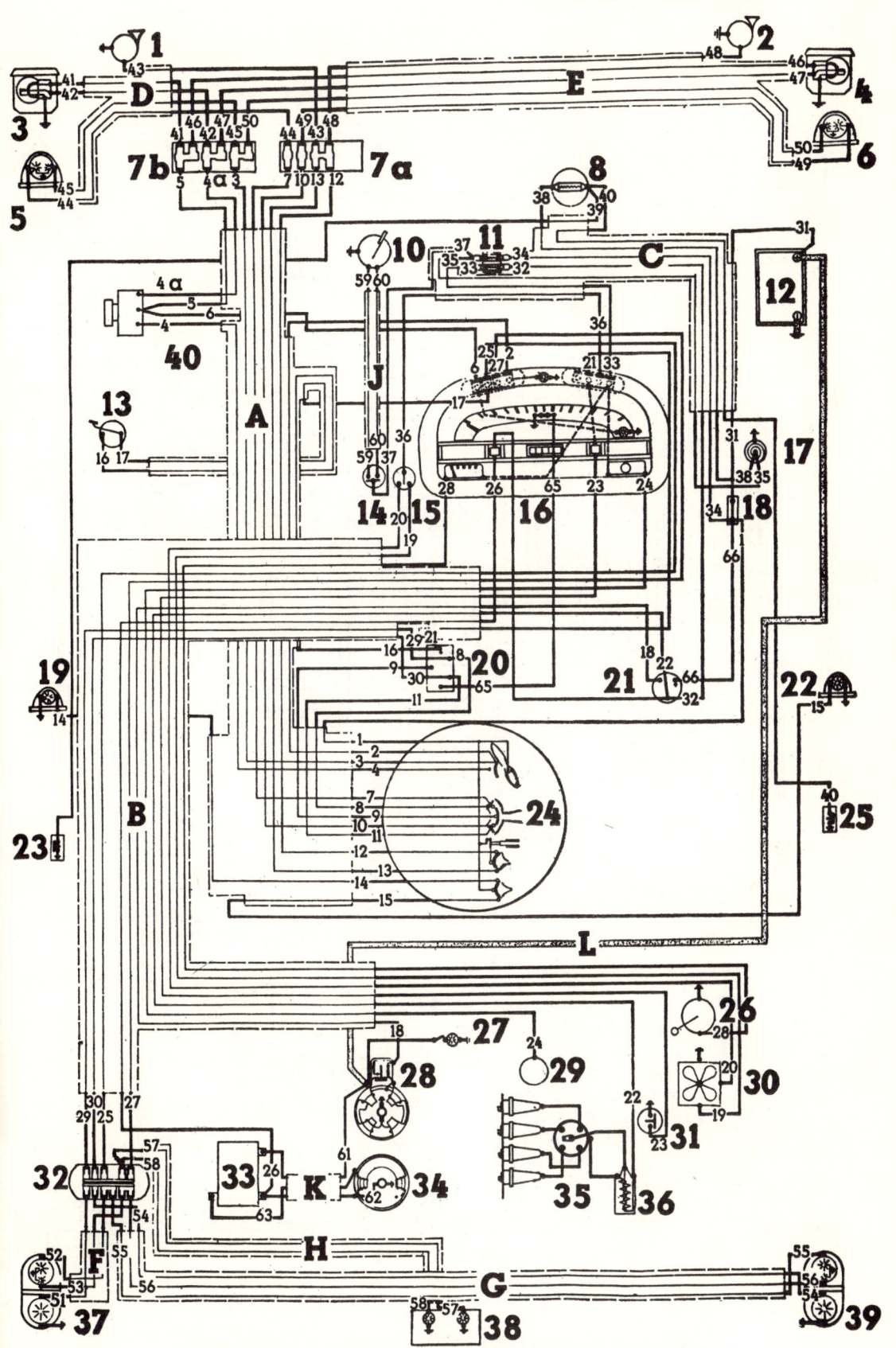

Wiring Diagrams 57

1963-64 Caravelle "S" chassis wiring diagram. (Courtesy of Renault, Inc.)

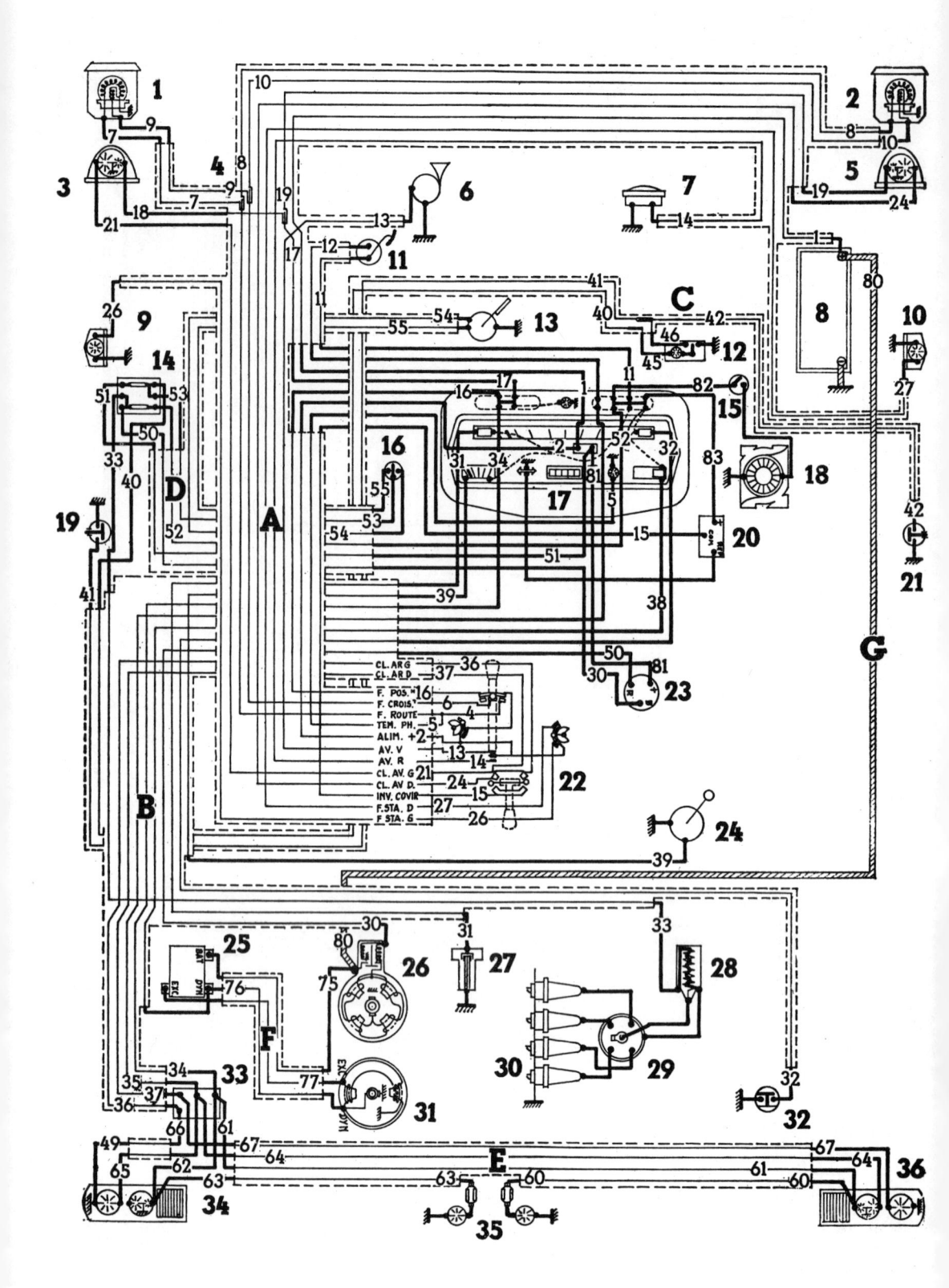

58 Electrical System

1963–64 R-8 chassis wiring diagram. (Courtesy of Renault, Inc.)

5
Engine Service

ENGINE SERVICE NOTES—4CV, DAUPHINE, GORDINI, AND CARAVELLE

The 4-cylinder engine is a replaceable, wet-type sleeve power unit that is attached to a trans-axle and mounted in the rear compartment to drive the rear wheels through live axles. The piston and sleeve assemblies can be replaced from the top by removing the head and the oil pan. The pan can be taken off without pulling the engine. The engine must be taken out of the frame to service the clutch, and the power plant must be removed to service the trans-axle.

CYLINDER NUMBERING SYSTEM

The cylinders are numbered from one to four, starting at the clutch end. The connecting rods are similarly numbered.

PISTON AND ROD ASSEMBLY

The piston must be assembled to the connecting rod so that the 0.138″ (3.5 mm.) hole in the skirt will face the clutch end of the engine when installed. The arrows are stamped on top of the pistons, which must face the flywheel end when installed.

The piston, ring, and rod assembly is inserted in its matching sleeve before the assembly is positioned in the cylinder block. Make sure that the rod bearing cap slants toward the camshaft side when installed. The numbers on the rods must face away from the camshaft side. *CAUTION: If installed backward, the rods will bind against the case.*

Adjusting the valve lash.

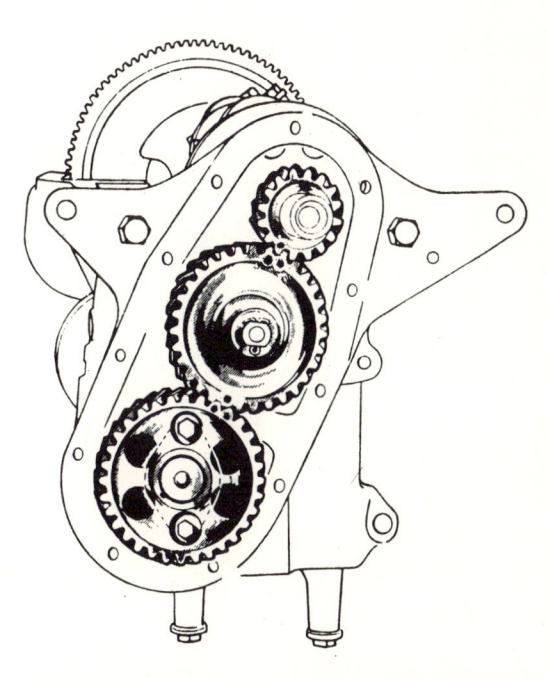

The engine compartment of the Renault Dauphine.

Three timing gears are used on the Dauphine, and each one is marked for alignment through the shaft centers. (Courtesy of Renault, Inc.)

59

Engine Service

The piston and rings are installed into the sleeve, and then the entire assembly is installed into the block from the top. The pan is easily removed without pulling the engine from the frame.

PISTON AND SLEEVE REPLACEMENT NOTES

If a piston or sleeve requires replacement, it is advisable to replace the entire set, because only then can you be assured that they are matched in weight and so maintain balance in the running engine. Then, too, a new piston and sleeve assembly will develop more compression pressure than a used unit. To obtain a good seal at the base of the sleeve, it is important that the sleeve protrude the correct amount and that the proper torque be applied to the cylinder head bolts. During removal of a sleeve, it is easy to change the position of the piston rings, in which case the rings will not seal properly and abnormal oil consumption will result. *Be sure to follow the manufacturer's instructions for installing this kit of parts.*

CYLINDER SLEEVE PROTRUSION

The top of the sleeve must protrude above the top of the block by 0.003"–0.006" (0.08–0.15 mm.). Cylinder base gaskets come in three thicknesses for an adjustment as follows: 0.035" (0.9 mm.), 0.037" (0.95 mm.), and 0.040" (1.0 mm.).

CYLINDER HEAD BOLTS

Cylinder head bolts are of different lengths as follows:

Bolts Nos. 4, 5, and 10	3.150" (80 mm.)
Bolts Nos. 2, 3, 6, 8, and 11	3.740" (95 mm.)
Bolts Nos. 7 and 12	4.134" (105 mm.)
Bolt No. 1	4.528" (115 mm.)

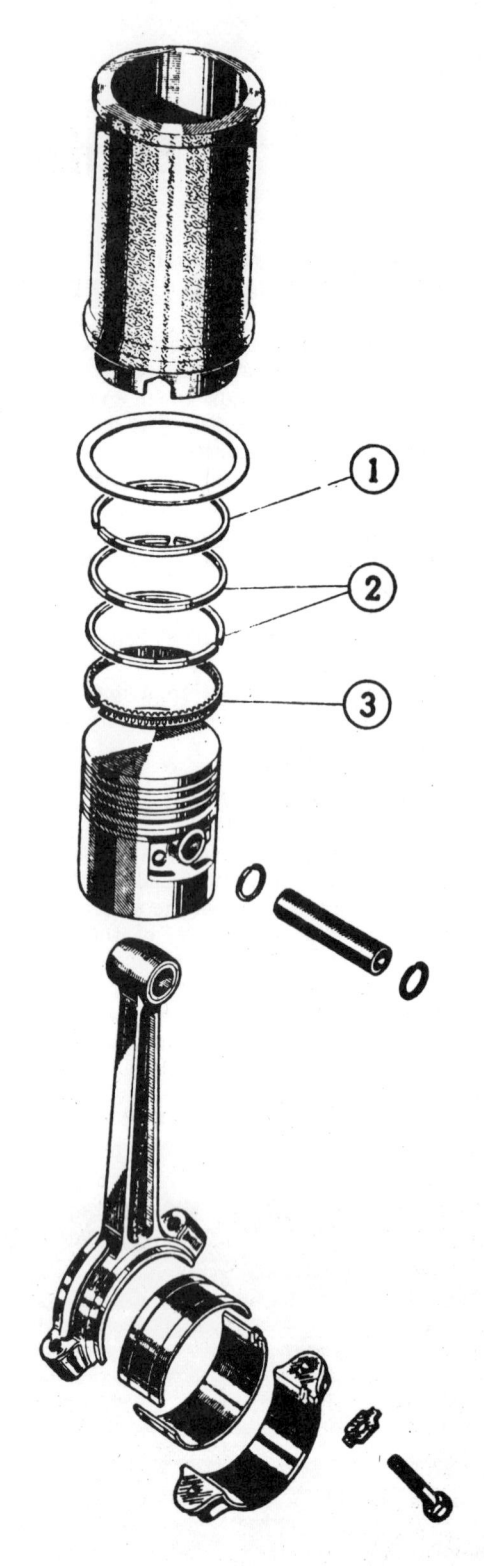

The sleeve, piston, and rod assembly. Late models come with a full-skirted, 3-ring piston. Be sure to follow the manufacturer's instructions when installing the new piston and ring kit. (Courtesy of Renault, Inc.)

4CV, Dauphine, Gordini, and Caravelle

MECHANICAL ENGINE SPECIFICATIONS—RENAULT

CRANKSHAFT

MODEL	CYL.	BORE In.	BORE Mm.	Con. Rod Journal In.	Con. Rod Journal Mm.	Main Brg. Journal In.	Main Brg. Journal Mm.	End Play In.	End Play Mm.
4CV	4	2.145	54.5						
5CV Dauphine	4	2.2835	58	1.4945-1.4951	37.959-37.975	1.5738-1.5744	39.991-39.975	.002-.004	.05-.10
Caravelle, Gordini	4								
R-8 and Caravelle "S"	4	2.5591	65	1.7310-1.7316	43.980-43.996	1.8110-1.8114	46.000-46.011	.0018-.0075	.045-.190

PISTON PIN

Diameter In.	Diameter Mm.	Fit in Rod In.	Fit in Rod Mm.	Fit in Piston In.	Fit in Piston Mm.
.5512	14	.0002F	.005F	.0008F	.020F
.7087	18	.0012P	.031P	.0002-.0005F	.005-.0127F

F = Free; P = Interference

VALVE SPECIFICATIONS—RENAULT

VALVE TIMING

MODEL	FACE ANGLE Intake and Exhaust (Degrees)	RUNNING CLEARANCE Intake In.	RUNNING CLEARANCE Intake Mm.	RUNNING CLEARANCE Exhaust In.	RUNNING CLEARANCE Exhaust Mm.	Intake opens before TDC	Clearance for checking valve timing In.	Clearance for checking valve timing Mm.	Lift Intake In.	Lift Intake Mm.	Lift Exhaust In.	Lift Exhaust Mm.	Number of teeth between sprocket marks
4CV													
Dauphine	30	.006C	.15C	.008C	.20C				.226	5.74	.236	6.0	O.C.
Caravelle, Gordini													
R-8 and Caravelle "S"	45	.005C	.12C	.008C②	.20C								O.C.

H — Hot; C — Cold

VALVE SPRINGS

Pressure Outer Lbs. @ in. of length	Pressure Outer Kg. @ mm. of length	Assembled height In.	Assembled height Mm.
31 @ .95	14 @ .24	1.220	31.0
29.8 @ 1.26	13.5 @ 32	1.259	32.0

VALVE STEM

Diameter Int. & Exh. In.	Diameter Int. & Exh. Mm.	Clearance Intake In.	Clearance Intake Mm.	Clearance Exhaust In.	Clearance Exhaust Mm.
.2362	6.0①	.0008-.0030	.02-.07	.0012-.004	.03-.10
.2756	7.0	.0008-.0030	.02-.07	.0012-.004	.03-.10

① In 1961, the valve stem diameter was increased to 0.2756" (7.0 mm.).
② Exhaust valves rotate.

62 Engine Service

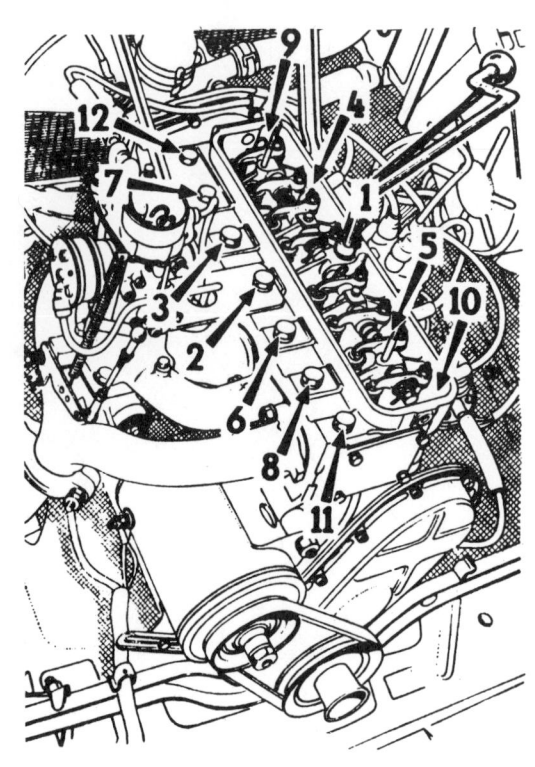

Cylinder head bolt tightening sequence. (Courtesy of Renault, Inc.)

ADJUSTING VALVES

The valves should be adjusted to 0.006" for the intake and 0.008" for the exhaust valve with a *cold* engine. To set the valves accurately, first make sure that the engine has not been run for the past six hours, and then turn it until the following valves are open:

Valve Open	Adjust
E-1	I-3, E-4
E-3	I-4, E-2
E-4	I-2, E-1
E-2	I-1, E-3

The rocker arm clearance can be adjusted after the engine has cooled exactly 50 minutes; clearances are then: 0.007" intake and 0.010" exhaust.

POWER PLANT, TRANS-AXLE, AND SUB-FRAME REMOVAL

① *From Inside the Engine Compartment:* Drain the cooling system and the oil pan. Remove the air filter and disconnect the wires leading to the engine. Pull off the flexible fuel line to the carburetor and pry off the carburetor throttle link. Disconnect the left splash pan at the back and remove the upper cardboard deflector.

② Disconnect the splash pan at the front and from the starting motor retaining bolt.

③ Remove the bolts holding the manifolds to the cylinder head, and then remove the splash pan, muffler, and manifold assembly as a unit.

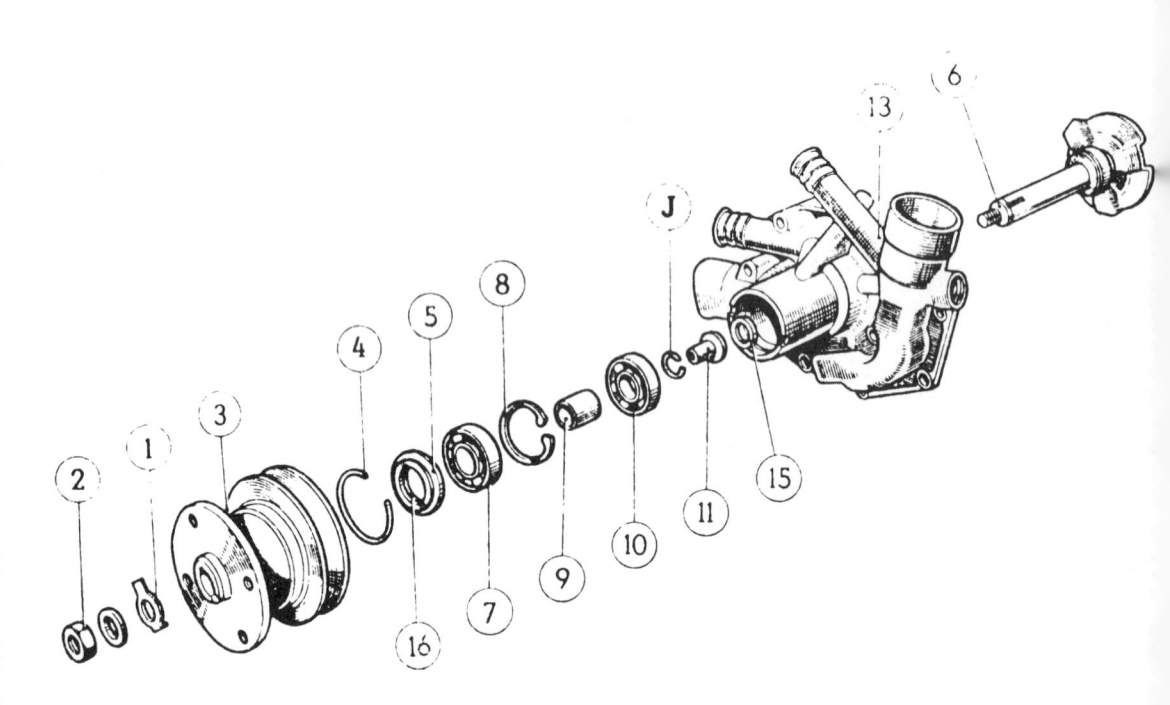

Parts of the water pump. (Courtesy of Renault, Inc.)

4CV, Dauphine, Gordini and Caravelle

④ *From Under the Car:* Remove the two bolts holding the fuel tank filler pipe, and then remove the tank retaining bolts (arrows) to drop the tank.

⑤ Disconnect the clutch control cable from its lever, the transmission shift control, the clutch and accelerator cable housings, the hand brake control, the speedometer drive cable, and the brake line at the 3-way connection on the crossmember.

⑥ Disconnect the travel-limiting strap and remove the pneumatic pad. Support the powerplant, and then disconnect the front and rear crossmembers.

⑦ Lift the rear end of the body and wheel the power plant and sub-frame assembly from under the car.

ENGINE REMOVAL

⑧ If the engine is to be removed without the trans-axle, it can be disconnected at the clutch bell housing, and steps ⑥ and ⑦ can be eliminated as the trans-axle remains in the frame. It is not neces-

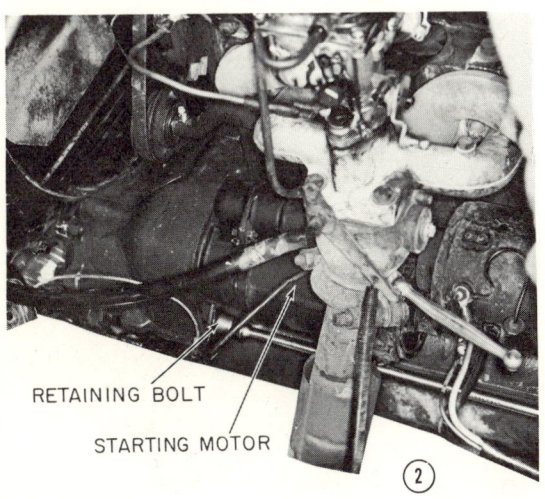

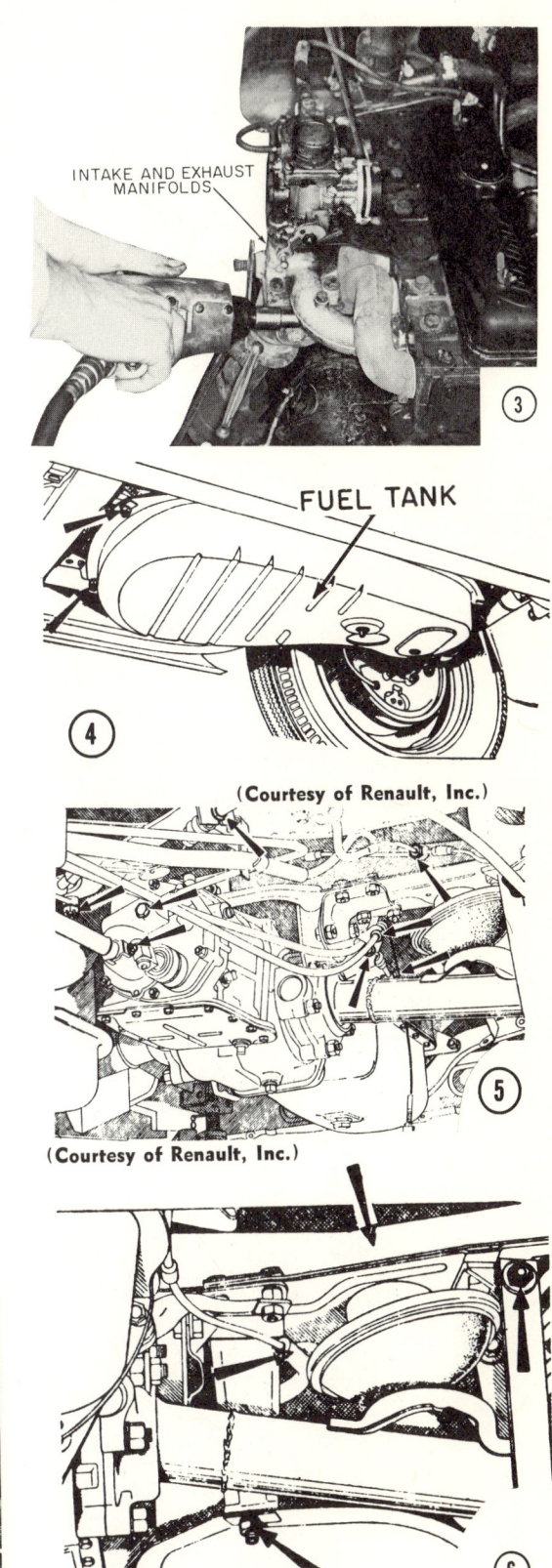

Engine Service

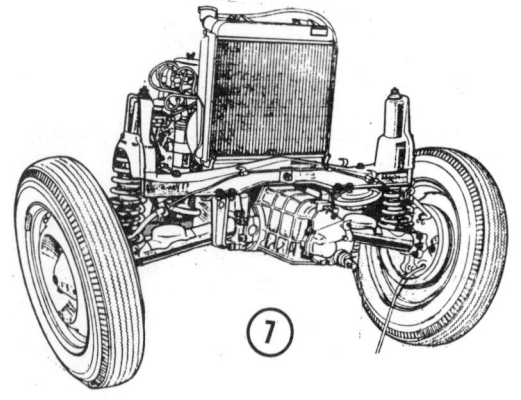

(Courtesy of Renault, Inc.)

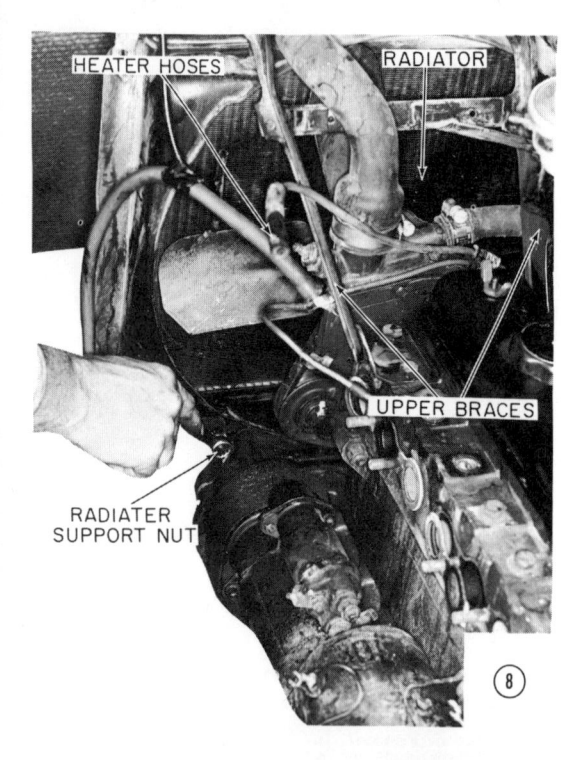

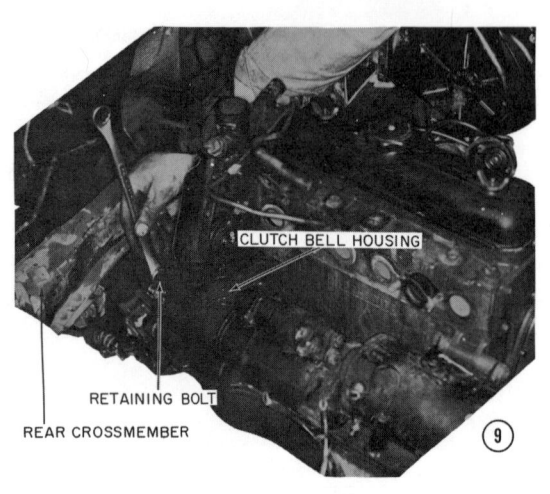

sary to remove the fuel tank, but the filler pipe must be taken off. The radiator must be removed by disconnecting it at the upper braces at the cylinder head and at the lower supports. Disconnect the radiator and heater hoses, and then slide the radiator assembly out from the left side. Remove the right splash pan.

⑨ Hook up a chain hoist to support the weight of the engine, and then remove the four bolts holding the engine to the clutch bell housing and the six bolts holding the rear of the oil pan to the bell housing.

⑩ Disconnect the engine at the front crossmember.

⑪ Remove the ignition coil (when it is installed on the timing gear cover), and then pull the engine back from the clutch shaft. Turn the engine crosswise in the compartment, and then lift it out.

⑫ The clutch pressure plate assembly can be serviced after the engine has been taken out.

⑬ The throw-out bearing can be serviced with the engine removed.

R-8 and Caravelle "S"

PILOT TOOL
CLUTCH PRESSURE PLATE

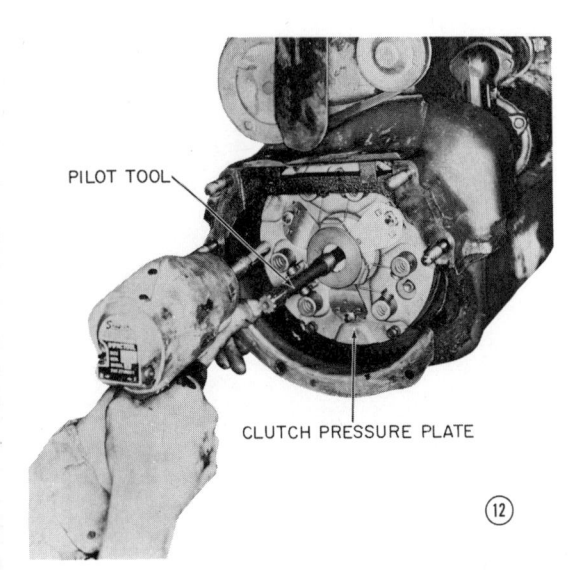

(12)

THROW-OUT LEVER

(13)

ENGINE SERVICE NOTES—R-8 AND CARAVELLE "S"

PISTON AND ROD ASSEMBLY

The piston pin is a press-fit in the rod. To assemble the piston to the rod, position the piston so that the arrow points up. The number on the rod cap must face the right-hand side. When installed in the engine, the arrows must face the front of the engine (flywheel end), with the connecting rod numbers facing the camshaft side of the engine. No. 1 piston and rod assembly must be installed in the cylinder closest to the flywheel end of the engine.

TIMING CHAIN TENSIONER

These new engines use a timing chain in place of the timing gears with which the older engines were equipped. On assembly, the marks on the timing

ENGINE TORQUE SPECIFICATIONS—RENAULT

MODEL	SPARK PLUGS Ft.-Lbs.	SPARK PLUGS M. Kg.	CYL. HEAD BOLTS Ft.-Lbs.	CYL. HEAD BOLTS M. Kg.	CON. ROD BOLTS Ft.-Lbs.	CON. ROD BOLTS M. Kg.	MAIN BRG. BOLTS Ft.-Lbs.	MAIN BRG. BOLTS M. Kg.	MANIFOLDS Center Ft.-Lbs.	MANIFOLDS Center M. Kg.	MANIFOLDS Ends Ft.-Lbs.	MANIFOLDS Ends M. Kg.	FLYWHEEL TO CRANKSHAFT BOLTS Ft.-Lbs.	FLYWHEEL TO CRANKSHAFT BOLTS M. Kg.
Renault, Gordini, & Caravelle	25	3.5	45	6.5	25	3.5	45	6.5	15	2.0	11	1.5	36	5.0
R-8 & Caravelle "S"	25	3.5	43	6.0	25	3.5	43	6.0					32	4.5

65

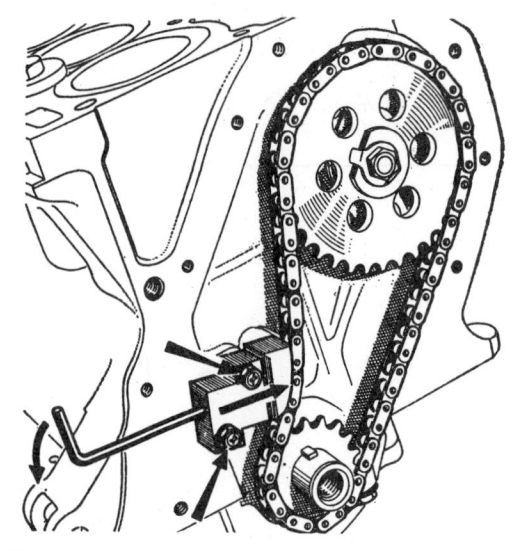

Engine Service

Turn the Allen wrench counterclockwise to position the slipper against the chain during assembly. (Courtesy of Renault, Inc.)

Cylinder head tightening sequence, Caravelle "S" and R-8. (Courtesy of Renault, Inc.)

gears should align through the centers of the shafts. When installing the chain tensioner, use an Allen wrench to turn the spring tensioner clockwise until the slide enters the support completely. Install the tensioner and friction plate on the block, and then turn the Allen wrench counterclockwise enough to clear the lug, which must enter the automatic play take-up groove.

CYLINDER SLEEVE PROTRUSION

These engines are equipped with wet-type, replaceable sleeves, as are the other Renault engines. However, the cylinder sleeve protrusion specifications differ in that the specifications for the new engine are 0.0020"–0.0047" (0.051–0.12 mm.). The base gaskets are supplied in thicknesses of 0.0028" and 0.004" (0.07 and 0.10 mm.).

ENGINE REMOVAL

The engine is removed without the trans-axle, but must be removed from the bottom as follows:

From the Left Side of the Engine Compartment. Remove the air cleaner and the manifold clamp. Disconnect the battery. Drain the coolant, saving the anti-freeze mixture. Disconnect the accelerator control, generator wires, and starting motor cables and wires. Remove the starting motor, splash pan and muffler, lower radiator hose, radiator shroud retaining bolts, and radiator retaining bolts.

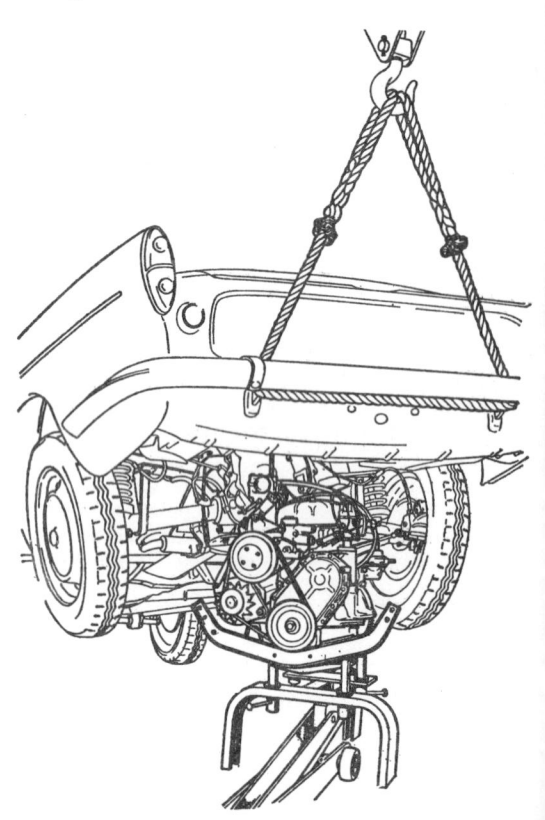

The Allen wrench must be turned clockwise to retract the slipper. (Courtesy of Renault, Inc.)

The engine is removed from below on the new models. (Courtesy of Renault, Inc.)

R-8 and Caravelle "S"

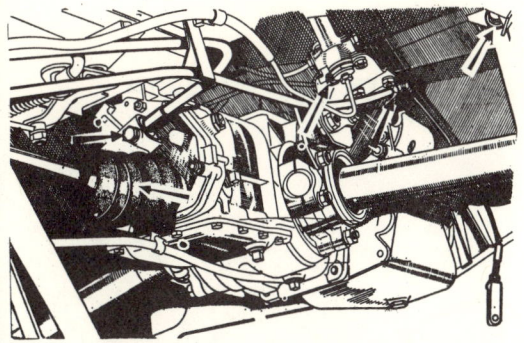

To remove the sub-frame assembly, disconnect the parts shown by arrows. (Courtesy of Renault, Inc.)

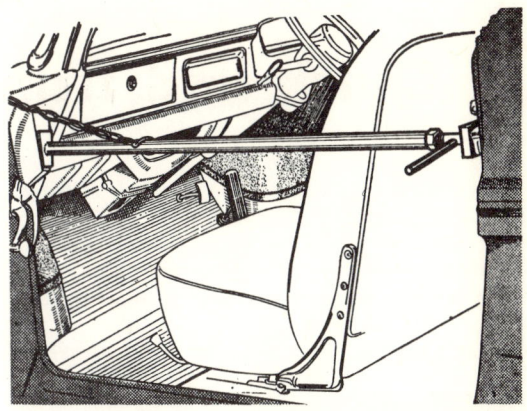

A special brace is available to prevent distortion of the frame and door openings when lifting the rear of the Caravelle body. In the absence of this brace, be sure to keep the doors closed for additional support. (Courtesy of Renault, Inc.)

From the Right Side of the Engine Compartment. Remove the upper radiator hose. Disconnect the heater hoses at the water pump, heat indicator wire, oil pressure indicator wire, fuel line at the pump, expansion chamber pipe at the radiator, and distributor primary wire. Remove the radiator shroud retaining bolts and radiator retaining bolts. Push the fan shroud back toward the fan, and remove the radiator from the bottom. Disengage the fan shroud and remove it. Remove the fan and engine splash pan.

From Under the Vehicle. Pass a sling around the rear bumper brackets and lift the vehicle. *CAUTION: Lifting the Caravelle convertible from the rear places an unusual strain on the frame, which can distort the door openings.* To prevent this, the factory supplies a special tool to place between the front and rear braces of the door opening. In the absence of this tool, be sure to keep both doors closed as they will act as a brace. Remove the clutch shield and disconnect the engine from the clutch housing. Support the engine with a jack and remove the engine rear support crossmember. Remove the two upper clutch housing retaining bolts, pull the engine toward the rear of the car, turn it approximately 30°, and lower it for removal.

6

Clutch and Transmission Service

The Renault trans-axle is a very compact unit, mounted in front of the engine. The entire power-plant, consisting of the engine, trans-axle, and rear sub-frame assembly, must be removed in all models, except the R-8 and Caravelle "S," in order to take out the trans-axle.

Renault makes three different trans-axles: a three-forward speed unit (type 314), a four-forward (type 318), and a three-forward speed unit (325) that is synchronized in all forward speeds. The first two are not synchronized in first gear. Inasmuch as the three units are very similar in construction, only the four-forward speed unit will be covered in detail herein. The fully synchronized unit was developed in 1963 for use with the optional automatic transmission (which is covered later in this chapter).

Until 1962, Renault offered a Ferlec clutch as optional equipment. This electromagnetic unit replaced the conventional clutch. Ferlec clutch service is covered in this chapter.

CLUTCH PEDAL ADJUSTMENT

The clutch throw-out mechanism is cable-operated. The pedal free play should be approximately ¾" (20 mm.), and is developed by adjusting the length of the control cable where it contacts the throw-out lever at the trans-axle. After loosening the locknut, turn the adjusting nut until there is a clearance of 5/64"–1/8" (2–3 mm.) between the adjusting nut and the lever. Tighten the locknut.

OVERHAULING A TRANS-AXLE

DISASSEMBLING—DIFFERENTIAL

① Mark and remove the differential carrier side covers, and then take out the universal joint bolts. From the carriers, remove the bearing cups, adjusting shims, and sealing washers.

② Slide the retaining spring out of its groove on the clutch shaft, remove the pin, and then the clutch shaft.

③ To remove the differential unit, turn it so that one boss enters one of the universal joint bores and slide it from the case.

DISASSEMBLING—TRANSMISSION

④ Remove the bottom cover. Remove the bolts holding the front cover in place and push it to the front as far as possible. Shift into first gear

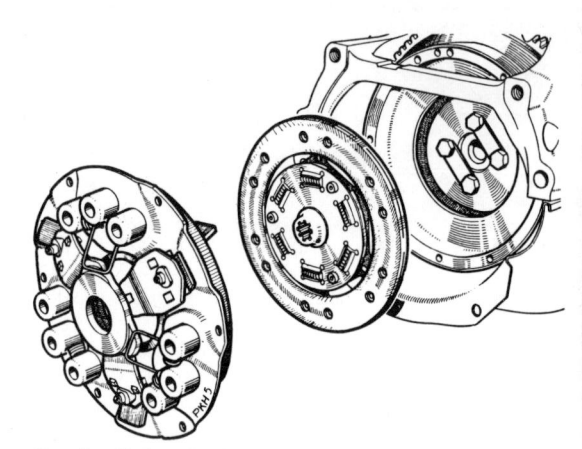

Details of the clutch assembly. (Courtesy of Renault, Inc.)

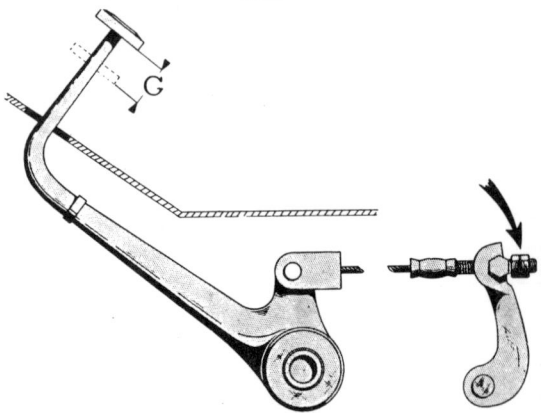

Clutch pedal play "G" should be 5/64"–1/8" (2–3 mm.) and is adjusted by turning the nut (arrow) where the cable contacts the throw-out fork. (Courtesy of Renault, Inc.)

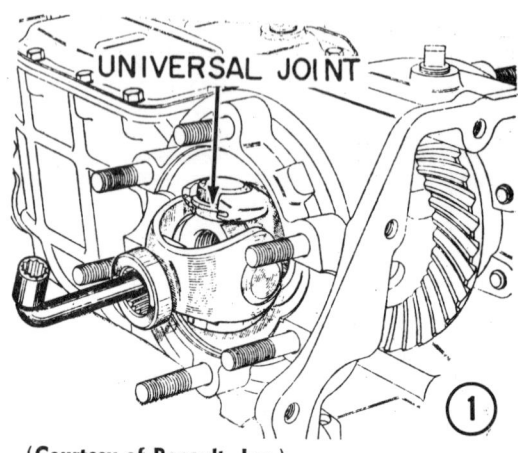

(Courtesy of Renault, Inc.)

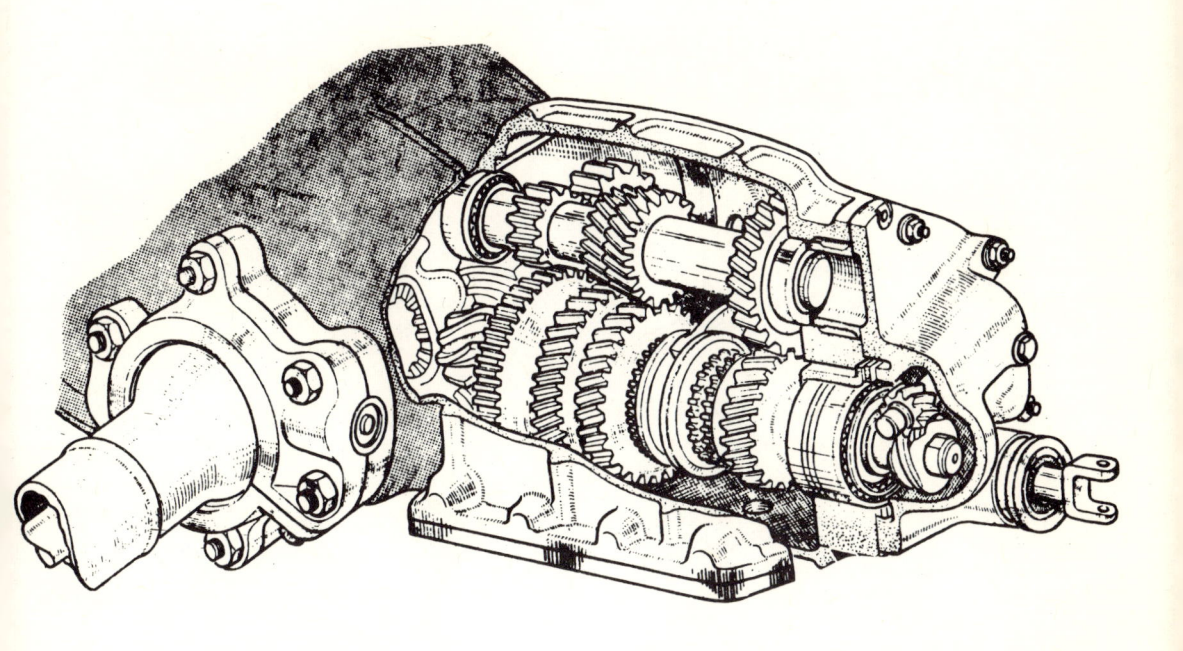

Trans-Axle Service

Sectioned view of the Renault transmission. (Courtesy of Renault, Inc.)

REAR AXLE SPECIFICATIONS—RENAULT

| MODEL | DRIVE PINION LOCK NUT || PINION BEARING PRELOAD |||| CARRIER BEARING PRELOAD |||| PINION & RING GEAR BACKLASH ||
| | || New Brgs. || Used Brgs. || New Brgs. || Used Brgs. || ||
	Ft.-Lbs.	M.Kg.	In.	Mm.	In.	Mm.	In.	Mm.	In.	Mm.	In.	Mm.
4CV, Dauphine, Gordini, and Caravelle	87	12.0			.0000	.00	.008	.20	.0000	.00	.005-.010	.12-.25
Caravelle "S" and R-8	87	12.0			.0000	.00	.008	.20	.0000	.00	.005-.010	.12-.25

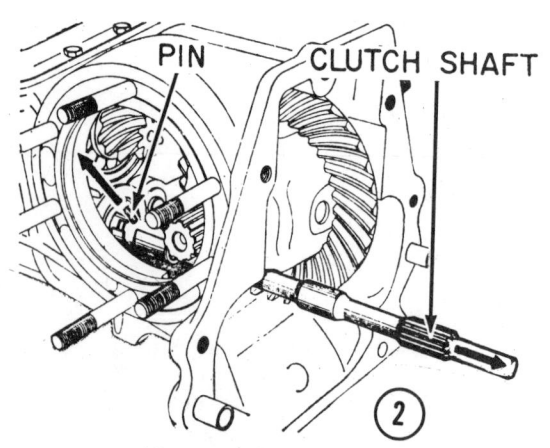

Trans-Axle

(Courtesy of Renault, Inc.)

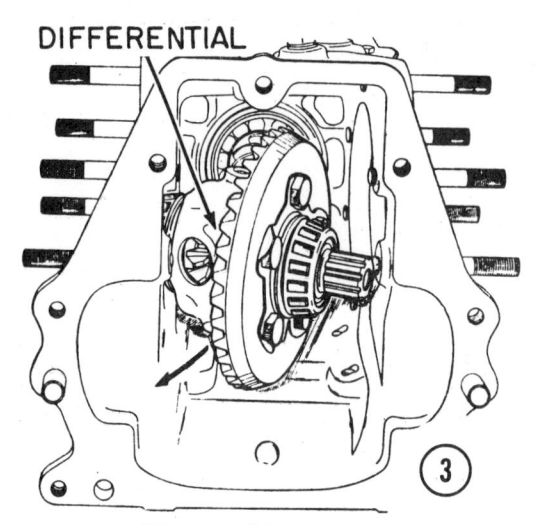

(Courtesy of Renault, Inc.)

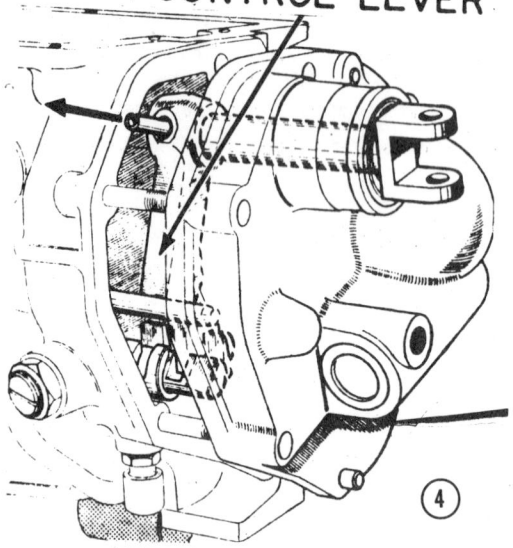

(Courtesy of Renault, Inc.)

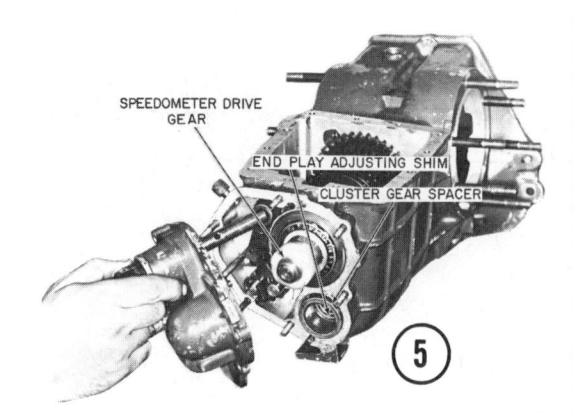

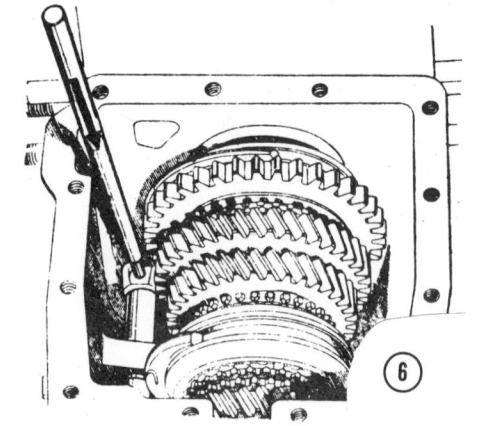

(Courtesy of Renault, Inc.)

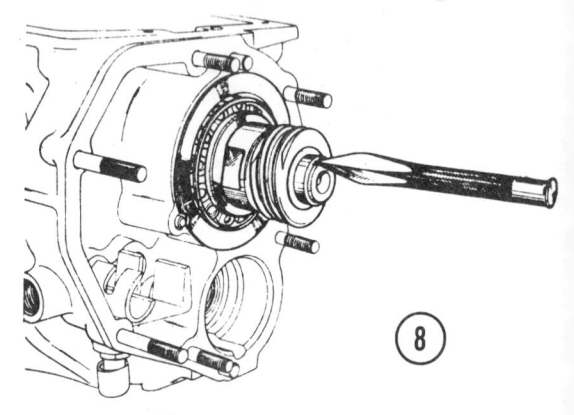

(Courtesy of Renault, Inc.)

Service 71

and drive out the pin holding the control lever to the shift shaft.

⑤ Remove the shaft and front cover assembly. Return the gears to neutral and remove the static eliminator, if so equipped, the cluster gear spacer, and the end play adjusting shim.

⑥ Drive out the pins holding the two forks to the shift shafts.

⑦ Remove the threaded plug from the outside of the case; extract the spring and locking detent ball. Remove the first-and-reverse shifter shaft. Remove the interlock, take out the interlock plunger, and then slide the second-and-third speed shifter shaft from the case. Catch the detent ball and spring.

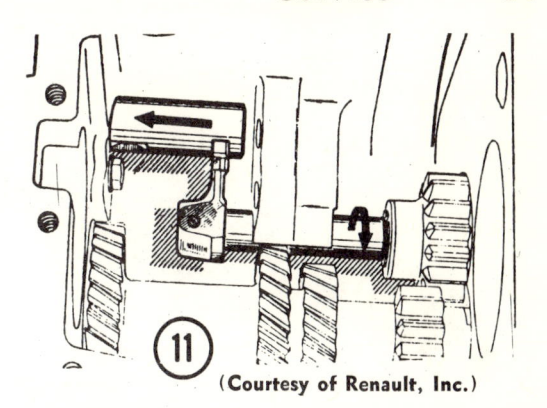

⑧ To disassemble the mainshaft, shift the transmission into any two gears to lock the shaft, and then remove the speedometer drive gear. It will be necessary to replace the speedometer drive gear as the locking flange has to be destroyed to remove it from the shaft. Return the gears to neutral.

⑨ From the rear of the case, pull out the double-cone roller bearing, the pinion-positioning washer, and the lock key.

⑩ To disassemble the mainshaft, it is necessary to remove two round splined washers (22) and (25) that hold the gears in position. The lock key has been removed in the previous step and it is only necessary to separate the gears, rotate the two washers to the unlocked position, and slide the gears from the mainshaft.

⑪ To take off the reverse shaft, remove the primary shaft and reverse shaft bearing thrust plate. Remove the lock stop, spring, and ball of the reverse shaft detent. Rotate the shaft until the control lever is completely disengaged from the reverse sleeve, and then remove the sleeve.

⑫ Drive out the pin and take off the control lever. Drive the reverse pinion retaining snap ring from its groove; and then take out the reverse

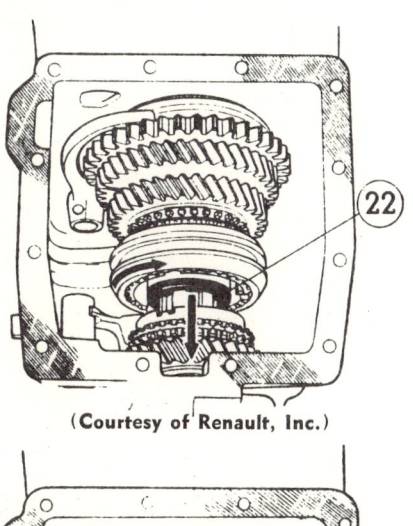

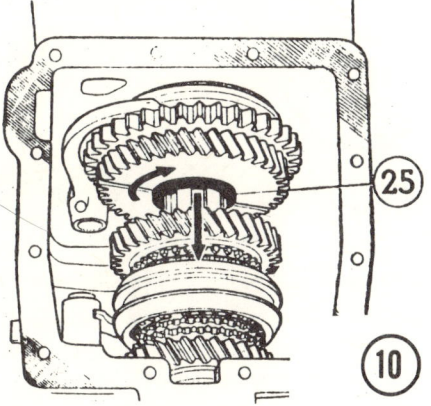

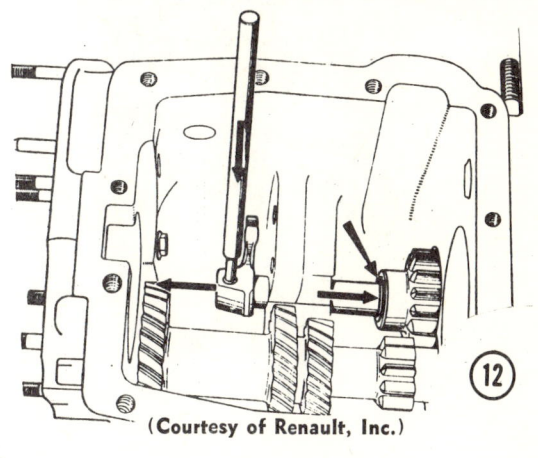

Trans-Axle

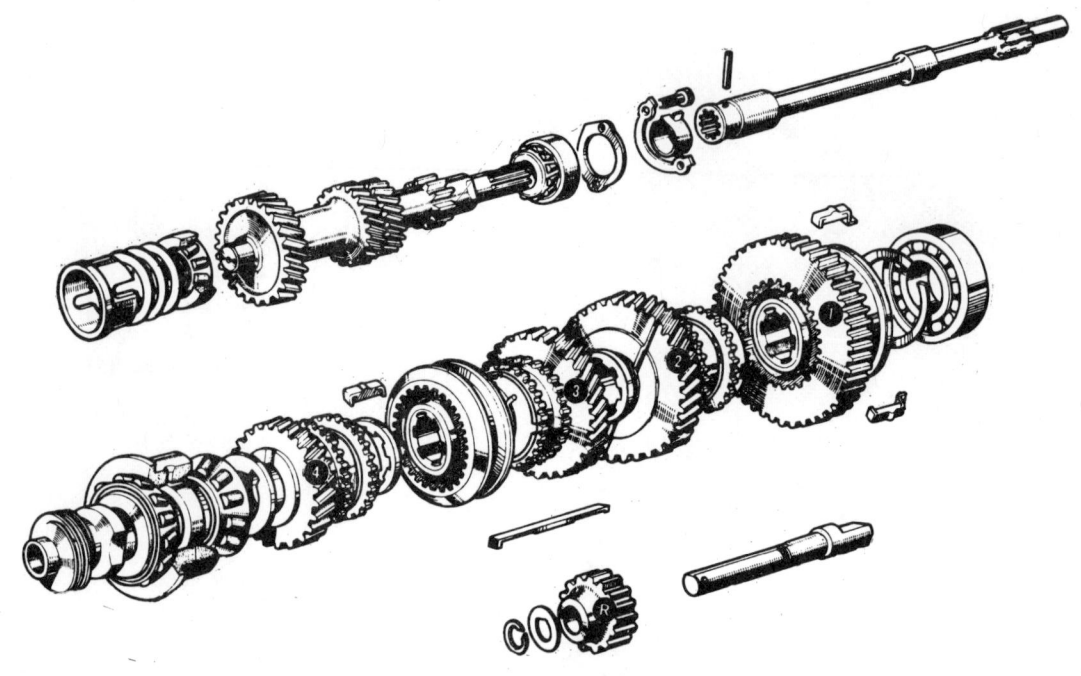

Exploded view of the transmission gears. (Courtesy of Renault, Inc.)

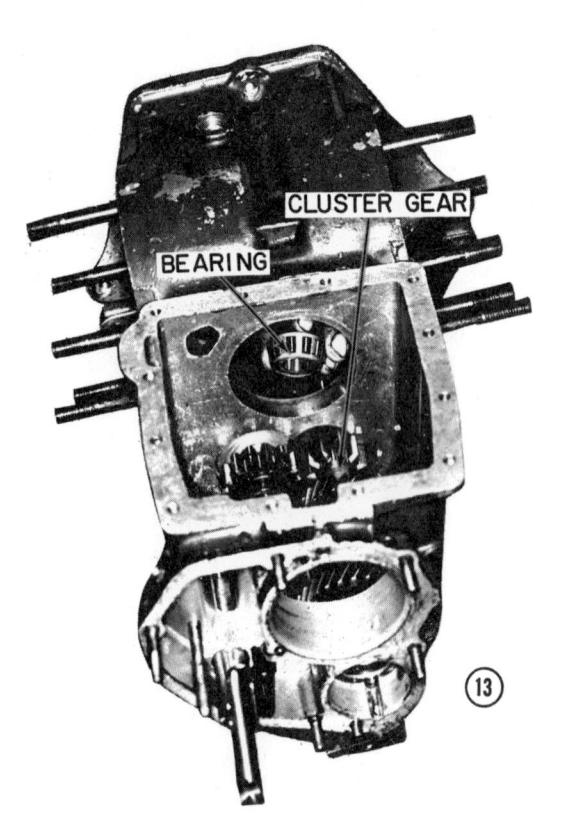

shaft, gear, washer, and snap ring. Remove the sealing plugs and extract the two detent plunger pins.

⑬ To remove the cluster gear (power input shaft), it is necessary to pull off the bearing at the differential end, and then lift out the shaft through the top of the case.

ASSEMBLING—TRANSMISSION

⑭ Before assembling the parts, it is important to establish the correct pinion position with reference to the centerline of the ring gear. The nominal assembly distance is 47.5 mm., and the pinion gear is marked in hundredths of a millimeter if it deviates from this dimension. In such a case, adjustment must be made to the pinion positioning shim. In this illustration, the pinion is marked 20 and if the new pinion is marked 20, then no change

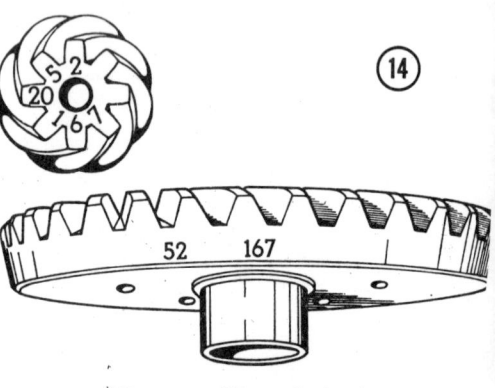

(Courtesy of Renault, Inc.)

Service

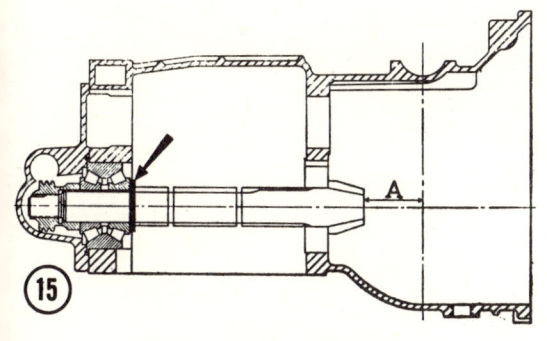

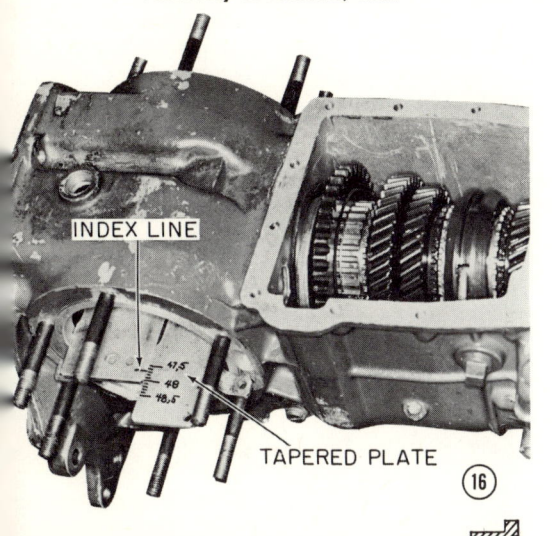

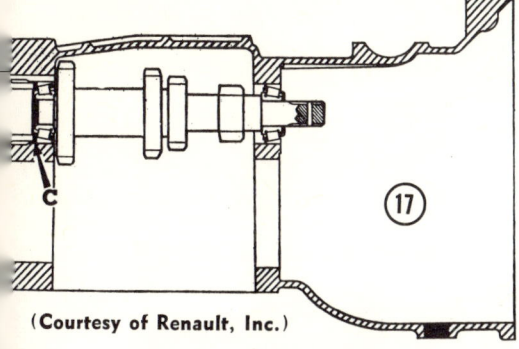

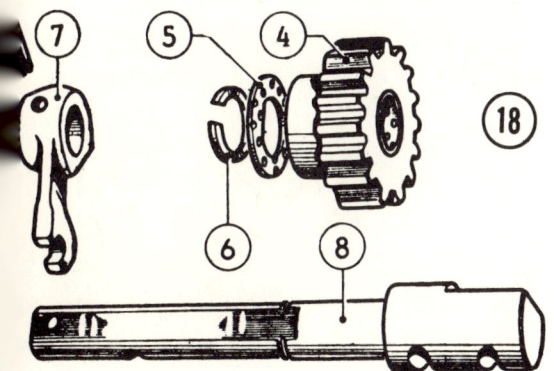

needs to be made in the pinion positioning shim. If, however, the new pinion is marked 40, then a 0.20 mm. change must be added to the shim to re-establish the correct pinion position. If the new pinion is marked in the negative direction, then a thinner washer must be substituted. The other numbers on the end of the pinion (52 and 167) are manufacturing matching numbers to show that the two parts are mated.

⑮ Replace the mainshaft (differential drive pinion), with the double-cone bearing, to test the position of the drive pinion (A). Replace the pinion-positioning washer (arrow) with the one selected, and tighten the speedometer drive pinion assembly on the shaft to 86 ft.-lbs. (12.0 m.kg.) torque, *but do not lock it*. Check the assembly for end play and replace the double-cone bearing if there is any play. Install the front cover to hold the drive pinion firmly in position for accurate measurement of pinion depth.

⑯ The position of the pinion gear can be checked with the illustrated gauge. The plate is tapered and can be slid in between the gauge and pinion until it fits tightly. Note the reference line on the plate, which should match up with the index mark at 47.5 mm. if the pinion has no correcting mark. If, however, the pinion gear is marked for a correction of 20, for example, the gauge indicator should line up with the 47.70 mm. mark (47.50 + 0.20 = 47.70 mm.), as shown. If the dimension recorded is smaller than it should be, change the washer to a thinner one, and vice versa. Spacers are available in increments of 0.05 mm. for adjustment. When the correct adjustment is obtained, remove the gauge and the drive pinion assembly.

⑰ To install the primary shaft (clutch shaft), replace the bearing on the short end of the shaft, slip the shaft into the housing, drive the bearing onto the primary shaft at the rear axle end, and then install the race. *The race must be flush with the edge of the housing.* Install the bearing race on the short end of the shaft so that the shaft turns freely, but without end play *with the cover in place*. If necessary, replace the adjusting shim pack (C) with one that will reduce the end play to zero. Adjustment shims are available in thicknesses of: 0.004″, 0.008″, 0.020″, and 0.037″ (0.10, 0.20, 0.50, and 0.95 mm.).

⑱ To install the reverse shaft (8), insert it through the rear axle end of the case. On the shaft side, replace the pinion (4) (with the teeth facing the rear axle end), thrust washer (5) (with its bronze side facing the pinion), and snap ring (6), which must be new. Temporarily, install the third-and-fourth speed shift fork shaft and turn the housing over.

⑲ Line up the keyway in the reverse shaft with the detent pin (3). Push in the reverse shaft fully. Turn the housing over again, and remove the third-and-fourth speed shift fork shaft.

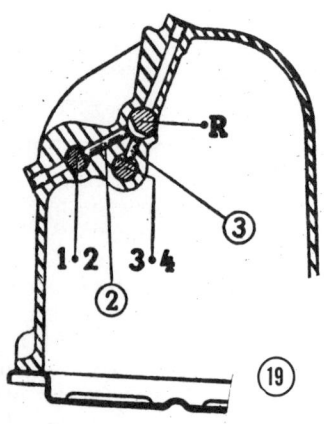

Trans-Axle

(Courtesy of Renault, Inc.)

(Courtesy of Renault, Inc.)

⑳ Position the control lever on the reverse shaft and insert a new lock pin. Replace the reverse sleeve, turn the shaft, and position the lever in the sleeve recess. Replace the primary-and-reverse shaft bearing thrust plate and lock it in position. Replace the detent pin and the threaded plug, which must be coated with sealer.

㉑ The reverse and the third-and-fourth speed detent springs are identical. The first-and-second detent spring is longer and made of thinner wire. It is rather difficult to replace the shafts and keep the detent balls in position. To do this, a special tool B.Vi. 34 is available. It is possible to press the detent balls in place with a screwdriver, but the assistance of a helper is required. To replace the shafts, position the spring (9), and then place the ball in the special tool illustrated. (1) Push the tool and ball into the shaft passage as shown at (A). (2) Turn the tool a quarter turn. (3) Use a thin rod as shown at (B) to push the ball toward the spring as you slide the tool toward the inside of the case.

㉒ Push out the tool by inserting the shaft (5) as shown at (C). Replace the interlock (1) and the detent ball with the tool (6) and push it into position with a thin rod (7) as shown at (D). Insert the first-and-second speed shifter shaft (8) and the fork as shown at (E). Replace the retaining pin.

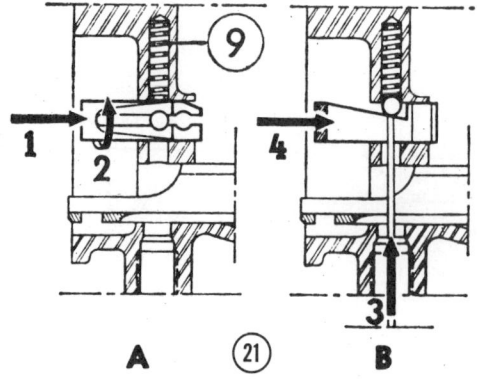

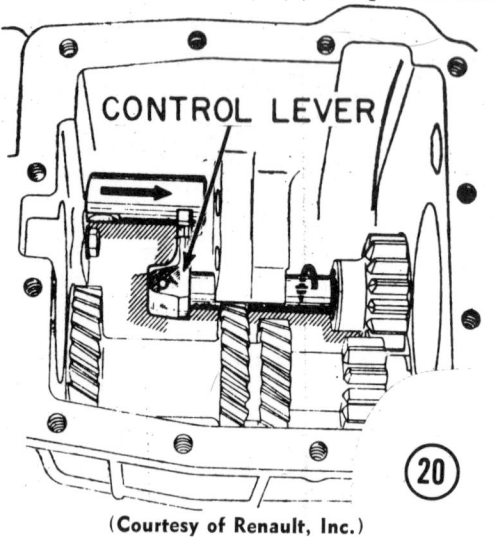

㉓ To assemble the secondary shaft (differential pinion), prepare the second speed synchronizer by positioning the retaining ring and the two springs on the hub.

㉔ Engage the ends of the locks under the retaining springs.

㉕ Position the hub in the sliding gear, with the groove toward the toothed end. Prepare the third-and-fourth synchronizer in the same manner. Slide the hub into the internal gear.

㉖ Slide the secondary shaft into the housing from the differential end.

㉗ Assemble the first-and-second speed sliding

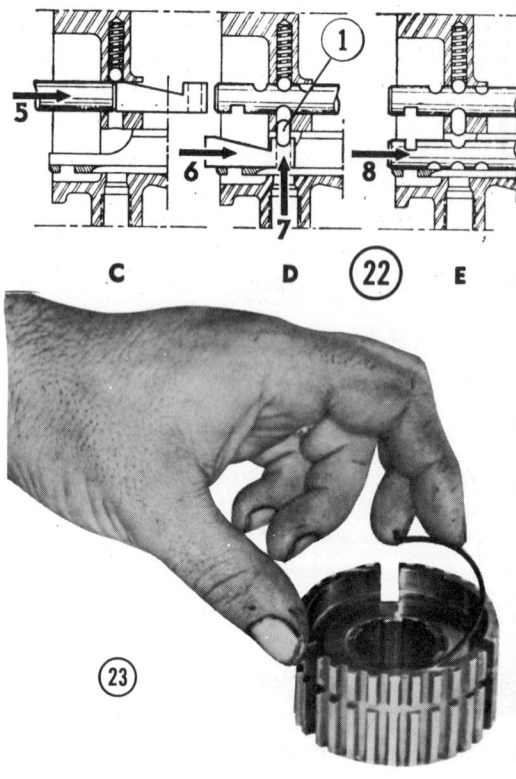

(Courtesy of Renault, Inc.)

Service 75

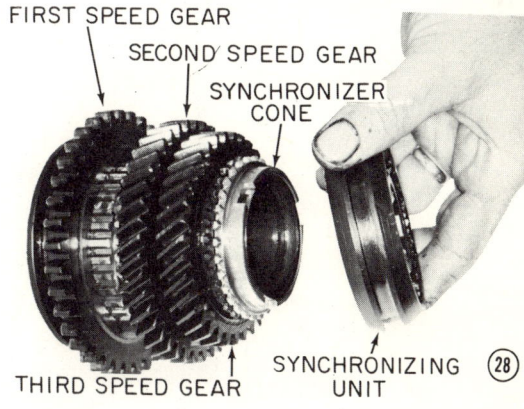

gear on its control fork (teeth facing the speedometer drive gear), and then the second speed gear, synchronizer cone, and splined washer.

㉘ Replace the third speed gear, the synchronizer cone, and the third-and-fourth speed synchronizer unit. *CAUTION: The synchronizer must be installed with the missing spline over the locking keyway.* Install the splined washer, the fourth speed gear, and the retainer ring synchronizer cone.

㉙ To insert the key, move the first-and-second

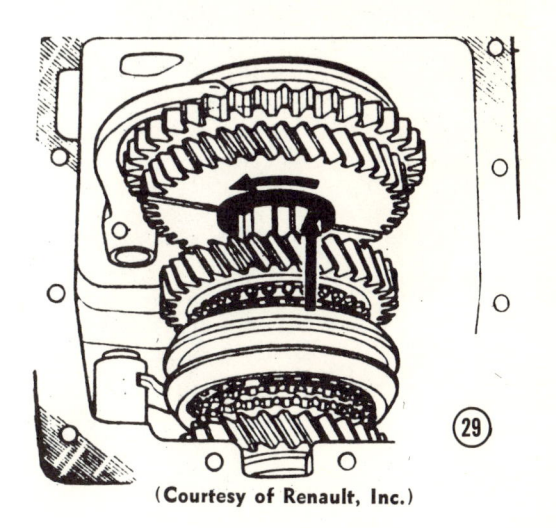

(Courtesy of Renault, Inc.)

Trans-Axle

(Courtesy of Renault, Inc.)

(Courtesy of Renault, Inc.)

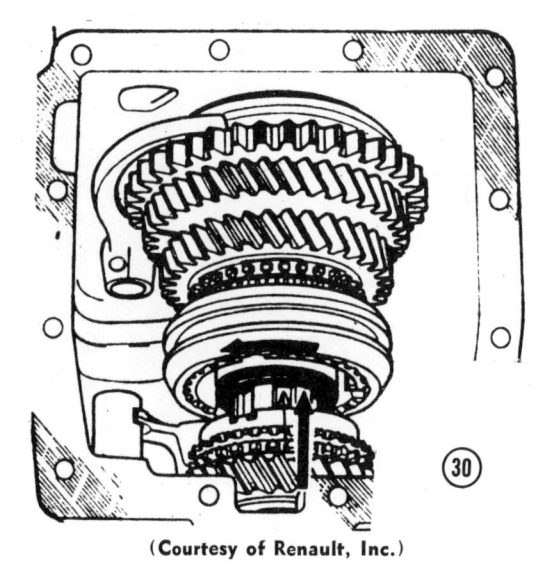

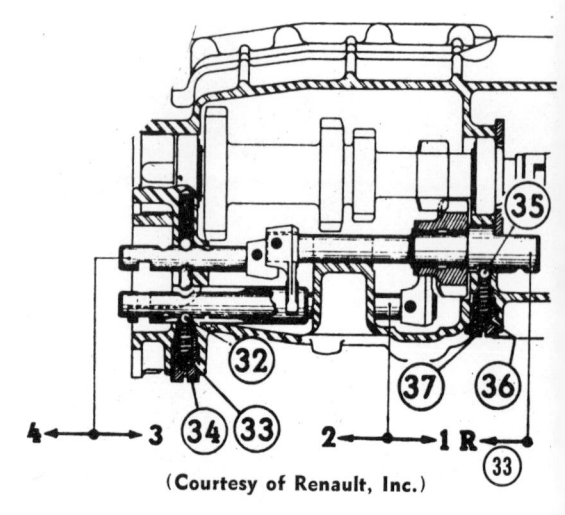

speed gear assembly toward the rear end to clear the splined washer, which should now be turned so that its keyway lines up with that on the shaft.

㉚ Move the third speed gear and the third-and-fourth speed synchronizer assembly toward the rear to clear the splined washer, which should now be turned to line up the keyway with the locking spline.

㉛ Insert the locking key fully into the groove. Replace the pinion positioning washer, with the keyway over the end of the locking key.

㉜ Replace the double-cone ball bearing and the speedometer drive pinion. Tighten the pinion to

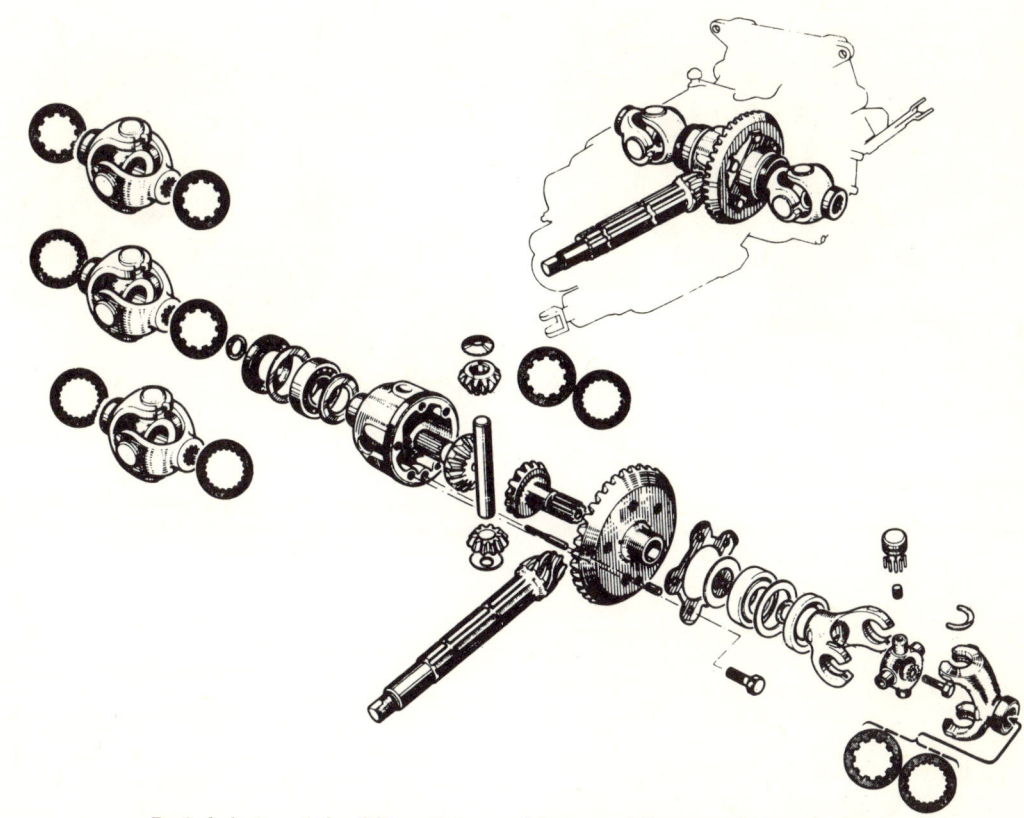

Service 77

Exploded view of the differential assembly gears. (Courtesy of Renault, Inc.)

86 ft.-lbs. (12.0 m.kg.) torque. Lock the speedometer drive pinion to the secondary shaft by staking it.

㉝ Push back the third-and-fourth speed shaft and replace the shifter fork. Replace the lock pin. Install detent ball (32) and the spring (33). Replace the threaded plug (34), after coating it with sealer. Install the reverse shaft detent ball (35) and spring (36). Screw in the threaded lock plug (37), after coating it with sealer. Tighten the locknut.

㉞ Replace the cluster gear shim pack and spacer. Engage second gear, install the fork shaft control lever, replace the front cover with a new gasket coated with sealing compound, and then install the lock pin to hold the control lever to the shaft. Return the gears to neutral and replace the transmission cover, using a new gasket and sealing compound.

㉟ Install the differential unit in the housing as shown. Replace the clutch shaft and lock it with the pin and retaining spring. Replace the differ-

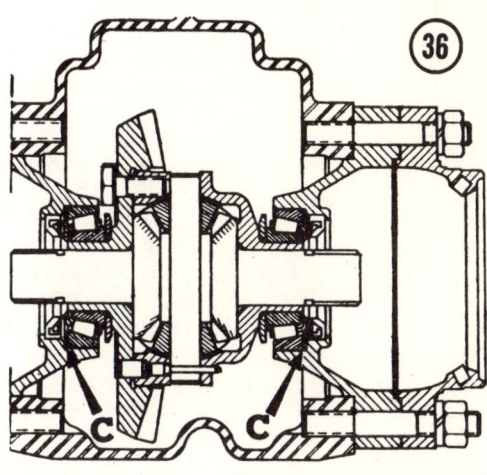

RING GEAR

(Courtesy of Renault, Inc.)

Ferlec Automatic Clutch

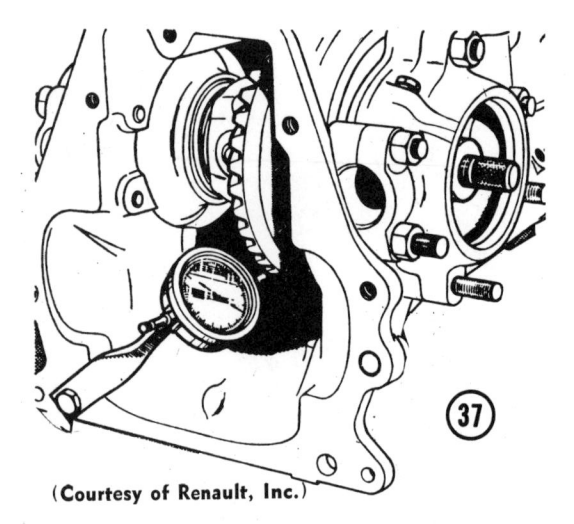

ential brackets as previously marked. Replace the universal joints and the half shells.

㊱ Check the carrier bearings, which should be assembled without any side play if the old bearings are to be re-used, or a total of 0.008" (0.20 mm.) pre-load if new bearings are used. The differential should rotate with a torque of 0.58–1.08 ft.-lbs. (0.08–0.15 m.kg.) with new bearings. The carrier bearing end play is controlled by shims at (C).

㊲ To measure the backlash between the pinion and ring gear, mount a dial indicator as shown. The backlash should be between 0.005"–0.010" (0.12–0.25 mm.). Adjustment can be made by changing carrier bearing shims from one side to the other.

FERLEC AUTOMATIC CLUTCH

The clutch operates by means of a magnetic field energized by the generator. When the engine is idling, the magnetic field is at its weakest and the clutch slips. When the engine is accelerated, the magnetic field is progressively strengthened until the clutch operates at maximum efficiency and there is no slippage.

The current necessary for operation of the clutch is taken directly from the armature terminal of the regulator, without passing through the regulator. In emergency cases, due to failure of the generator, the dashboard switch can be moved from its GEN position to BAT position to energize the clutch until the unit can be serviced.

A rheostat (7) is connected to the throttle linkage so that depressing the accelerator pedal decreases the resistance in the circuit. Thus, as the generator charging rate increases through increased engine rpm, the clutch circuit resistance decreases, making the magnetic circuit more effective.

A switch (11) is incorporated in the shift lever to ground the clutch and ignition circuits whenever the lever is moved, thus allowing the gears to be shifted without clashing. Release of the shift lever restores the clutch circuit.

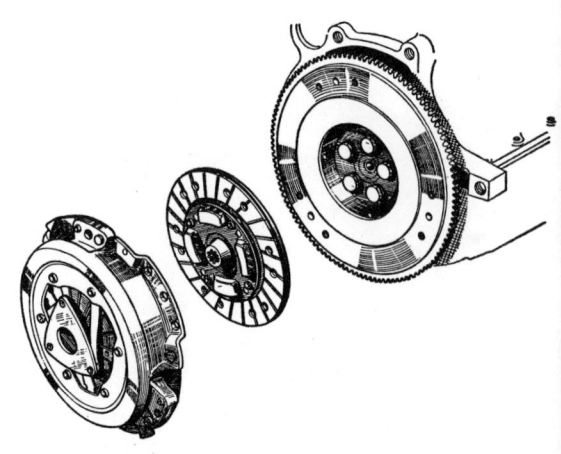

(Courtesy of Renault, Inc.)

Exploded view of the Ferlec clutch. The clutch disc offset side must be assembled facing the trans-axle. (Courtesy of Renault, Inc.)

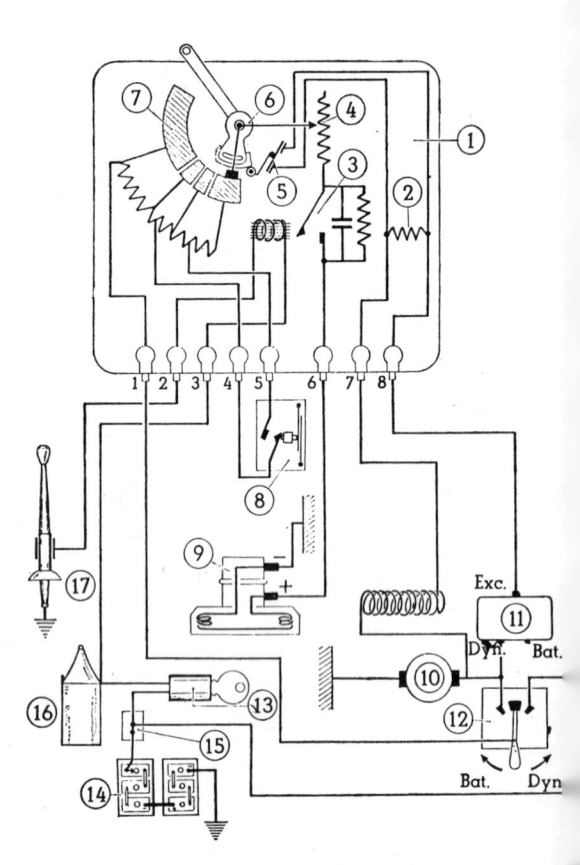

Wiring diagram of the 12-volt Ferlec: (1) Control case, (2) field current limiting resistor, (3) clutch release relay, (4) adjustable resistor, (5) field resistor by-pass switch, (6) by-pass switch cam, (7) rheostat, (8) short-circuiting switch, (9) clutch, (10) generator, (11) gear shift lever switch, (12) dash switch, (13) ignition switch, (14) battery, (15) terminal plate under dash, (16) ignition coil, (17) gear shift lever. (Courtesy of Renault, Inc.)

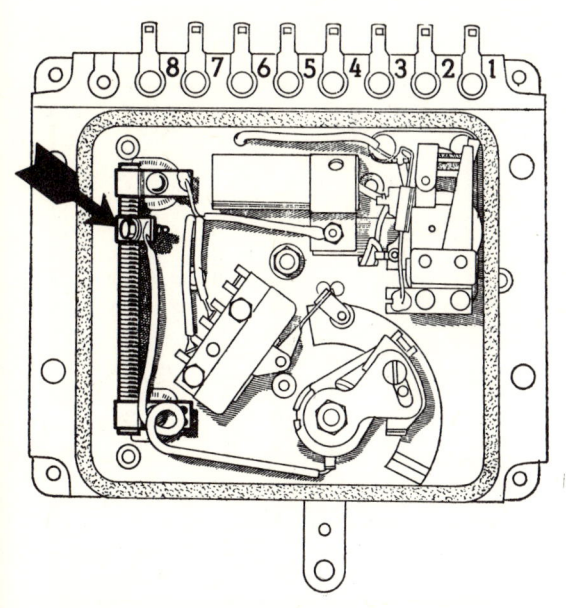

Service

Details of the control case. The arrow points to the adjustable slide on the resistor mentioned in the text. (Courtesy of Renault, Inc.)

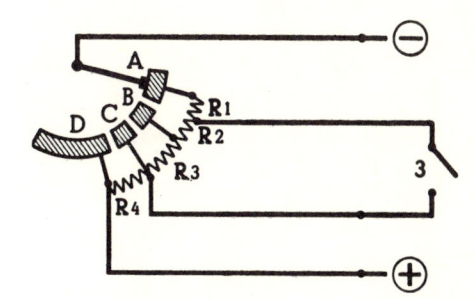

Operation of both the 6-volt and the 12-volt Ferlec clutches is controlled by inserting or removing resistance in the operating circuit through the action of rheostat (9). With the car in either first or reverse and the micro-switch open, the resistance of the rheostat decreases from terminal "A" (idle speed) to terminal "D" (acceleration) by successive elimination of resistances R-1 + R-2, R-3 and R-4. (Courtesy of Renault, Inc.)

OVERHAULING

In general, the greatest difficulty is caused by the accumulation of oil on the surfaces of the operating parts, which soon pick up enough dirt to interfere with the motion of the armature toward the flywheel. To clean the unit, soak it in carbon tetrachloride *(CAUTION: Be sure there is ample ventilation)* or use a rag saturated with lacquer thinner. Dry the unit with air.

To replace the trailing links, make identification marks on each piece for proper assembly. Unlock and remove the three stop nuts (20) which hold the armature. Remove the three bolts (21) which hold the trailing links (11) to the flywheel (1). If the armature, spider plate, or pressure plate is damaged, the entire unit must be replaced. If the trailing links are worn, they must be replaced as a set of three. Install the set of trailing links, tightening nuts (22) finger-tight. Position the armature against the flywheel. *NOTE: There is only one position in which the units will fit together properly.* Insert the tips of the trailing links in-

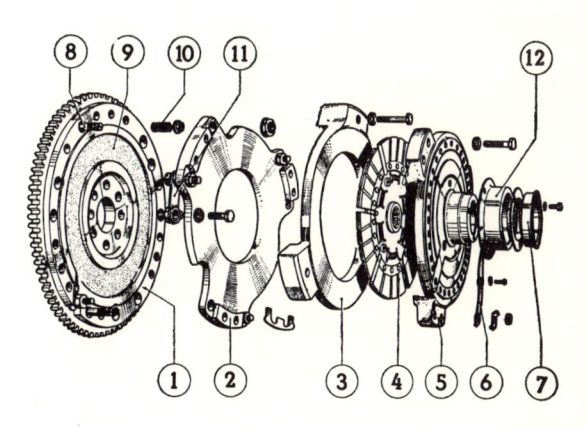

REMOVING

Disconnect the clutch release relay lead from the ignition coil and the lead from the positive brush. Remove the powerplant. Punch-mark the relative positions of the flywheel with respect to the crankshaft, and each part with respect to the others in order to ensure proper balance when reassembling. Remove the brushes and brush holders. Disconnect the flywheel conductor strap (7) and remove the pressure plate. Save the adjusting shims (6), if any were used, and then remove the clutch disc.

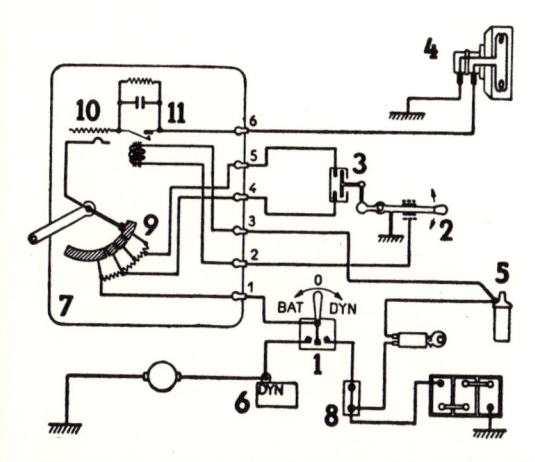

Wiring diagram of the 6-volt Ferlec clutch. (1) Dash switch, (2) shift lever, (3) micro-switch under floorboard, (4) clutch, (5) ignition coil, (6) regulator, (7) case, (8) terminal plate on dash, (9) rheostat, (10) adjustable resistor (see text for adjustment), and (11) clutch release relay. (Courtesy of Renault, Inc.)

Exploded view of the parts of the clutch. (Courtesy of Renault, Inc.)

80 Ferlec Automatic Clutch

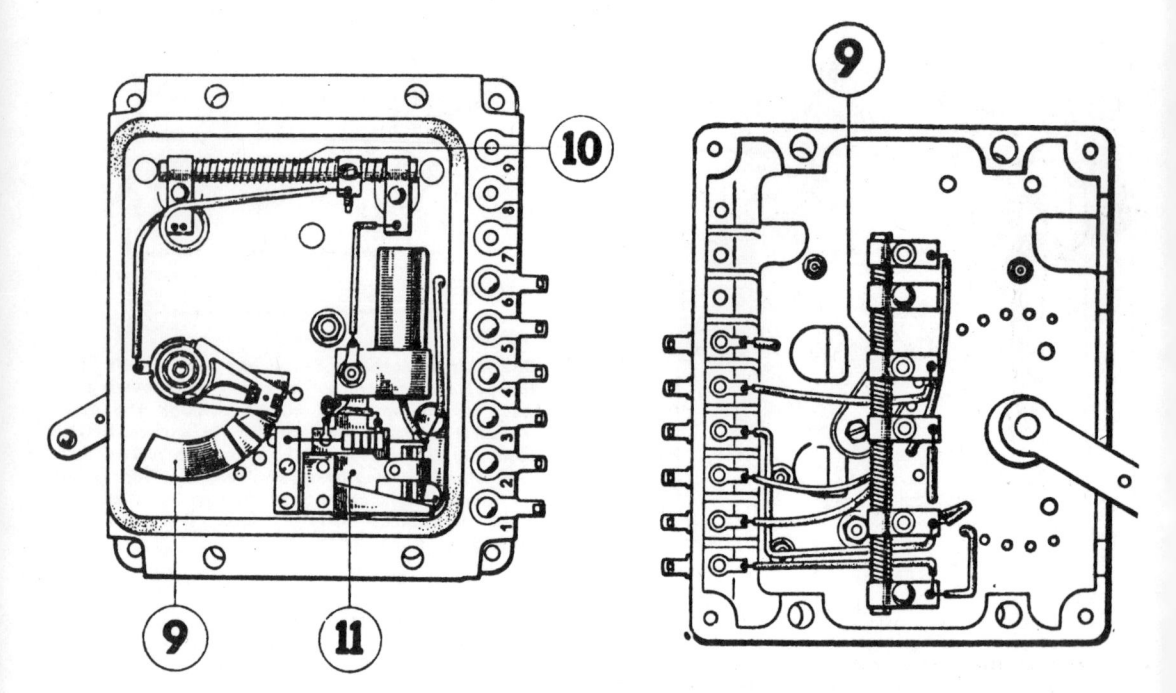

The control box of the 6-volt Ferlec clutch. The adjustable resistor (10) is discussed in the text, as it is the method of adjusting the smoothness of clutch engagement. (Courtesy of Renault, Inc.)

side their housings in the flywheel. Replace bolts (21), with the flat and lockwashers. Tighten the bolts (21) and nuts (22) to 7 ft.-lbs. torque.

ADJUSTING

If the old disc is to be used again, position a 0.008″ shim under each ear of the pressure plate, *provided that these shims had been used before.* If a new disc is to be used, it is imperative that these 0.008″ shims be used. Check the air gap at three different points, 120° apart. With a new disc, the air gap must be from 0.014″–0.018″, with a difference between readings of not over 0.0015″.

If the old disc is re-used, the air gap must not be less than 0.008″. If it is close to 0.008″, remove the three 0.008″ shims that were installed on assembly to restore the gap to the new specifications.

To Adjust the Armature Stop Nuts. Remove the clutch disc and replace the pressure plate, with the 0.008″ shims, if they are part of the assembly. Insert a 0.115″ feeler gauge between the pressure plate (6) and the spider plate (4), as close as

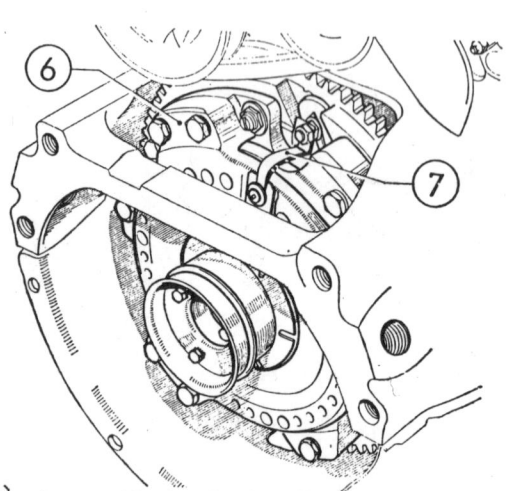

Clutch assembly details. (6) Clutch attaching bolts and (7) conductor strap. (Courtesy of Renault, Inc.)

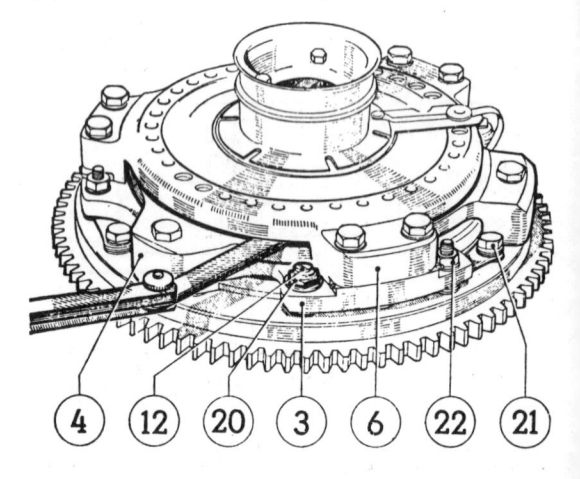

Adjustment procedure is to turn the stopnut (20) down until it just contacts the armature (3), with a 0.115″ (2.90 mm.) gauge positioned as shown, and then stake the nut to keep it from turning. Repeat for the other two stopnuts. (Courtesy of Renault, Inc.)

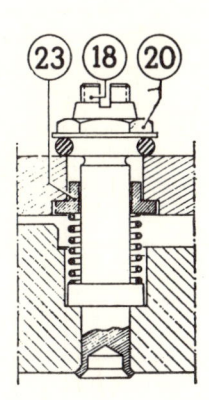

Details of the stopnut (20) mentioned above. (Courtesy of Renault, Inc.)

possible to the stop nut (20) which you are adjusting. Turn the stop nut until it just touches the armature and repeat for the other two stop nuts. To lock the three stop nuts, make a small punch mark in the upper collar.

Installing

Clean the mating surfaces. Bolt the flywheel on the crankshaft in the same position as removed. Tighten the four flywheel-to-crankshaft bolts to 33–36 ft-lbs. torque. Clean the slip rings with alcohol. Position the clutch disc with the longest side of the hub facing the crankshaft. Bolt the pressure plate in position, according to the punch marks made during disassembly, to 7–9 ft.-lbs. torque. Place the 0.008" shims under the ears of the pressure plate, if they are part of the assembly. Connect the conductor strap and coat it with varnish. Replace the brushes in their holders. Check to be sure that they are free to slide up and down. Connect the purple lead (6) to the positive brush. Insert a clutch alignment tool, energize the clutch, and then tighten the bolts holding the engine to the trans-axle unit. Switch off the clutch current.

Adjustments

As the clutch disc wears, the air gap between

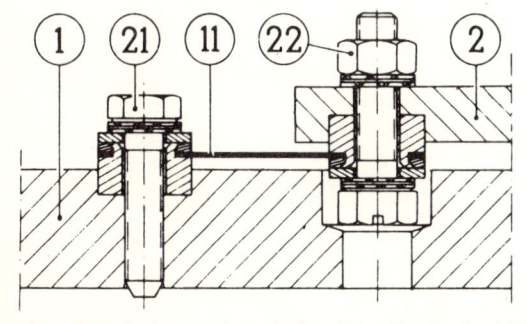

Details of the trailing link. (1) Flywheel, (2) spider plate, and (11) trailing link. (Courtesy of Renault, Inc.)

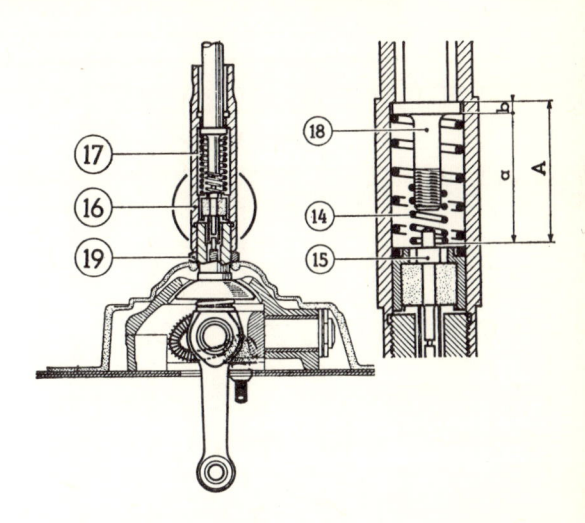

Gear shift lever switch details. Turn bushing (16) in tight, and then back it off ½ turn. When replacing spring (14), adjust bolt (18) until distance "A" is 1" (25.4 mm.). (Courtesy of Renault, Inc.)

the flywheel and the armature diminishes. A point will be slowly reached where the clutch will begin to chatter or grab. When this happens, the resistance of the adjustable resistor (4) can be increased to reduce the flow of current to the flywheel and thereby weaken the strength of the magnetic field. *CAUTION: This adjustment cannot be made to compensate for a clutch air gap of less than 0.008".* The resistance of the adjustable resistor will increase when the sliding contact (arrow) is moved away from the terminal side of the control case. The sliding contact should be moved only a small amount, and then the car road-tested for proper clutch operation as follows:

Road Test

Accelerate slightly to get the car rolling, and then depress the accelerator fully with the shift lever in first gear. If the engine stalls, the adjust-

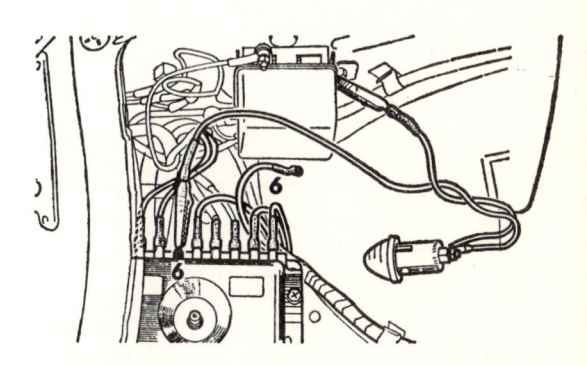

To check the declutching relay, disconnect No. 6 wire and connect a test lamp between the terminal and ground. With the 3-way switch and ignition switch turned on, the lamp should light. The lamp should go out when the shift lever is moved. (Courtesy of Renault, Inc.)

82 Ferlec Automatic Clutch Troubleshooting Chart

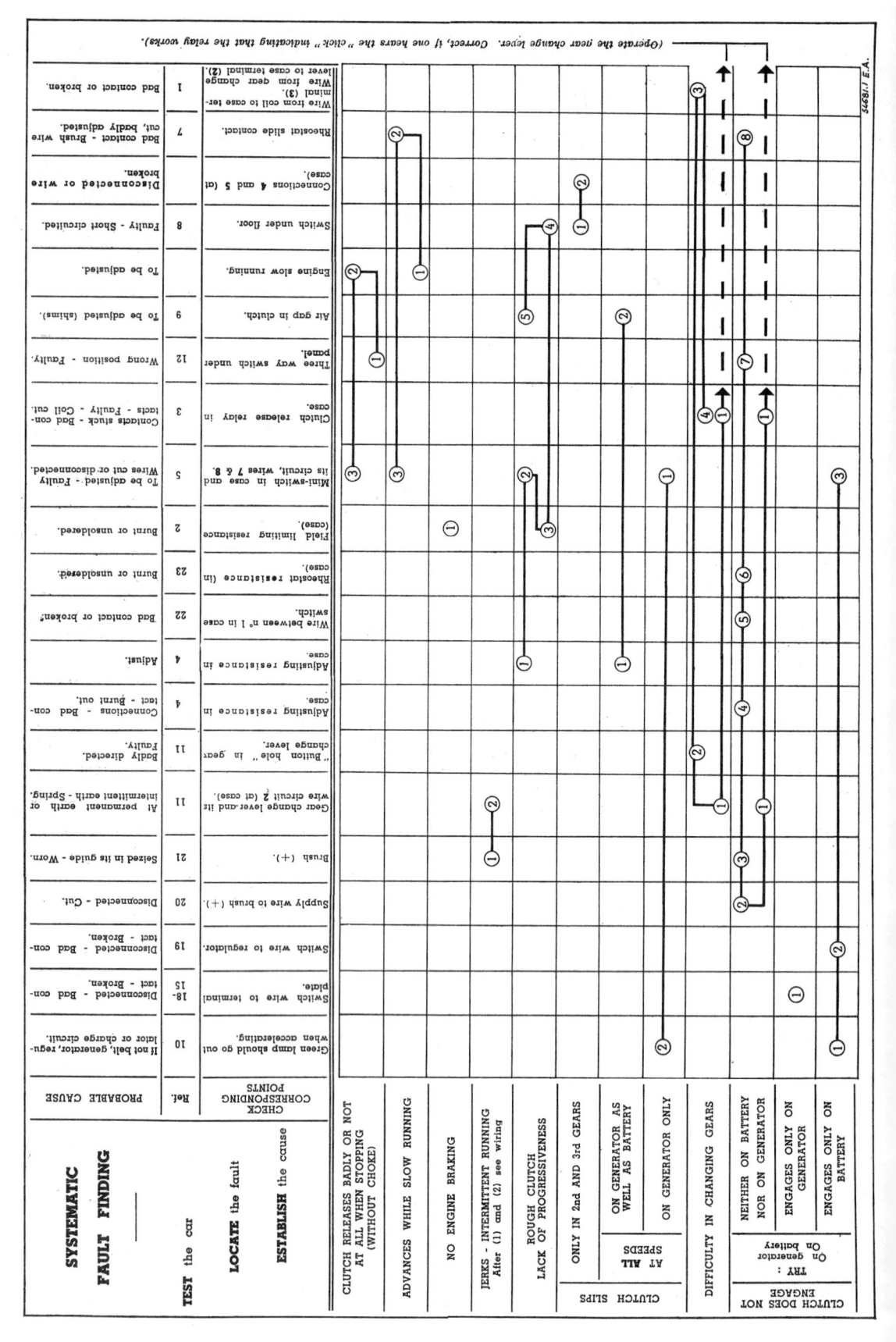

Automatic Transmission

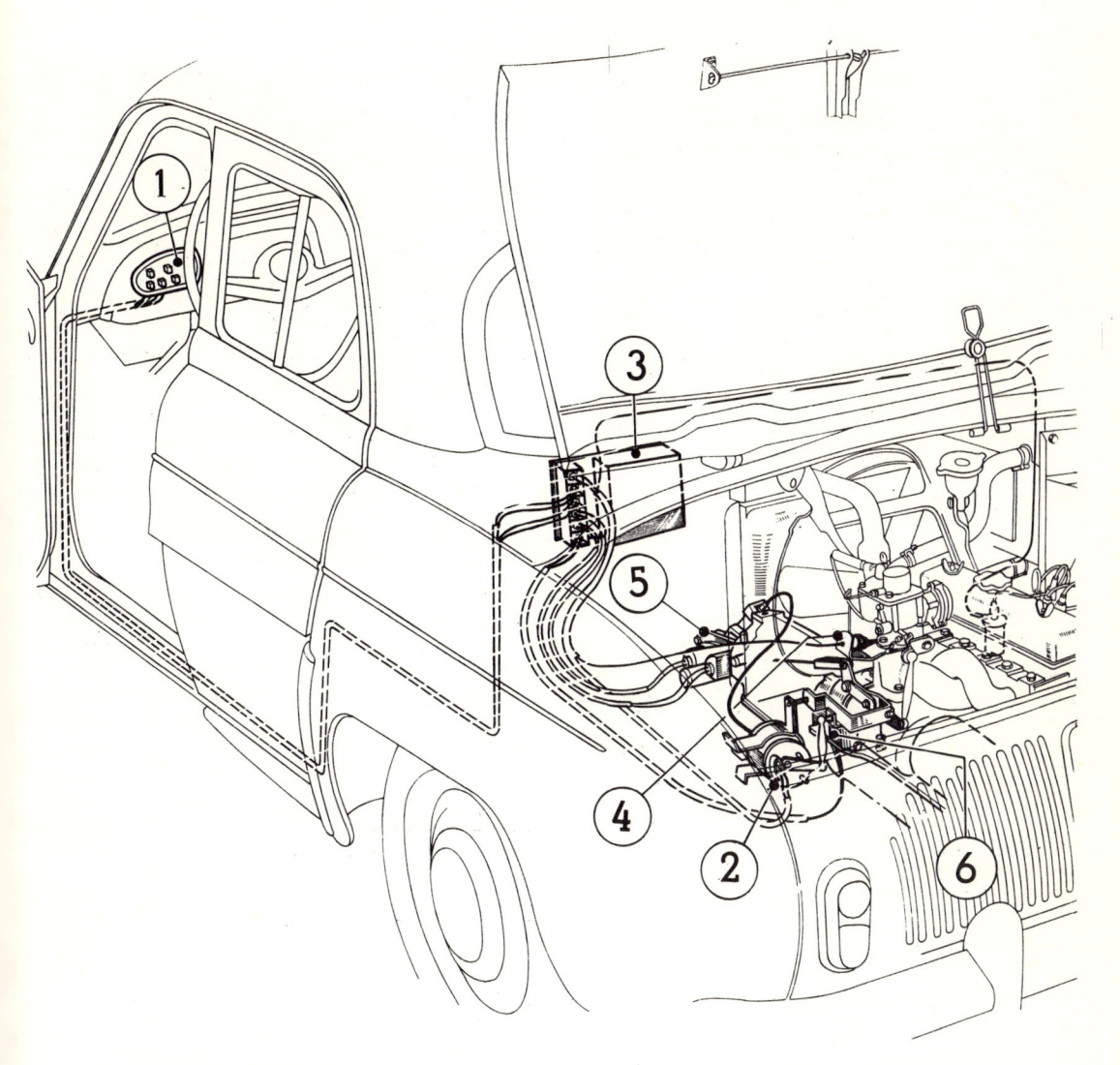

Placement of the various control units for the Renault automatic transmission. (1) Push-button panel, (2) governor, (3) relay case, (4) decelerator, (5) actuator and servo motor, and (6) the coupling link. (Courtesy of Renault, Inc.)

able resistor (4) is set too low. If the engine races, the resistor is set too high. Repeat the procedure in second gear, and the same results should occur.

If lowering the adjustable resistor does not correct racing, then the short-circuiting switch (8) may have high internal resistance. This can be checked by driving the car in first gear at 12 mph. Move the gear shift lever to release the clutch, but do not shift. Release the accelerator and the shift lever, and the car should slow down. If the car does not slow down, the short-circuiting switch (8) is not operating properly. If the car slows down abruptly, the adjustable resistor is set too low.

AUTOMATIC TRANSMISSION

In 1963, Renault introduced an automatic transmission for the Dauphine. The gear shift lever is replaced by push buttons and the shifting procedure is automatic after the driver selects the desired range. The clutch is replaced by an electromagnetic powder coupling, and the shifting is done by an electric servo motor, which is attached to the front of the standard three-speed, fully-synchronized transmission. The entire shifting procedure is timed by an electrical relay box in conjunction with a governor.

RELAY CASE

The relay case is the brains of the system. It contains relays to actuate the various shift and clutch controls. It transmits the orders of the governor and push button control panel to the clutch coupling, decelerator, and actuator. The unit is composed of relays, transistors, and time-delay circuits.

Automatic Transmission

The relay case is behind the cardboard deflector, which must be removed to service the unit.

Positions of the governor and decelerator. Note the throttle connecting link.

Governor

The governor is driven by the transmission output shaft. It contains two sets of contact points to signal the shift points according to car speed. At the same time, it signals the relay control box for clutch disengagement or engagement.

Decelerator

During a gear shift, it is necessary to reduce engine speed. This is accomplished by a solenoid-controlled valve in the intake manifold, just under the carburetor. When the governor signals that a shift is to take place, the relay case actuates the solenoid and the control valve under the carburetor shuts off until the shift is completed.

Coupling Unit

The coupling is a powder-type, electromagnetic clutch, which takes the place of the conventional disc clutch assembly. Its operation depends on electric current solidifying the ferro-magnetic powder between the driving and driven units. With the engine idling, current is supplied by the battery. As the engine speeds up, current is supplied by the generator at a higher voltage. This increased voltage with speed, plus compensating voltages sent from the control relay case, changes the speed of clutch engagement.

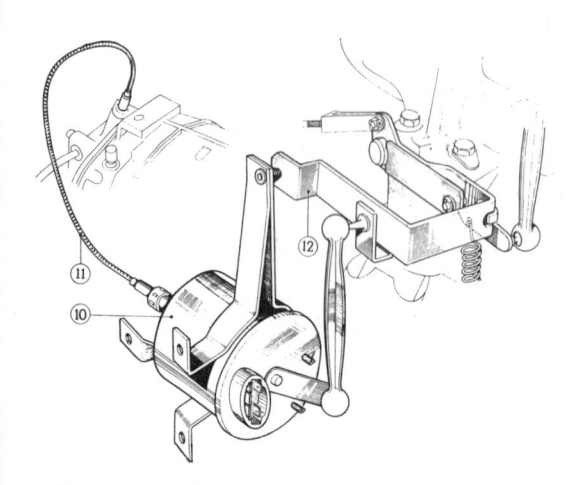

The governor (10) is mounted on the wheel panel. The governor is controlled by the speed of the car and the position of the accelerator pedal. It is connected to the transmission through a drive cable (11) and to the carburetor throttle valve through link (12). (Courtesy of Renault, Inc.)

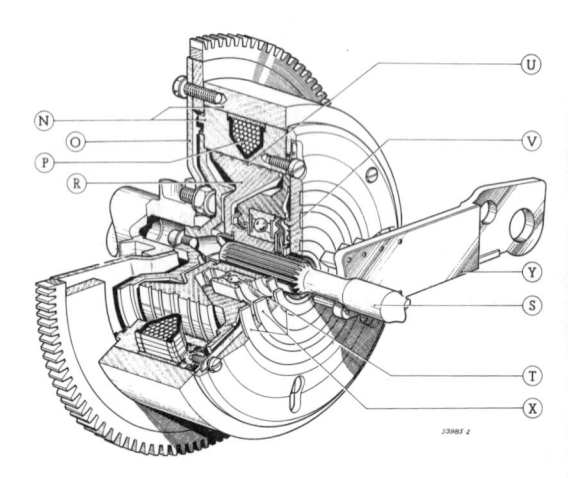

The coupling is a powder-type, electromagnetic unit. (N) Outer pole piece, (O) starter gear plate, (P) coil, (R) inner pole piece, (S) input shaft, (T) ball bearing, (U) air gap, (V) contact ring, (X) slip rings, and (Y) brush carrier. (Courtesy of Renault, Inc.)

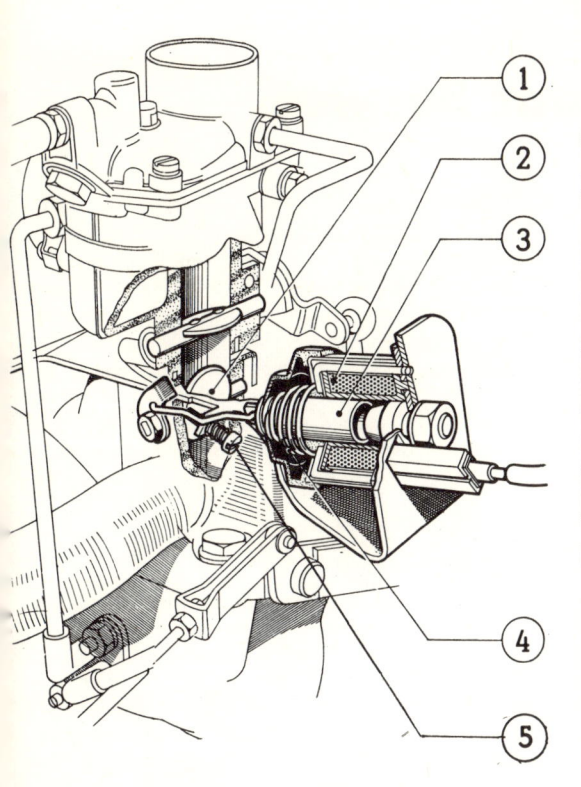

Service 85

The decelerator unit actuates a flap valve (1) during shifts. The adjustment screw (5) is to prevent stalling the engine, (2) is the coil, and (3) is the solenoid plunger. (Courtesy of Renault, Inc.)

The mechanic must have this test panel to check the various units. It contains all the basic units and is equipped with switches which allow substitution of each unit, one at a time, until the defective one is uncovered.

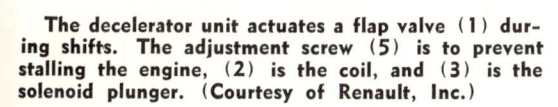

Actuator

The actuator is an electrical servo motor attached to the front of the standard three-forward speed transmission. A solenoid chooses the correct shift fork, and then the motor moves it in the proper direction as signaled by the governor and relay case.

Shift Points

Position of Foot on Accelerator	Gear Change Speed in mph (Km./h.)			
	Accelerating		Decelerating	
	1st to 2nd	2nd to 3rd	2nd to 1st	3rd to 2nd
Depressed	12 (19)	24 (41)	18 (31)	8 (16)
Lifted	21 (33)	42 (68)	36 (58)	16 (26)

SERVICE PROCEDURES

Except for the one adjustment to the decelerator, no service procedures to the control units of the transmission are permissible in the field. The factory has established a replacement policy in which the defective unit is returned for repair, and a new unit is installed on the car. The only service adjustment that can be made is to the decelerator flap valve. Turn in adjusting screw (5) so that the engine rpm is reduced to 2200 maximum when the solenoid shuts the flap valve during gear changes. *CAUTION: Under no circumstances should the ignition coil feed wire or the wire to the decelerator be grounded, or damage to the relay case will result.*

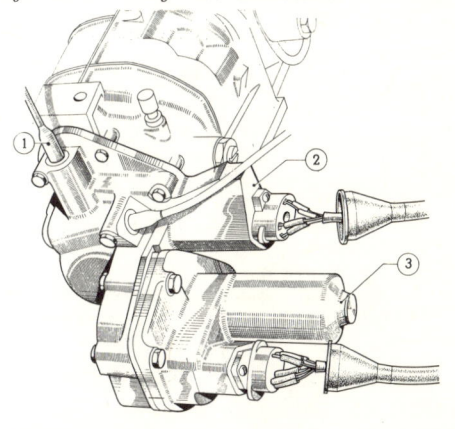

The actuator consists of a shift rail selector solenoid (2) and an electric motor (3) which shifts the gears. The flexible cable (1) sends car speed information to the governor. (Courtesy of Renault, Inc.)

7
Running Gear Service

STEERING GEAR OVERHAUL

DISASSEMBLING

① Clamp the unit in a vise. Remove the steering arm bolts (1).
② Unscrew locknut (2) and the end fitting (3). Remove the rubber sleeves (C).
③ Remove the lock ring (4), thrust washer (5), spring (6), and plunger (7).
④ Remove the flange retaining screw, and then take off the flange (9), upper lock ring (10), washer (11), and spacer (12). Pull the seal (13).
⑤ Remove the lock ring (14) and lubrication nipple (16).
⑥ Drive out the pinion and bearing assembly (18).
⑦ Remove the seal (19) and lock ring (20), and then press off the bearing (17).
⑧ Remove snap rings (21) from both ends of the spring by using a small screwdriver to lift and clear the snap ring at the smooth end of the rack. With a wrench holding the milled flats on the toothed end, rotate the rack so as to release the snap ring from its groove. To remove the snap ring from the toothed end, pull on the rack, and the snap ring will pop out when the rack contacts the bushing. CAUTION: *The snap rings, re-*

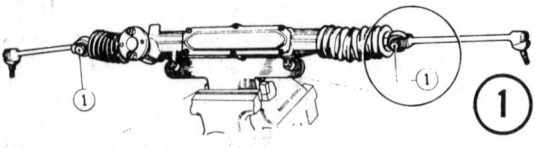

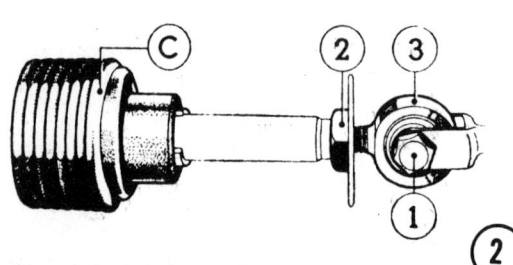

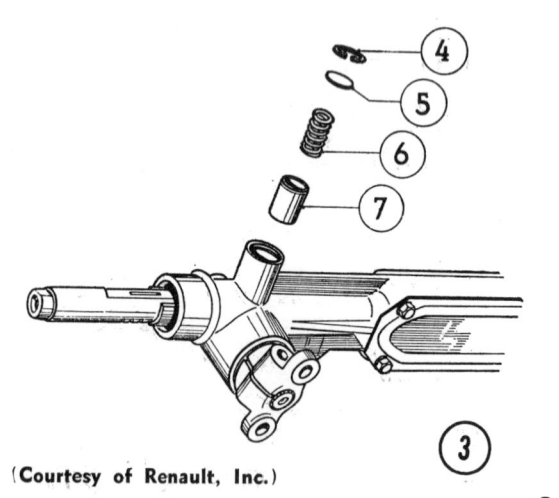

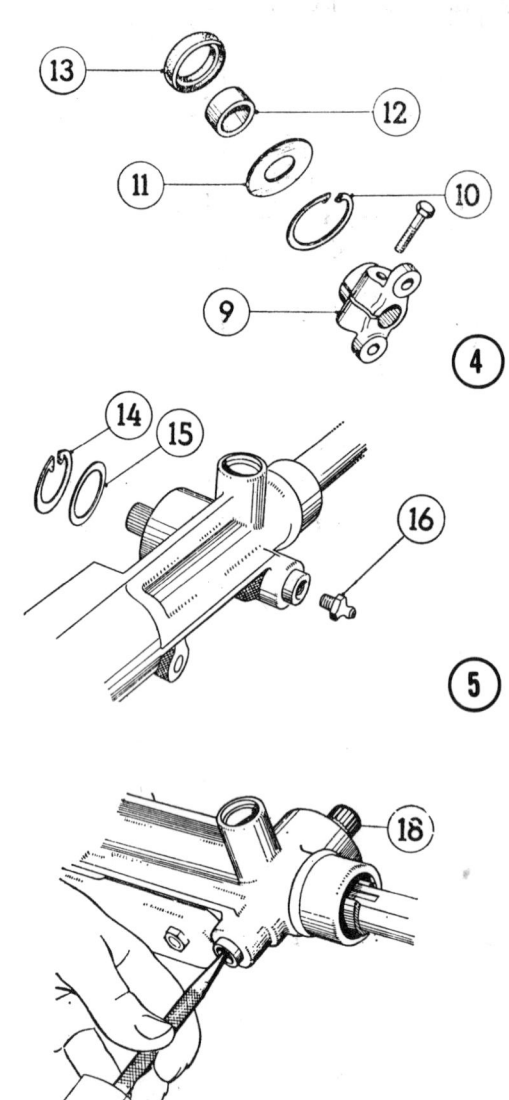

86

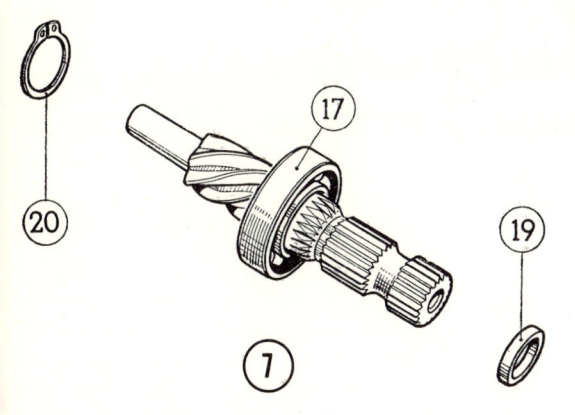

Steering Gear Overhaul 87

tainers, and seal must not be re-used. Remove the return spring, cups, and the rubber bushing.

Assembling

⑨ From inside the housing, install the lower bushing (26). Place a small amount of grease in the back of the rack bushing (27). Insert rubber bushing (25) into spring (24), and then compress the spring, with its two cups (22), into the housing. Insert a new snap ring (21) and make sure that it is tight in its groove. Insert the rack (23), toothed end first, into the housing until the end piece reaches the middle of the spring, and then lead it into the rubber bushing (25). Place the second snap ring (21) in position.

⑩ Slip a retaining fork in position to hold the spring, and then slide the rack in until the snap ring (21) slips into its groove. Remove the retaining fork. Using a tube, drive in a new bushing at the opposite end of the pinion and install a new snap ring. Replace the cover and gasket.

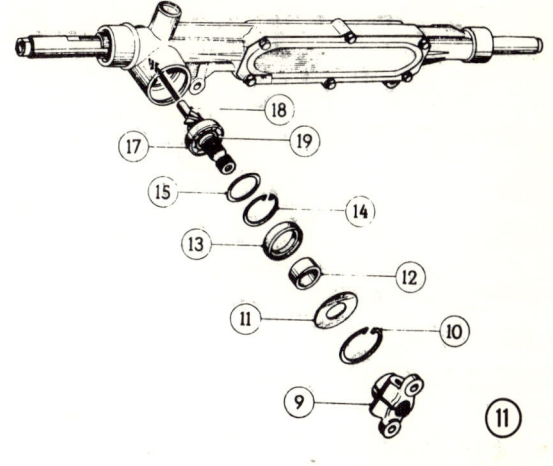

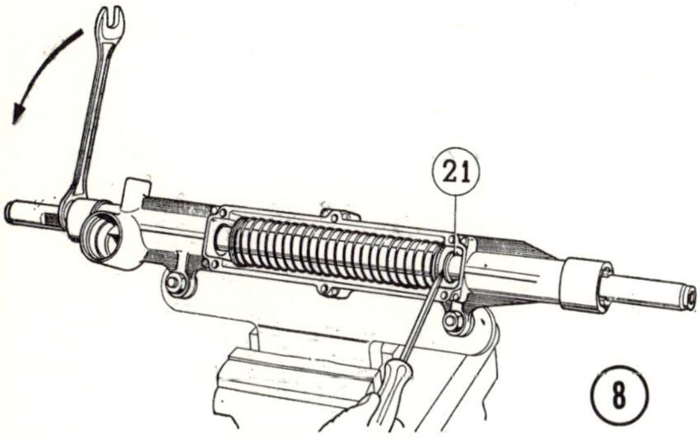

⑪ Position a new thrust washer on the pinion, and then press the bearing into place. Install a new seal washer (19) into its groove on the pinion. Position the shaft end of the pinion (18) opposite the pressure spring, and then install the parts in the following order: thrust washer (15), new snap ring (14), new and lubricated seal (13), spacer (12), washer (11), and new upper snap ring (10). Position the drive flange (9), with the center line of the two holes perpendicular to the axis of the rack. Tighten the retaining bolt.

⑫ Install plunger (7), spring (6), and thrust washer (5). Compress the assembly, and then install a new inner shaft snap ring (4). Install the lubrication nipple into the lower bushing, and then install the dust covers.

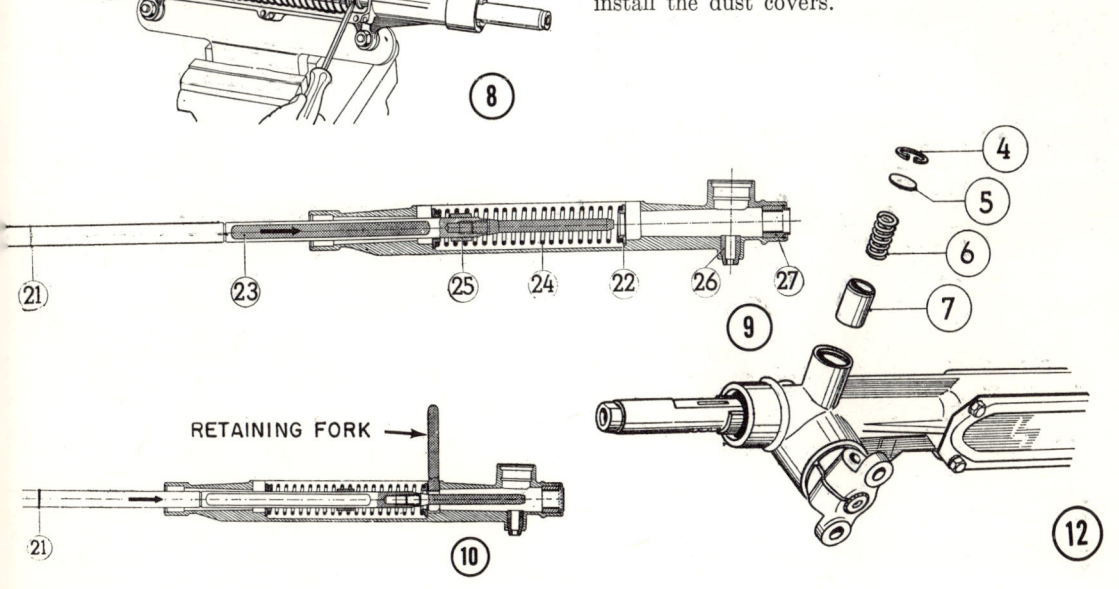

Brake Service

FRONT AXLE SPECIFICATIONS—RENAULT

MODEL	CASTER (Degrees) P = Positive N = Negative	CAMBER (Degrees) P = Positive N = Negative	STEERING AXIS INCLINATION (Degrees)	TOE-IN In.	TOE-IN Mm.	TOE-OUT ON TURNS (Degrees) Inner Wheel	TOE-OUT ON TURNS (Degrees) Outer Wheel
4CV	P10	P1⅓	10	11/64–13/64	4.5–5.0	25	20
Dauphine	P10	Nil	10	⅛–3/16	3.1–4.7	24½	20
Caravelle	P10	Nil	11½	⅛–3/16	3.1–4.7	24½	20
R-8	P9	P1⅔	9½	¼	6	24½	20
Caravelle "S"	P9	P1	10¼	¼	6	24½	20

BRAKE SERVICE—4CV, GORDINI, DAUPHINE, AND CARAVELLE

These models use conventional two-shoe brake assemblies that are hydraulically actuated, with cable-operated parking brake on the two rear wheels. Since 1960, a pressure limiting valve has been installed on the rear crossmember to limit the maximum hydraulic pressure that can be applied to the rear wheel brake cylinders. This device helps to maintain a more equalized brake application during sudden stops.

BRAKE SHOE ADJUSTMENT

Adjust the brake shoes by turning the cams marked "C" and "T" in the indicated direction to move the shoes closer to the drum. Always adjust the primary shoe "C" first. Turn each adjustment until the shoe just touches the drum, and then back it off slightly until the wheel is free. Depress the pedal several times after each adjustment to check that the wheel is free.

Details of the rear brake assembly of the Dauphine. To remove the drum, remove the two nuts holding the axle bearing retainer to the backing plate, and then pull the drum and axle assembly as a unit.

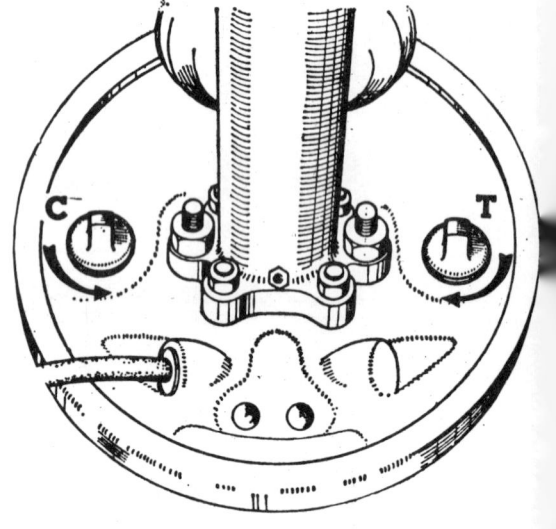

The shoe adjustment is made by turning the square-headed eccentrics (C) and (T) in the indicated direction to move the shoes closer to the drum. (Courtesy of Renault, Inc.)

4CV, Gordini, Dauphine, and Caravelle

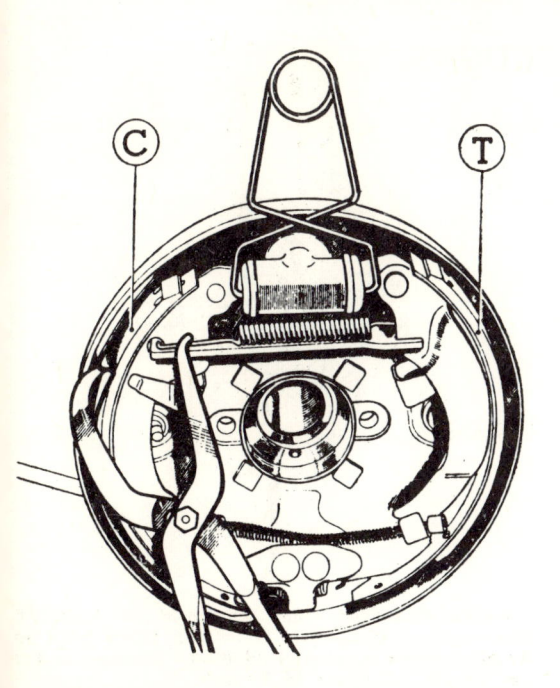

When installing the shoes, the one with the longest lining (C) must be installed in the front. A special tool is available to protect the lining from damage when using the brake spring pliers. (Courtesy of Renault, Inc.)

HAND BRAKE ADJUSTMENT

After the brake shoes have been adjusted, tighten the cable sleeve until three teeth on the sector are passed before brake application begins. Check that the wheels are free with lever in the *off* position.

MASTER CYLINDER, R&R

Disconnect the battery, then remove the spare wheel and the front tunnel. Disconnect the stop light switch wires, close the reservoir outlet with a plug, and then disconnect the hydraulic inlet tube. Remove the switch and the three-way union. *NOTE: Save the seals.* Remove the master cylinder retaining bolts, and then move it forward.

After reinstalling the master cylinder, adjust the push rod until the brake pedal can be depressed 13/64" (5.0 mm.) before the push rod makes contact with the master cylinder piston. Bleed the brakes, starting at the one farthest from the master cylinder and finishing at the one closest to the cylinder.

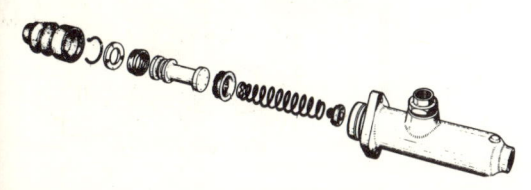

Exploded view of the master cylinder. (Courtesy of Renault, Inc.)

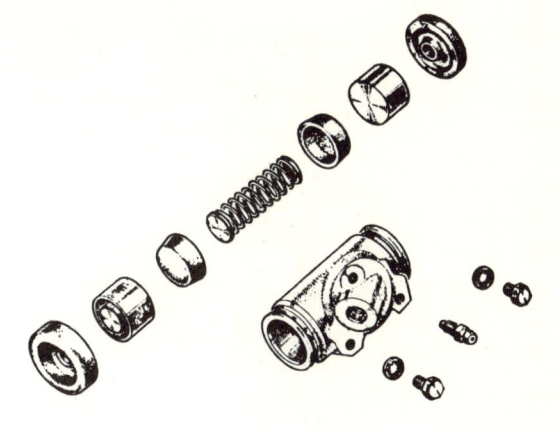

Parts of the wheel cylinders. (Courtesy of Renault, Inc.)

BRAKE PRESSURE REGULATOR

Late models have a pressure regulator installed in place of the "T" fitting to limit the maximum pressure applied to the rear wheels in order to compensate for the forward shift of the center of gravity as the vehicle is brought to a sudden stop.

Testing the Regulator

Connect a 1,500 psi gauge to the bleeder fitting at one of the rear wheel cylinders. Bleed the lines by loosening the hose fitting and pressing slowly on the brake pedal. *CAUTION: Make sure that the master cylinder reservoir has enough fluid for this operation.* Have a helper press on the brake pedal slowly so that it takes at least two seconds to reach maximum pressure. The gauge should rise to 710 psi (50 kg. cm^2) for drum brakes and to 1070 psi (75 kg. cm^2) for disc brakes *and remain there even though more pedal pressure is applied.* If it continues to rise, or if fluid is detected on the valve, the unit must be replaced.

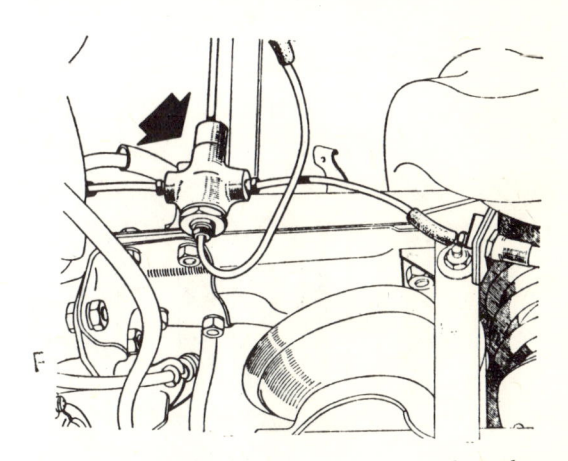

The pressure regulator (arrow) is used on later models in place of the "T" fitting. Its purpose is to limit the pressure which can be applied to the rear brake shoes on a sudden stop. (Courtesy of Renault, Inc.)

Brake Service

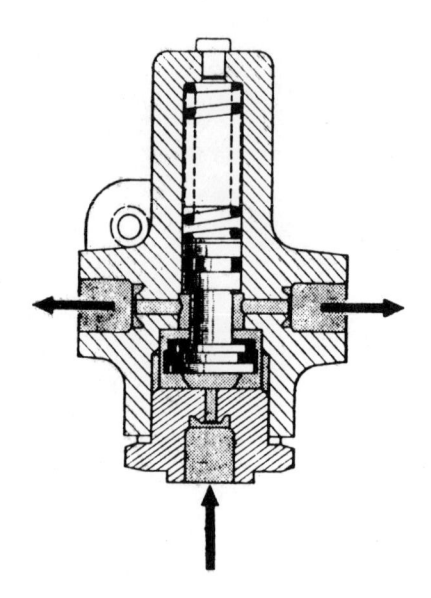

For normal braking, the unit is inoperative. (Courtesy of Renault, Inc.)

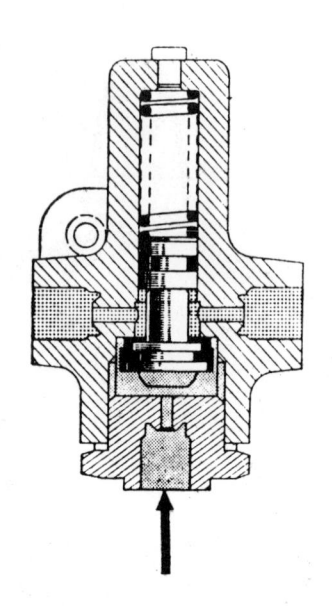

During a sudden stop, movement of hydraulic fluid to the rear cylinder forces the piston back to the point where it restricts additional pressure to the rear wheels. (Courtesy of Renault, Inc.)

DISC BRAKE SERVICE—R-8 AND CARAVELLE "S"

The braking system has been completely redesigned, both models having disc brakes on all four wheels. The new braking system differs from conventional disc brakes in the use of a fully floating caliper with a single piston. The automatic adjustment device consists of a rubber "O" ring (1) in the accompanying illustration. On brake application, the "O" ring is distorted in its groove which keeps it in a state of tension. When the driver releases pedal pressure, the "O" ring returns the brake pad to its normal position, which is just clear of the disc.

Special Assembly Notes. The brake pads must be changed when the total thickness of the plate-pad assembly reaches 0.197" (5.0 mm.). The normal clearance between the lining and the edge of the caliper should be 0.012" (0.3 mm.). After adjusting the parking brake, the clearance between the lever boss and the pad back plate must be 0.008" (0.2 mm.). *Caution: When installing a piston in the caliper, it is essential to install the gap of the automatic play take-up device in line with the bleed screw; otherwise, it will not be possible to bleed the caliper.* The piston stud has a punch mark to indicate the gap of the automatic play take-up device and the piston face is marked with a line to indicate the same position, and these must face the bleed screw on assembly.

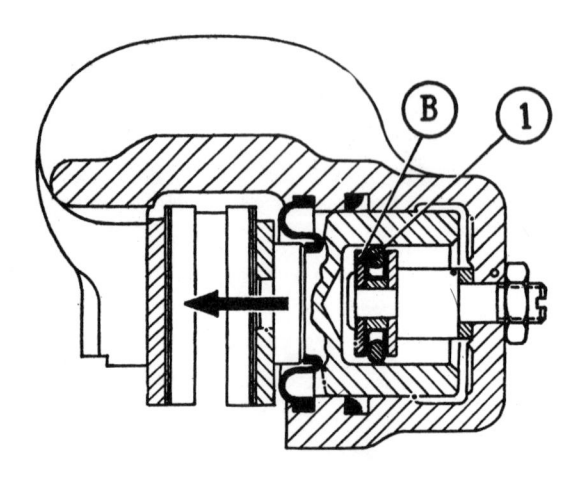

The brakes are adjusted automatically. On brake application, the rubber "O" ring twists, setting up a strain.

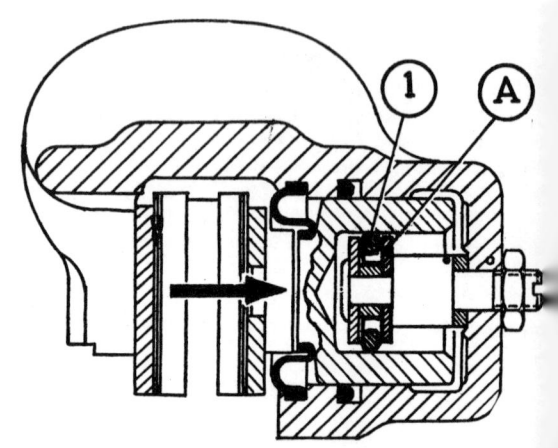

When pedal pressure is released, the distorted "O" ring (1) returns the piston from the disc. (Courtesy of Renault, Inc.)